DATE		

© THE BAKER & TAYLOR CO.

MURDER IN THE MILLIONS

Erle Stanley Gardner
Mickey Spillane
Ian Fleming

J. Kenneth Van Dover

With photographs

FREDERICK UNGAR PUBLISHING CO.
New York

Copyright © 1984 by Frederick Ungar Publishing Co., Inc.

Printed in the United States of America

Library of Congress Cataloging in Publication Data

Van Dover, J. Kenneth.
  Murder in the millions.

  Bibliography: p.
  Includes index.
  1. Detective and mystery stories, American—History
and criticism.   2. Popular literature—United States—
History and criticism.   3. Gardner, Erle Stanley, 1889–
1970—Criticism and interpretation.   4. Spillane,
Mickey, 1918–   —Criticism and interpretation.
5. Fleming, Ian, 1908–1964—Criticism and interpretation.
6. Spy stories, English—History and criticism.
7. American fiction—20th century—History and criticism.
I. Title.

PS374.D4V36   1984   813'.0872'09   84-2493
ISBN 0-8044-2946-4
ISBN 0-8044-6944-X (pbk.)

To SA

Contents

Clues to the Reader   ix

Introduction: Three Superselling Giants   1

1 Erle Stanley Gardner   15
  High Relief Life, Low Relief Prose   16
  A Jack London Come Lately   25
  The Case of the Velvet Claws   33
  The Case of the Sulky Girl   54
  The Case of the Eighty Encores   70
  The D.A. and the Hard-Boiled Op(ess)   76
  Happy, Healthy, and . . . Rich   88

2 Mickey Spillane   91
  The Plot Thins: *I, the Jury*   94
  My Typewriter Is Quick   115
  Tough Guys and Spies   139
  One Lonely Knight   150

3 Ian Fleming   153
  Dionysiac of the Atom Age   156
  Banco: *Casino Royale*   160

Damsels and Dragons 173

Notes 215

Bibliography 219

Film and Television 227

Index 231

Clues to the Reader

The working title of this study was "Supersellers." The term seemed most clearly to indicate the peculiar common achievement of the three writers under consideration. Erle Stanley Gardner, Mickey Spillane, and Ian Fleming did not merely produce a "bestseller" or two. Again and again they produced books that sold over two million copies. The quantity and the consistency are remarkable. Gardner published twenty-five novels that sold an average of somewhat over two million copies each; eight of Spillane's novels averaged over five million; and eleven of Fleming's averaged over three million. Their unequaled salesmanship justifies treating these three writers together in a single volume.

A second shared characteristic is implied in the title *Murder in the Millions*. In very different ways, each of the three writers chose to work within the broadly defined genre of crime/suspense literature. A lawyer, a private eye, and a secret agent have in common an interest in solving (or, in the instance of the secret agent, in preventing) murder. All three act dramatically to resolve the most radical threat to the moral stability of the human community.

I have tried to explore the implications of a mass-produced moralistic literature by identifying the stereotypes employed by each of the superselling authors and by analyzing the moral, social, and political prejudices they exploited. Doubtless there are other equally fruitful approaches, but these seem to me to be the central issues in understanding the art of the superseller.

The organization of the study is straightforward. I have treated each author separately, and within each section have proceeded chronologically through the author's works. I have followed a pattern of concentrating fullest attention upon the inaugural novel, and then discussing the later novels primarily as they diverge from or develop the formulas of their prototype. The eighty-two cases of Perry Mason conform so closely to a single type that I confined myself to a detailed examination of the first two and a very cursory review of later developments. I have also included short accounts of the non-superselling novels and novel series by Gardner and Spillane.

I should confess that I thoroughly enjoy the works of all three writers. I was a fan before I proposed to become a critic. After reading and rereading, annotating and analyzing, I remain a fan. Still, I have not made the argument that the reader *ought* to enjoy mass-produced entertainments. *De gustibus non disputandum est.* Nor have I presumed to judge the prejudices of the authors or of their mass audiences. I have merely tried to present fair statements of the ideas and attitudes embodied in the novels. Certainly Spillane's portraits of communists, blacks, and—especially—women will offend the sensibilities of many. Many more will disagree with them. I was not offended; I have kept my disagreements largely to myself.

Gardner and Spillane wrote mysteries. Inevitably I have had to reveal some surprise endings. With regard to Gardner, I offer no apologies. If I have ruined the surprises in three Mason novels—*The Case of the Velvet Claws, The Case of the Sulky Girl,* and *The Case of the Horrified Heirs*—and of one Lam-Cool novel—*Spill the Jackpot*—there remain unspoiled seventy-nine of the former and twenty-eight of the latter. The difficulty with Spillane is more acute. The shock ending is a Spillane trademark.

With some reluctance, I have limited myself to revealing explicitly the villain in only two, but these two are among the most famous surprise villains in literary crime. I can only urge readers to complete *I, the Jury* and *Vengeance Is Mine!* before they refer to my accounts.

I must claim the privilege of expressing my gratitude to a number of people. Bruce Cassiday has been a most helpful and encouraging editor throughout the conception and gestation of *Murder in the Millions*. Daniel Williams, a scholar devoted to a much earlier period of American popular literature, has also been an important and supportive friend. Other friends at the Abteilung für Amerikanistik at the Universität Tübingen—especially Hartmut Grandel, Hans Borchers, Siegfried Neuweiler, and Zoe Hartmann—helped by conferring academic legitimacy on the study of popular literature. The genesis of *Murder in the Millions* may be indirectly traced to a seminar on The American Detective Story which these colleagues encouraged me to offer during my tenure as Fulbright *Gastprofessor* at Tubingen. I cannot let pass this opportunity to thank my parents and the many other friends here and in Germany for their all too often unprovoked kindnesses. Finally, I must mention what I cannot fully express: my gratitude for the endless support (and patience) of my wife, Sarala.

J.K.V.D.

Introduction:
Three Superselling
Giants

No man but a blockhead ever wrote except for money
—Dr. Johnson

However he might rate the quality of their writings, Dr. Johnson could hardly fault the motives of Erle Stanley Gardner, Mickey Spillane, and Ian Fleming. They are among the most roundheaded writers in literary history. The success with which they manufactured profitable fictions was unprecedented. At a time when no novel could expect to sell a million copies in America, they produced million-sellers and multi-million-sellers and they did so again and again. They revolutionized the industry: they were to popular literature what Henry Ford was to the automobile. The vehicle that rolled off Ford's assembly lines may have lacked the poetry of a Bugatti, but it took people where they wanted to go. The pioneering supersellers also provided a basic sort of transportation, carrying their readers into a fictional world where prose simplifies problems and plot solves them.

Ford is reported to have said that his customers could buy their Model Ts in any color they wanted, so long as they wanted black. Gardner, Spillane, and Fleming were equally disinclined to indulge in experimental variations on a proven theme. Consistency—predictability—not innovation or customization was their trademark. Perry Mason's career stretched over forty years, yet the progress of

1

his eighty-second *Case* in no significant way differed from that of his first. Mike Hammer resumed his practice after a ten-year hiatus, but the '62 Hammer remained essentially identical to the '52 model. Though his antagonists change their allegiance, James Bond always fights the same battle and in the same style.

In 1928—the twentieth year of production—the Model T was discontinued. Having invented the market for middle-class cars, Ford saw it develop its own momentum. Automobile sales moved into numbers as inconceivable in 1908 as Model T sales would have been in 1907. A similar explosion has occurred in the sales of the second generation of supersellers. Every year since the late sixties seems to have produced a novel or two which has sold more than six million copies—*The Godfather* and *The Exorcist* (both over twelve million), *Love Story, Valley of the Dolls, Jaws, Shogun, The Thornbirds*. Of the three original supersellers, only Mickey Spillane reached the six million mark, and he made it only with *I, the Jury*.[1]

Nonetheless, the accomplishment of the Gardner-Spillane-Fleming triumvirate was a remarkable one. Working within the broad limits of a single literary genre—crime/suspense—they totally dominated the literary marketplace during the middle third of the twentieth century. Gardner launched Perry Mason in 1933, and his popularity remained unparalleled throughout the depression and on into the war years. Spillane burst upon the scene in 1947, and over the next five years—the era of Levittown and McCarthy—published seven novels, each of which sold more than five million copies. James Bond, debuting in 1953, dazzled the decade of the cold war. Separated by personality as well as by geography—Los Angeles, New York, and London—the three authors were hardly acquaintances, yet successively they stereotyped the fantasies of a crucial period of American history.

Fleming died in 1964; Gardner survived until 1972, productive to the very end. Spillane's last Hammer novel appeared in 1970, and his most recent book, *The Day the*

Sea Rolled By (1981), was written for children. The seventies saw the emergence of the record-breakers like Peter Benchley, James Clavell, and Colleen McCullough, none of whom have been as regular or as prolific as the original triumvirate. Even such steady practitioners of the craft of superselling as Harold Robbins, James A. Michener, and Robert Ludlum have tended to concentrate their efforts into substantial, intermittant volumes. Whatever their productivity, these later supersellers are a diverse lot; they do not, as did their remarkable forebears, share a common world view implied by the genre they are exploiting.

The conventions of crime/suspense made sense to Gardner, Spillane, and Fleming and to their readers. Three variations on a single form preoccupied American readers from FDR to JFK. But the form and its variations are not merely historical curiosities. They continue to have an effect; they continue to find an audience. Forty Perry Mason titles are still in print; fourteen (of fourteen) Bond volumes and twenty-three (of twenty-three) thrillers by Spillane are still available.[2] Bond continues to attract predictably large audiences in the cinema; that *two* Bond films opened in 1983 suggests that any obituary would be premature. And following the success of a Mike Hammer telemovie in 1983, Spillane has undertaken to supervise a new television series for his hero of the forties. The appeal of the supersellers has not yet been exhausted. They still speak to and for America.

The superseller offers a unique insight into the ideological assumptions of the literate population of a country. The Soviet Union, for instance, has consumed more than half a billion volumes of Lenin since 1917. By 1979 some sixty-five million copies of the works of Leonid Brezhnev were in print.[3] This occurred in a country where paper shortages have severely restricted the availability of books.

By comparison, the American mass market has been far less unanimous in its endorsements. Still, an examination of the record in *80 Years of Best Sellers, 1895–1975* by

Alice Payne Hackett and James Henry Burke reveals interesting trends. Editions of the Bible (like those of Marx) are omitted from consideration as incalculable. America's periennial favorite is Dr. Spock's *Pocket Book of Baby and Child Care* (23,285,000 copies as of 1975). *Better Homes and Gardens Cook Book, Webster's New World Dictionary of the American Language, The Guinness Book of World Records,* and *Betty Crocker's Cookbook* round out the top five bestsellers. None are works of fiction. The nation's highest priorities lie elsewhere. Three books are related to the generation and sustenance of the family; a fourth—the dictionary—represents the education of youth; and the *Guinness Book* may serve as a vulgar emblem of an oft-noted national drive to be first and most. Useful books—reference works, self-improvement guides (e.g., *How to Win Friends and Influence People*), motivational tracts (*The Power of Positive Thinking*)—figure prominently throughout the list.

But fiction prevails. Two hundred and one of the three hundred sixty-six books that have sold over two million copies in America are classified as fiction (and this does not include nineteen books classified as juvenile fiction). Mario Puzo follows directly behind Betty Crocker. William Peter Blatty, Harper Lee, Grace Metalious, Erich Segal, Jacqueline Susann, Peter Benchley, Richard Bach, Margaret Mitchell, and Erskine Caldwell comprise the remainder of the top ten novelists (Caldwell's *God's Little Acre* ranking twenty-first among all books).

The Soviet taste for Marxian dialectics may seem relatively creditable. And if the eleventh American novel is Orwell's *1984* (a reminder that compulsory reading affects sales figures in America too), the thirteenth is Harold Robbins's *The Carpetbaggers* and the fourteenth is *The Happy Hooker* (7,141,156 copies) by Xaviera Hollander. Americans would seem to be attracted to melodramatic themes that emphasize violence, sex, and sentimentality.

Of the top-selling fifteen novelists in America, only two can be considered consistent performers. Erskine Caldwell has sold over two million copies of ten different books;

Harold Robbins has produced eleven such titles by 1975, and since then he has surely extended his record. These are remarkable achievements, and a study of the works of Caldwell and of Robbins will have much to say about writing and about America. But there is an essential difference between these two and the next category of supersellers— the Gardner-Spillane-Fleming triumvirate. Like all popular writers, Caldwell and Robbins catered to their audiences, each separate fiction fulfilling certain expectations. But each fiction was original in itself. Caldwell and Robbins tailored "bespoke" novels. Gardner, Spillane, and Fleming sell off the rack. The most fascinating aspect of their imaginative art is its deliberate lack of imagination, its assumption (vindicated by sales) that redundancy is a literary virtue. Even Harold Robbins demonstrated a certain versatility. The character types and the plot situations may be the same in all his novels—his readers demand as much—but the contexts of the action at least are varied. The virtuosos of the superseller are those writers who can hit upon a prototype—defined in its characters, its plots, its scenes, and its attitudes—which can be endlessly duplicated with only nominal variations and yet continue to attract extremely large audiences. Preeminent among these extraordinarily limited artists, extraordinarily successful sellers are Gardner, Spillane, and Fleming.

Statistics substantiate their claim to superior salesmanship. Spillane owns the best sales-per-book record. His total sales amount to over one hundred fifty million—over twice that of Chairman Brezhnev. Spillane's first novel, *I, the Jury*, occupies the eighteenth place among novels in America; he also claims numbers 21, 25, 26, 27, 28, 29, and 184. The sales of his first seven novels are as almost unbelievably consistent as are their contents. Ian Fleming's bestselling novel, *Thunderball*, ranks forty-third among novels, followed by numbers 54, 70, 76, 78, 79, 89, 101, 102, 105, 112, and 125. The only Bond novel *not* to sell two million copies was the posthumous *Man With the Golden Gun*. Erle Stanley Gardner's top-selling novel, *The Case of the Sulky Girl,* places a relatively unimpressive sixty-fourth on the American fiction list. But of the 201 titles which make the fiction list, Gardner alone accounts for twenty-five. Figures in 1980 credited him with worldwide sales of over three hundred million—even Lenin must be looking over his shoulder.

Sales figures such as these suggest that a study of the works of Gardner, Spillane, and Fleming might reveal as much about the mind set of literate America as the study of the works of Lenin and Brezhnev would reveal about that of literate Russia. None of the three authors explicitly proposes a dogmatic analysis of social reality; none presumes to advocate any comprehensive political interpretation of the contemporary world. But there is an implicit coherence to the progress of their manipulation of formulas. Ideological and esthetic natural selection have resulted in a meaningful evolution of values in the works of the three authors. Gardner, Spillane, and Fleming are the fittest who have survived—have triumphed—in the jungle of the literary marketplace. The record of their imaginative adaptations reveals much about the art of the common man in midcentury America.

The most obvious evidence of coherence is, of course, the shared genre. All three writers are inevitably shelved in the same library ghetto—variously labeled mystery, suspense, detective, crime, or thriller. Whatever its name, this category of popular literature has been a prominent and profitable one for more than a century. It has attracted some of the best minds of our time and some of the most enterprising. But no artist and no hack has approached the sheer popularity of Gardner, Spillane, and Fleming. Of the fifty-five crime and suspense novels which sold more than two million copies between 1895 and 1975, Gardner, Spillane, and Fleming produced forty-five. This overwhelming dominance in such a competitive field is astonishing.

Crime/suspense also enjoys the distinction of being the most definitely moral of literary categories. Events must end in discovery of innocence and guilt, and normally end in the punishment of the latter. Whatever the superficial pleasures of the text—and these may include sex, sadism, and snobbery—the form of literature practiced by Gardner, Spillane, and Fleming remains fundamentally concerned with the issue of justice and security. This concern further distinguishes their performances from those of a non-genre superseller like Robbins. Robbins's theme—the monotone of his fiction—is power. His protagonists inhabit a relatively amoral world where individuals create values only through self-assertion. Even Spillane and Fleming, far nearer to the Robbins ethic than Gardner, assume some superior source of values. The depression pieties of Erle Stanley Gardner passed into the postwar paranoid patriotism of Spillane and then into the remorseless nationalism of Fleming. The egocentric realpolitik embodied in Robbins's novels represents a new departure in mass consumption in the sixties and seventies.

In addition to sharing a genre, Gardner, Spillane, and Fleming exploited with unequalled success a familiar popular literary device, the series character. Mario Puzo's *The Godfather* heads the list of bestselling crime/suspense novels, having sold twice the six million copies of the number two book, *I, the Jury*. The popularity of the movies derived from it dwarfs that of the not inconsiderable fame of the Bond films or the Mason television series. And yet the name most often associated with the novel is Marlon Brando, not Don Corleone. Who is the protagonist of *The Exorcist? Peyton Place? Love Story? Valley of the Dolls? Jaws?* These are trivia questions. But Gardner, Spillane, and Fleming have each contributed proper names into the common American vocabulary. Perry Mason, Mike Hammer, and James Bond are individuals as autonomous as Don Juan, Faust, or Hamlet. Just as pipefitters who have never read Tirso de Molina, Marlowe, or Shakespeare recognize the latter, so professors of English who disdain to read Gardner, Spillane, and Fleming recognize the former.

The art of these three supersellers has thus had a uniquely pervasive influence. A writer's influence is usually measured by the degree to which his literary contemporaries and heirs consciously or unconsciously imitate him. He is judged by his contribution to the continuing tradition. The superseller generally exercises no such productive influence. Not surprisingly, his simplicity and his success encourage imitators. The basic stock of formulas which he relies upon repeatedly may be copied by any close reader. And yet who can name the fake Gardners or fake Spillanes or fake Flemings? More difficult still, who can name successful fakes? The bestseller list discloses none. Raymond Chandler, an inimitable (and much imitated) stylist, once confessed his debt to Gardner. A host of Spillane-manqués expired in the paperbacks of the fifties. Fleming spawned a host of pastiches and parodies, and certainly affected the careers of Donald Hamilton, Len Deighton, even John le Carre. But such inconsequential or tangential influences only confirm the paradox of mechanical originality of the true superseller. Other writers may absorb certain techniques or build upon an established audience, but the essential achievement—a literary construct which can be mass-produced and will be consumed by masses—belongs inalienably to the superseller.

To return to the issue of influence: the superseller speaks not to his fellow artists, but to their antitheses; not to writers, but to inarticulate readers. His audience consists of men and women who demand from literature direct entertainment and unambiguous instruction. They demand an art which clarifies, and they know—maugre the professors of English—that clarity and subtlety are antagonistic. The superseller must stroke the commonest sentiments and prejudices. He does not so much speak to his reader as speak for him. He represents the man who cares enough to send Hallmark's very best.

The analogy is an apt one. The greeting-card industry enjoys its enormous prosperity because modern man has

difficulty formulating the sentiments which society periodically expects him to. (Even the very articulate sometimes
share this awkwardness: professors of English are known
to patronize both Hallmark and Gardner.) The superseller
offers a similar satisfaction with regard to the common
need to reaffirm the meaning of existence. All art makes
such an affirmation—demonstrates some sort of
coherence—but usually on its own often esoteric terms.
Popular literature imposes no terms. It accepts the intuitions of its readers and arranges them in a straightforward
drama that proves the world does proceed in an orderly
fashion—that there is an intelligible plot concealed in current events, that character is knowable, that good and evil
are definite opposites, and that we are good. The superseller merely accepts and arranges these commonplaces most
effectively. He may do this naively or cynically, but in
either event he acts as the ventriloquist for his dumb audience.

Mysteries and thrillers are often dismissed as "escape
literature," but this only begs the question: escape from
what? The answer, already implied, would seem to be,
escape from ambiguity. Both the detective story and the
spy story depend upon explicit moral and political standards. There is always action, but more importantly there
is always unequivocal judgment of action. The reader's
interest lies as much in escaping the uncertainties of daily
life as its banalities. Obviously, exotic scenes and extravagant actions are a factor in the appeal of the genre. But
reassurance is its primary function.

It is noteworthy that the popular appetite for fictional
figures who can derive meaning from a chaos of corpses,
cigarette ashes, and eventually communist conspiracies
coincided with the acceptance of Darwinian principles in
the 1880s. As people began to doubt the solicitous omnis-
cience and omnipotence of God, they began to be attracted
to imaginary heroes who commanded a comparable
authority. If murder must occur, there is some consolation
in the expectation that someone may collect the detritus of

the victim's life, infer from it vital facts, and finally orga-
nize an infallible interpretation of whodunit and how and
why. When special providences have been disallowed by
the mechanism of natural selection, there remains some
relief in the faith that a mortal intelligence may make the
necessary deductions from the fall of the sparrow.

The crime/suspense story, thus, serves as a fable for
modern adults, reassuring them that the apparently pointless ambiguities and nuances of their existences may indeed be ultimately meaningful. "Fable" suggests the moral
direction of this reassurance, but "fairy tale" may offer an
even more accurate insight into the nature of the appeal of
the genre, especially as practiced by the supersellers.

The fairy tale, like the mystery and the thriller, is governed by familiar formulas. It begins "once upon a time"
and ends "they all lived happily ever after." The interval
between is full of surprising and often violent incidents.
Frequently there is a quest motif, a search not for the
true murderer, but for the true parent. Identity is a crucial problem; self-realization is an inevitable conclusion.
The wicked stepmother is displaced (more than once
by being rolled down a hill inside a nail-studded barrel);
Cinderella's virtue is recognized; order is restored. These
generic imperatives underlie the periennial appeal of the
fairy tale and apply equally to that of the superselling thriller. The one centers on birth, the other on death. The one
relies upon magic and innocence, the other on ratiocination and power. The one emphasizes fantasy, the other
verisimilitude. The one is a folk art, the other a calculating
manipulation of sophisticated clichés.

Still, the similarities in motive and form are remarkable.
These may be further clarified by reference to Bruno Bettelheim's recent analysis of the structure and function of
the fairy tale in *The Uses of Enchantment* (1975). Bettelheim
notes that the fairy tale, unlike myth, depicts a distinctly
ordinary world: ". . . although the events which occur in
fairy tales are often unusual and most improbable, they

are always presented as ordinary, something that could happen to you or me or the person next door when out on a walk in the woods."[4] Substitute "streets" for "woods" and you have a fair description of the tone of a superseller. The concatenation of events in a Gardner novel may be quite incredible, but the narrative remains resolutely reasonable. Fleming even attempts to make the robbing of Fort Knox or the highjacking of an atomic bomb seem plausible. Elements of the grotesque and the macabre have been admitted into the genre since "The Murders in the Rue Morgue," but the supersellers never indulge in them. The action may be contrived or spectacular, but never unnatural. Bettelheim also notes the unflagging optimism of the fairy tale and its tendency to simplify situations and figures into easily recognizable types. Both features characterize the crime/suspense novel as well. Perry Mason's inexhaustible invincibility became the object of jokes, but it was also the source of his amazing longevity. Ian Fleming has an eye for the evocative detail, but he employs it on his backgrounds, not on his characters. The most important connection between fairy tales and crime/suspense novels derives from their common moral function. Bettelheim argues that it is not the ultimate distribution of rewards and punishments that comprises the moral force of the fairy tale, but rather the continuous opportunity for the child to identify with the hero of the tale in all of his struggles: "Because of this identification the child imagines that he suffers with the hero his trials and tribulations, and triumphs with him as virtue is victorious."[5] A similar process of identification occurs in the crime/suspense novel, and this helps to explain the necessary and memorable preeminence of the protagonist. Mason and Hammer and Bond survive as autonymous individuals in part because their millions of readers have been invited to invest themselves in the hero's sufferings and his triumphs.

Bettelheim proceeds to observe that "the figures in fairy tales are not ambivalent":

> A person is either good or bad, nothing in between. One brother is stupid, the other is clever. One sister is virtuous and industrious, the others are vile and lazy. One is beautiful, the others are ugly. One parent is all good, the other evil. The juxtaposition of opposite characters is not for the purpose of stressing right behavior, as would be true for cautionary tales. . . . Presenting the polarities of character permits the child to comprehend easily the difference between the two which he could not do as readily were the figures drawn more true to life, with all the complexities that characterize real people.[6]

Even the superselling novelist cannot afford to be as obviously simplistic as the teller of fairy tales. But he does tend to portray uncomplicated stereotypes. These may be as unsubtle as Fleming's bizarre villains and pliant females, or as familiar as Gardner's earnest working girls and unreasonable guardians. The superseller has no use for psychological chiaroscuro. The members of his cast are healthy or they are psychotic; they are rarely troubled by the mild neuroses that afflict ordinary life.

In part his reliance upon stock characters is a matter of economy. The superseller's schedule permits him little time to fill in the nonessential nuances of character. In part, too, his simplifications—unlike those of the fairy tale—do carry an explicit moral burden. The reader wants his villainy unrelieved by mitigating considerations. He finds enough "troubled" criminals in his newspapers (and enough sympathetic commentators); he expects from his fiction inexcusable malignity and unapologetic heroism.

But this reaffirmation of the reality of moral extremes is related to Bettelheim's larger point. The crime/suspense genre offers more than just clear-cut vices and virtues. It offers a clear-cut world. The protagonist—the detective or the spy—masters not only the crucial matter of innocence and guilt, he masters all forms of social behavior. Perry Mason knows how to comfort the hysterical and how to blackmail the blackmailer, how to bribe a cop and how to tip a hatcheck girl. He controls all situations; he is as self-possessed in a restaurant as in a courtroom. He knows to advantage the rules of etiquette as well as the rules of law. He sees what must be done, and he does it. The reader, conscious of the insecurities and resentments that arise from coping with the incomprehensible rules and rituals of life in modern society, admires both qualities—the hero's self-confident vision and his consequent actions. Mike Hammer's iconoclasm—his contempt for arty types, the idle rich, bureaucrats—and James Bond's brand-name snobbery are contrary poses that work to the same end: the hero knows the "real" thing as well as he knows the good thing. That there are indeed real things and good things may be a comforting proposition in this uncertain century.

Bettelheim sees the role of the fairy tale as transitional: "Ambiguities must wait until a relatively firm personality has been established on the basis of positive identifications."[7] The superselling crime/suspense novel suggests that for millions of twentieth-century readers "a relatively firm personality" is not a secure achievement. Adults remain in need of "positive identifications," and the superseller is contrived to fulfill that need. In this age of anxiety, readers are willing to pay again and again to hear retold a reassuring tale about someone who does all the right things and does them not once upon a time, but here and now, in a radically simplified but still recognizable version of the reader's own oppressively unsimple world. In their own ways and for their own times, Gardner, Spillane, and Fleming provided the right sort of hero and the right sort of world.

1

Erle Stanley Gardner

The point is that a writer in starting a story should first decide what lowest common denominator of public interest, or what combination of common denominators he is going to put in the story. Once he puts them in the story he knows he is starting on a firm foundation. If he doesn't have them in the story he doesn't have anything.[1]

—Erle Stanley Gardner

Erle Stanley Gardner began to package fiction for the masses in 1921. His motives were admittedly mercenary; his skills were conscientiously developed; his success was enormous. For many of the next forty-nine years, Gardner was less than a full-time writer, yet the bibliography of his works compiled by Ruth Moore lists well over a thousand titles—novels (nearly 130), non-fiction books, "novelettes," short stories, and articles. In addition, he edited hundreds of scripts for other media—film, radio, television, comic strips. Gardner was the first and by far the most prolific of the three supersellers.

Of the thousand-plus items that issued from his "fiction factory" certainly the most important were the eighty-two Mason novels (there are, as well, three Mason novelettes). Upon these his reputation rests: of the twenty-five Gardner novels to sell more than two million copies, twenty-three belong to the Mason series. Although some attention should be paid to Gardner's subsidiary novels series—D.A. Doug Selby and detectives Bertha Cool and Donald Lam can be considered unpopular only relative to Perry Mason—and to the formative period of his apprentice work in the pulp market, the final estimation of the nature and the merits of Gardner's superselling craft of fiction must be based upon an analysis of the "common denominators" which he contrived to embody in the cases of Perry Mason.

High Relief Life, Low Relief Prose

Three authors are primarily responsible for the fact that most readers think of Los Angeles as one of the ideal settings for a detective story. None of the three was native to the area. Raymond Chandler was born in Chicago and, as he never ceased to remind his correspondents, was educated at an English Public School and in the literary circles of Georgian London. Ross Macdonald, born Kenneth Millar in San Francisco, was raised in Vancouver and took his degrees from the University of Western Ontario and the University of Michigan. Yet both men, arriving in Southern California in middle age, found in the environs of Los Angeles the appropriate scenes for their fictional analyses of life in modern America: neighborhoods, slums, freeways, nightclubs, gambling, cults, brushfires, corruption, old fortunes, and new frauds. The westward course of empire had reached its conclusion at Hollywood and Vine. These phenomena—this place—epitomized twentieth-century America, and so offered Chandler and Macdonald the material with which to reform a popular genre into a thoughtful, even subversive criticism of a way of life. Neither Chandler nor Macdonald was a superseller.

The ambitions of the third stranger to seize upon the scene were simultaneously both more and less grand. Erle Stanley Gardner was content to repeat all of the most trite and the most flattering truisms concerning the character of Americans, and his depictions of the California cityscape/landscape generally lack the evocative precision of those of Chandler and Macdonald. Indeed, he rarely attempts to reproduce nuances of any sort—descriptive, social, psychological, linguistic. Where others are disturbed, Gardner is confident; where Chandler and Macdonald found concrete cause to doubt the oft-proclaimed

triumph of the American experiment—found, that is, in
the specific conditions of California lives sufficient reason to question the doctrine of manifest destiny—Gardner
saw and reported in capital letters clear proofs of the vin-
dication of the original errand into the wilderness. Chandler and Macdonald etched the close details of their
portraits in anger and in sorrow; Gardner's broad strokes
and bright colors paint a simplified and optimistic portrait
of an era. The era—one of depression and world war—
liked what it saw in Gardner's sketches, and it made him a
superseller.

Gardner is easily dismissed for his facility and his naivete. But in several respects, his personal engagement with
the people and the land of California was far more pro-
found than that of either Chandler or Macdonald. His
birthplace was the most distant of the three, in space and
in tradition. Gardner was born in Malden, Massachusetts
in 1889. He was as much the heir of the Puritans as was
Nathaniel Hawthorne. Family records trace his descent to
the early days of the colony, the maternal line going back
to the *Mayflower*. All his life Gardner subscribed to the
popular notion of the Puritan ethic, with its emphasis
upon self-reliance, diligence, and industry, and he un-
ashamedly honored these virtues in his fiction. They are a
pervasive presence in the Mason novels.

In 1899 Gardner's father, an engineer, moved his family
to Oroville, a mining town in northern California, and for
the rest of his life Gardner considered himself a Californian. When he graduated from high school in 1909,
Gardner had already begun to read law with a local attorney. An experiment in formal instruction at Valparaiso
University in Indiana was soon aborted when Gardner devoted more time to practicing boxing than to studying law.
He returned to California, continued his informal reading, and was admitted to the bar in 1911. He married the
following year and a daughter was born in 1913. (Gardner
and his wife, Natalie, separated amicably in the 1930s;
Gardner did not remarry until her death in 1968.) From

1911 until 1933 he practiced law, first in Oxnard and then in Ventura.

Chandler's decade of wheeling and dealing as an oil-company executive, 1922–32, helped to educate him in the psychology and the morality of the capitalist entrepreneur, and his work with Paramount Studios may have offered similar enlightenment regarding the mechanisms of cinema and moguls. But Chandler was essentially a private person, and his sensitive depictions of American characters were usually based on observation made from a distance. Similarly, Ross Macdonald's lifestyle seems to have offered him limited opportunities for intimate acquaintance with the population he depicts. His knowledge of the ambitions and the habits of his characters is more analytic (and introspective) than empirical. Distance, introspection, and an ear for language are the main components of Chandler and Macdonald's art.

Gardner was much more directly involved in the lives of Californians. His experience was almost unlimited; he was familiar with a broad range of individuals, excepting only the two extremes—the very rich and the very poor, the millionaires who didn't need to work and the indigent who couldn't find work—and about these he wrote very little. As a criminal lawyer, he became acquainted with what he called "the underclasses"; he even complained to his father that they comprised most of his clients. Nonetheless, he served them well, and at a time of considerable racial prejudice, he became notorious for his inventive defenses of his many Chinese clients. In 1918 Gardner assumed the position of president in a friend's company, Consolidated Sales, and for three years he crisscrossed the state, button-holing enterprising executives and developing an effective sales psychology. Gardner thus came to know the doers and the done-tos.

Later, as his fame as a writer grew, Gardner devoted considerable energy to pursuing and correcting what he believed to be miscarriages of justice. In 1948 this concern was institutionalized in The Court of Last Resort, a committee of experts headed by Gardner who regularly investigated charges that an innocent man had been convicted. The Court was in part a publicity stunt for *Argosy* magazine, but it also reflected a genuine and philanthropic impulse. And it brought Gardner into close contact with a wide variety of victims, criminals, and professionals. He memorialized many of the latter in the dedications he began to add to his novels in 1945. As a result of his range of connections, Gardner's correspondence in the 1950s often averaged 20,000 words a day. Finally, mention must be made of Gardner's large number of friendships with Mexicans and Mexican-Americans, which found partial expression in his several books about the Baja. Gardner's hale-fellow-well-met image was not a pose. He seems to have impressed men from all walks of life with his honesty and his generosity; he liked people and he was interested in them. As readers responded to the writer, so acquaintances responded to the man.

Gardner's vast experience of self-reliant men (his coterie of devoted secretaries seems to have comprised his primary knowledge of women) provided him with ample warrant to appoint himself their spokesman. Self-made and self-making men may not fairly epitomize America, but they do epitomize the American ideal, and Gardner, self-made himself, related to them immediately when he met them and represented them uncritically when he came to place them in his fictions. Gardner rarely slipped into the obtrusive homiletics of Horatio Alger, but he always implied the normalcy and the value of making one's own way. He knew—better than Chandler or Macdonald—that the social and commercial environment of modern America might systematically deform the behavior of its citizenry, but he preferred to focus his attention and the attention of his readers upon generally decent characters intent upon earning their livelihood in a country of opportunity, characters for whom crime is an aberration, not a commonplace. Perhaps Gardner lacked the ability to see deeper into the human heart; certainly he would have concealed any discouraging insights from his creative art.

Gardner's settings are as flat as his characters. This too, at first glance, seems a paradox, for he was a man intrigued by the topography of California. His days as a lawyer and a businessman provided him with an equally intimate knowledge of the layout of a Chinese ghetto and an industrialist's headquarters. Moreover, he was throughout his life fascinated by the natural beauties of California. Gardner was even something of an explorer, and he composed several books about his expeditions in the Sacramento River delta and in the deserts of the Baja. In 1937 he began to accumulate the acres that eventually comprised his Rancho del Paisano in Temecula, a hundred miles southeast of Los Angeles. This became his permanent base of operations, but the pressures of society even here frequently drove him to load up one of his campers and set out for a day or a week in the wilderness that surrounded his fiction factory.

Little of this sensitivity to the natural or social environment survives in his fiction, and for several reasons. He refused to clot the carefully sustained pace of action with extended passages of non-functional description. He was also disinclined to recognize the environment as an effective accomplice in his moral dramas: a man is responsible for his own actions, and should not consider shifting blame onto his parents, his economic class, his diet, etc. (The contrary conviction, of course, encouraged Chandler and Macdonald to attend more scrupulously to the influences of environment.) But Gardner does seem to have been simply unable to articulate a sense of place. Even his travel books tend to concentrate upon the mechanics of his undertakings and to slight his impressions of the natural world that was his ostensible object. Gardner himself supplied many of the photographs that illustrate these narratives. Nearly all seem to be snapshots of Gardner himself, his companions, his pets, the people he meets. The splendor of the mountains and the deserts are almost accidental backgrounds. The snapshot may serve as an accurate metaphor for the style and purpose of Gardner's prose. His fictional world is anecdotal, superficial, and happy. Chandler and Macdonald create their portraits of California and Californians by seeking out crucial images, arranging perspectives and sidelights, fiddling with the technology of lenses and films to achieve the most revealing focus and depth of field. Gardner simply compiles album after album of flash photos of ordinary people caught off guard. The only unusual aspect of his collections is that the occasion for which his subjects are gathered is a murder, not a vacation or a wedding.

Character and scene, then, are deliberately stereotyped by Gardner. The third element of his craft—the one of which he was most proud—is also rigidly defined. Once Gardner had plotted out the prototype of a given series, he never varied the essential combination of conventions. He once recalled how, after the second or third Mason novel, his publishers had advised him to vary the restrictive formula. "Now, after nearly seventy Perry Mason books, when I even talk about an element of novelty, the publishers have kittens. Tell a kid the story of the 'Three Bears' and the child wants to hear it over and over again. Try to change it and the kid has a fit."[2] The superseller cannot afford to alienate his audience of big kids, and Gardner never did change his story.

Gardner was aware of the fairy-tale factor. In a substantial analysis of the Mason formula composed as a guide for television script writers, he made some even more revealing comments. In this piece he noted the necessity of realizing and exploiting "the lowest common denominator of public interest." He further observes that "there are three major characters who have been virtually indestructible in the course of fiction: Robin Hood, Sherlock Holmes and Cinderella."[3] Of the last, he writes,

> The Cinderella story has been told and retold many, many thousands of times. It is a common denominator which has the greatest public appeal. It is a soothing syrup to the unfortunate. It leads people to believe that there is some-

where a magic power, a fairy godmother, which will make their dreams come true—therefore it isn't simply a waste of time to have dreams.[4]

Gardner directly relates the work of fiction to his readers' dreams, not to their realities. And he finds in Perry Mason "the fairy godmother touch of Cinderella, in which justice is brought to the downtrodden."[5]

Gardner's most suggestive comments are made in connection with the Robin Hood paradigm:

> People are oppressed in many ways. . . . Yet people instinctively desire freedom and there is a vast yearning on the part of the people to be reassured that God is in His heaven, that all is right in the world and that justice will triumph over tyranny. . . . In a good story the audience identifies itself with the hero and when the audience feels that it is identified with the hero and the hero does something truly heroic the audience feels inspired accordingly.[6]

"Reassurance"; "identification": these are the natural effects of the fairy tale and the self-conscious aim of the superseller.

In his discussions of Cinderella and Robin Hood and Perry Mason, Gardner always speaks of what his readers desire, not of what they have. His goal is not, like that of Chandler and Macdonald, to hold a mirror up to nature, but rather up to fantasy. Precisely because his readers' lives have been cramped and distorted by environmental pressures, the lives of his characters are fabulously self-controlled. Gardner's creatures are accidentally entangled in a murder plot that threatens their liberty, but this does not disturb their self-possession. Even his murderers are never pathological personalities. They are wrong-minded, not insane.

Thus the reader is encouraged to identify not only with the hero—though that is a primary effect—but also with his supporting cast, with a world of autonomous, responsible individuals. Philip Marlowe, walking down his mean streets, often appears to be a last resort, an isolated refuge of decency in a darkening landscape. Perry Mason's world is permanently sunlit; the only obscurity results from a single cloud which his penetrating intelligence regularly disperses. The reiteration is part of the reassurance.

Francis and Roberta Fugate, in *Secrets of the World's Best-Selling Writer,* report that Gardner referred to another popular pastime to explain the appeal of his repetitious fiction: He

> used a baseball analogy to answer critics of the formula story. The basic plot of a baseball game is the same day after day, year in and year out, he pointed out. The conflicts are the same, yet the spectators return time after time because, as in the well-plotted formula story, they never know what combination of events is going to occur during a game. They learn the identities of players and know what to expect of them, just as readers learn about the recurring characters in books and buy more books about them in order to see them perform.[7]

There is practical wisdom in this comparison. Series characters do build a momentum of reader interest. But there is also a point for speculation.

Baseball was indeed America's sport, particularly in the thirties and forties, and the source of its appeal may indeed be related to that of the detective story, which was then enjoying its golden age. Baseball is a peculiar game in the degree to which it is rulebound. The mound and the plate are exactly positioned sixty feet and six inches apart. The base paths are carefully drawn, and transgression is prohibited. An umpire evaluates every pitch and every slide. Every movement of ball or man must be judged: strike or ball, out or safe. In football, or basketball, or hockey, the referee intervenes in the power struggle only when he observes an infraction; in baseball the umpire's calls are omnipresent.

The detective story genre is famous for its rules—S. S. Van Dine's "Twenty Rules for Writing Detective Stories," Father Knox's "A Detective Story Decalogue." The golden-age writers made something of a fetish of fair play.

Gardner's supersellers are rulebound in a slightly different sense, but to the same effect. If the reader seeks from fairy tales and from the detective story to be reassured that there are objective rules of behavior—real rights and wrongs—then Gardner's baseball analogy may indeed indicate a fundamental source of his appeal. His refusal to vary even apparently nonessential formulas responds to that inarticulate desire for an unequivocal order which is felt by millions who are conscious that they inhabit a world without umpires or detectives.

It also expedites the writing of fiction, and this is the final point to be made before turning to examples of that fiction. Formulas are easy to fill in. (Easy at least for Gardner, if not for his would-be imitators). "The fiction factory" was Gardner's own phrase for his enterprise. The factory consisted of one generator—Gardner—and up to six or seven secretaries, some of whom stayed with him for thirty-five years (and one of whom he married in 1968). Gardner developed the practice of dictating his stories onto recording cylinders and then quickly reviewing a typescript before it was mailed to the publishers. Rather than write his fiction, Gardner talked it. His reliance upon carefully indexed formulas obviously facilitated this largely extempore procedure.

On occasion Gardner even experimented with devices called "Plot Genie" and "Plotto." The latter, for example, consisted of a set of diagrammed wheels which the storyteller turned to provide himself with random new combinations of character types, settings, and conflicts. Gardner even attempted to customize the Plotto method by constructing his own wheels covering "Acts of Villainy as Story Base," "Complicating Circumstances," "Setting," "Motive," Blind Trails by Which Hero Is Misled or Confused," etc. The efficacy of such devices was unsatisfactory even for the ingenious Gardner, but they indicate his notion of the art of fiction. *Secrets of the World's Best-Selling Writer* reprints in an appendix Gardner's "Fluid or Unstatic Theory of Plots," an exhaustive analysis of the possible variations in the plot sequence of a detective story. Gardner's genius for manufacturing stories was unprecedented, but it was not untutored; he was a most self-conscious craftsman.

A Jack London Come Lately

Gardner's apprenticeship was served in the pulp magazine market of the 1920s. Before he mass-produced novels, he mass-produced short stories. For twelve years—1921–1932—he developed his skills by parceling fiction into neat, marketable units of ten- to thirty-thousand words. The twenties saw a great proliferation of cheap periodicals targeted at the aggressive postwar generaton of middle- and lower-class readers. Magazines with titles like *Top Notch, Triple X, Clues,* and *Black Mask* consumed a prodigious number of short stories and novelettes at a penny or two a word. They provided Gardner with a definite audience with definite expectations, and they also supplied him with tested formulas which satisfied those expectations. Gardner did not abandon those formulas when he began to expand into novels, and his audience did not abandon him. The economies he learned producing fiction for the pulps—the mechanics of a series concept, the stereotypes of character, the conventions of plotting, the rhythms of dialogue—served him equally well when pressed to the larger scale of the novel. For Gardner, the transition to novelist meant merely delivering more of the same.

But he seems to have found something especially congenial about the shorter form. Long after the profitability of his novel series was established, Gardner continued to issue short pieces for the pulp market. Even at the end of his career, the annual two or three novels would be supplemented by an occasional novelette and up to half a dozen articles. The shorter forms—fictional and nonfictional—suited his temperament. They provided him with an immediate access to his audience, but they also enabled him to capitalize on his two special advantages: a broad range of interests and a fertile imagination. Gardner's sense of adventure and his knowledge of and attitudes toward the ways of the world coincided with those of his readers. He could demonstrate an easy mastery of those matters which interested him—from criminal law to archery—and could with equal facility convey that mastery in concise dramatic or expository prose.

The fecundity of Gardner's imagination is legend; he could, it seems, spontaneously generate endless variations on a given theme. The form of the short story and novelette rewards such inventiveness. Recalling the premise of a certain series, Gardner could effortlessly contrive a set of appropriate complications, flesh out the plot as he dictated the narrative to a secretary, and not be concerned with editing out the inconsistencies creeping into a composition stretched over days. A complete action, with its predictable cast of characters and its unique sequence of entanglements, could be finished in a single sitting and then dismissed from his mind as Gardner moved on to another established premise and a new permutation of plot.

Gardner's talents were such that he was able to sustain simultaneously an improbably large number of these pulp serials. To conceal his embarrassing prolificacy, he resorted to pseudonyms: Charles M. Green, Kyle Corning, Grant Holiday, Robert Parr, Carleton Kendrake, Charles Kenny, Arthur Mann Sellers, Les Tillray, Dane Rigley, Charles M. Stanton, and A. A. Fair. Drawing upon letters from Gardner, Ellery Queen has compiled a summary account of the major serials attributed to these nom de plumes: "Señor Arnaz de Lobo, the professional soldier of fortune; Sidney Zoom and his police dog; the suave and sinister Patent Leather Kid; the firm of Small Weston & Burke; Ed Jenkins, the Phantom Crook (one of Gardner's personal favorites); Whispering Sands; Speed Dash, a human fly with a photographic memory (Gardner's earliest series character); Major Brane, free-lance secret-service man; El Paisano, who could see in the dark; Larkin,

a juggler who used only a billiard cue as his weapon; Black
Barr, a two-gun Western avenger; Ken Corning, the slick
lawyer who antedated Perry Mason; Hard Rock Hogan;
Fong Dei; Crowder; Rapp; Skarle."⁸ These colorful characters with their attention-grabbing quirks and their distinctive names—Zoom, Brane, and Dash anticipate Mason,
Cool, and Lam—sometimes lasted through scores of adventures. The bibliography of Gardner's pulp titles represents thousands of pages of fiction. By the end of 1925, his
fifth year of writing, Gardner had sold approximately a
half million words. His carefully tabulated income from
his writing in the year 1925–6 amounted to $5838.15. By
the early thirties, he was making fifty thousand dollars a
year, in addition to his income as a lawyer.

   Most of these works are now relatively inaccessible,
locked away in specialist collections. But one of Gardner's
most popular pulp series has recently been made available
in Ellery Queen's edition of *The Amazing Adventures of Lester Leith* (1980). Queen has reprinted five of the sixty-five
Leith novelettes which originally appeared between 1929
and 1943. Even for Gardner, such longevity was unusual.
Lester Leith was an ideal pulp hero; as Gardner wrote to
Queen, he was "a typical character *of* the pulps, and written *for* the pulps."

   Lester Leith, dilettante, has definite antecedents in the
detective story genre. At the time of his conception, the
two dominant writers in the field were S. S. Van Dine and
Dorothy Sayers. Both had introduced their aristocratic detectives in the years immediately preceding Leith's debut:
the first Philo Vance novel appeared in 1926, the first
Lord Peter Wimsey in 1927. Leith is an American Wimsey,
a west-coast Vance. Although Gardner could not pretend
to imitate the substantial erudition of Van Dine and
Sayers, he could credit his protagonist with the same
supercilious mannerism as those of his models. Leith is the
elegant amateur: (speaking to his butler) "Tut, tut, Scuttle,
how often must I tell you that my interest in crime is
purely academic? That's why I never make personal inves-

tigations. I only study the reports published in the newspapers . . ." ("In Round Figures," p. 12). He condescends in a genteel manner to the police: "Lester Leith said, in a slow drawl, 'Of course, Captain, you know this is an inexcusable outrage. I should resent it, only I'm rather tired tonight, and being resentful consumes a lot of energy, don't you think?'" ("A Thousand to One," p. 116).

The drawl is not Gardner's normal voice; he assumes it here to satisfy expectations, and the affectation becomes something of a strain. Escapism has many directions to choose from. The roaring twenties delighted in visions of leisure class self-indulgence and superciliousness; the thirties returned to a preference for more explicitly reassuring fables of the survival of the earnest. Gardner was equally adept at packaging middle-class illusions about the aristocrats or about itself, but despite Leith's long run, he was most comfortable and most successful with the latter.

If Leith's character was designed to profit from the vogue for Vance and Wimsey, the operative conceit of his adventures is derived from an older tradition, that of the gentleman-thief, a tradition which extends back to Gardner's third "indestructible" character, Robin Hood. Nearer precedents may be found in A. J. Raffles by E. W. Hornung (introduced in 1899, last appearance in 1909) and Arsène Lupin by Maurice Leblanc (1907–1925). The criminal activities of Lupin and Raffles are presumably excused at least in part by the elegance of their deportment, their fidelity to a certain code of behavior, and ultimately even to their patriotic loyalty to their countries. Nonetheless, Hornung's brother-in-law, Sir Arthur Conan Doyle, strongly disapproved of the notion of a socially acceptable villain: "You must not make the criminal a hero." Gardner's commitment to middle-class morality was no less strong than Sir Arthur's, but the demands of the pulp market pushed him into deviations. His novels tend to reflect a natural sense of the accepted parameters of fair play and decency that is neither priggish nor subversive. But for the pulps, Gardner could embrace startling extremes. Speed

Dash, the human fly with the photographic memory, invariably attributed his powers to his "pure life": "The things he did could only have been done by one who never inhaled the faintest wisp of tobacco smoke, never touched his lips to a beer glass or looked at a woman's neatly turned ankle."[9] Gardner was equally willing to exploit a popular appetite for the exotic and the illicit. He wrote about conspiratorial Chinese and fiery-tempered Mexicans, and he created rogue heroes like Ed Jenkins, "outlaw, desperado, and famous lone wolf," and Lester Leith. Yet even the latter are tamed by an eminent streak of civic-mindedness.

A summary of one of Leith's early adventures may illustrate both the typical esthetic and the typical ethic of one of Gardner's pulp stories. "In Round Figures" was published in *Detective Fiction Weekly,* August 23, 1930. The tale opens with Scuttle, an undercover policeman who serves as Leith's butler, drawing his master's attention to newspaper accounts of a recent jewel robbery. The crime was committed by a fat lady who crashed a high society party, faked a faint, and then knocked unconscious the two hired guards who came to her assistance. She and her accomplices collected the jewelry and escaped in an ambulance which mysteriously passed through police roadblocks.

Leith's first task, then, is to discover how the fat lady obtained her forged invitation to the party and how she escaped after the robbery. He succeeds in this and devises a counterplot which requires the baffled Scuttle to purchase imitation jewels and to hire a jovial fat lady, a human skeleton, and the disgraced social secretary of the party's hostess. The criminal mastermind proves to be the sign-painter who engraved the invitations and who contrived removable panels for the side of the "ambulance." Leith tricks him into revealing the location of the safe hidden in his factory, and he tricks Scuttle and his police superior, Sgt. Ackley, into believing that Leith has passed the recovered jewels to the fat lady and sent her off on a train journey. The police halt all trains and take into custody five suitably dressed fat ladies, all of whom have been hired by Leith and none of whom is carrying jewels. By the time that Ackely and Scuttle realize that the original fat lady has returned to Leith's apartment, Leith has already distributed the loot.

The plot is obviously a dense one. All the complications transpire within thirty-seven pages (and there are even subplots—the fat lady marries the human skeleton). Leith is both a ratiocinative detective (the device of deductions from newspaper reports can be traced directly to Poe's "The Mystery of Marie Roget") and a confidence man. He is also, in his exchanges with the police, something of a humorist, a quality missing in most of Gardner's protagonists. (And judging from the samples in the Leith series, one not much missed.) That the victims of his depredations are themselves criminals helps to exonerate Leith's own provocative disregard for legal niceties. Leith is a selfless villain; he scrupulously steals only from thieves, and as a matter of course he transfers his proceeds—less 10 or 20 per cent "costs of collection"—to his favorite "charitable trusts." In effect, Gardner offers his readers a welfare-state Robin Hood who steals indirectly from the rich and gives indirectly to the poor.

Leith makes further excuses for his criminal behavior. "It has always seemed to me that the best way to check crime is to deprive the criminals of their ill-gotten spoils" ("A Thousand to One," p. 118). Despite these sophistical justifications, Leith's pattern of action implies a fundamental disregard for the rights of private property. He never cooperates with the police, and he never attempts to restore the "spoils" to its rightful owner. This theme evidently appealed to readers throughout the depression, but Leith's repeated avowals of benevolent disinterest suggest that Gardner's conscience was troubled by this subversive fantasy.

Despite their irregular morality, the Leith novelettes anticipate several features of Gardner's more prominent novel series. The most important is the basic theme of conflict. The process of detection is merely prologue to the main action which pits Leith against both robbers and cops. Gardner's protagonists are men of action and argument, rather than men of detached, conclusive analysis. They never indulge in what Sherlock Holmes called his "three pipe problems"; instead they are continuously rushing into action.

This feature resulted from a conscious decision on Gardner's part. In a letter to his publisher, Thayer Hobson, he wrote: "Frankly I think there is more of an opening for a conflict type of detective story than for an intellectual type of detective story. There hasn't been any real Jack London style of conflict developed by detective writers."[10] The reference to the proto-superseller, London, is significant, especially in connection with Gardner's pulp career. Gardner was, in several ways, the heir of his fellow Californian. Both engaged in the mass production of short and long fictions, both developed a fast, efficient prose style, both enjoyed travel and travel writing, both loved the terrain of California and both operated ranches there, both championed—from quite different perspectives—the lower classes. Gardner writes most in the spirit of London when he organizes his material around a contest of wills. Strenuous competition between individuals has an esthetic and moral value in the works of both writers. Gardner's later protagonists may not defy conventional morality as Lester Leith does (with crucial reservations), nor do they attempt to transcend it as do London heroes like Wolf Larsen, but they do strenuously assert themselves against the opposition of powerful forces. If they do not break the rules, they do survive and prosper by stretching them.

The Leith series illustrates Gardner's faith in the intrinsic value of conflict: it serves as a primary source of entertainment and instruction. Lester Leith must compete not only with clever criminals, but also with the potent organization of the police. A parallel structure underlies the Perry Mason series. Mason too has two strong adversaries constantly pressing him into action—the actual murderer and the precipitate forces of justice, embodied in the police and district attorney who are determined to convict Mason's client. Leith's Sgt. Ackley might even be viewed as a crude prototype of Hamilton Burger—overconfident, blundering, indulging a personal animosity against his opponent that leads him to violate decorum, always wrong and always humiliated by the revelation of his error. Both Mason and Leith triumph by avoiding the self-defeating arrogance of their antagonists—flexibility is a necessary virtue in Gardner's world.

And both Mason and Leith equivocate their own observance of the rules. Gardner—and presumably his audience—was fascinated by the borderline between virtue and vice. Mason and Leith stand somewhat ambiguously between their antisocial and their social antagonists. Leith is a thieving thief-catcher, Mason a lawbreaking lawyer (Leith, of course, being the more serious offender). And in both series the competition and the transgressions are supervised by an impartial higher authority whose private sympathies clearly lie with the protagonist. A judge presides over Mason's courtroom contests. Captain Carmichael performs the analogous role in the Leith series. Carmichael is a "true" policeman, gentlemanly and fair. In "The Exact Opposite" he becomes "terribly upset" at Sgt. Ackley's brutality in striking Leith. In "A Thousand to One" he seems actually to enjoy Ackley's final discomfiture at being outwitted by Leith: he fights back "a twinkle which persisted creeping into his frosty eye." Perry Mason frequently earns a similar twinkle from the judge after a clever cross-examination. The captain and the judge are just and dispassionate referees of the essential conflict, but they can appreciate a deft jab.

A final point regarding the Leith series can be made by returning to the Raffles precedent. Hornung's narrator for these stories is Raffle's old school chum, Bunny. The two men share a quasi-homosexual intimacy. The upstanding Bunny worships the "amateur cracksman" even as he deplores his delinquencies, and his devotion testifies to Raffles's fundamentally all-right character. Leith adopts a comparably precious nickname for his confidant— "Scuttle"—but the relationship is inverted. Bunny adores; Scuttle detests. Yet a similar effect is achieved. Scuttles's fawning and futile efforts to betray his employer serve in some sense to excuse Leith's ingenious immorality. A man beset by household spies and in constant danger of entrapment may well be allowed an unusual latitude for action. And in the end, even Scuttle evinces a sneaking satisfaction in Leith's ability to outthink Sgt. Ackley.

There is no hint of homosexual attachment in the Leith series or in any other of Gardner's works. Although male friendships appear occasionally, nearly all of Gardner's masculine protagonists (and nearly all of his protagonists are masculine), like Lester Leith, lack intimate male friends. The loyalty of Della Street, not that of Paul Drake, means most to Perry Mason. Leith comes to an understanding with the various women he encounters (such as the fat lady and the social secretary in "In Round Figures") more readily than with any man. This is an extraordinary phenomenon in a genre famous for its male pairs: Dupin and his narrator, Holmes and Watson, Nero Wolfe and Archie Goodwin, Hammer and Chambers, Travis McGee and Meyer. Other men in Gardner's fiction may be respected and even trusted, but never embraced. Scuttle, ever ready with his Judas kiss, represents a hazard that all of Gardner's protagonists avoid.

The Case of the Velvet Claws

The purities of Speed Dash and the impurities of Lester Leith helped Gardner to earn superseller status within the limited context of the pulps. By 1932 his ten-year bibliography comprised over three hundred and thirty titles— articles, short stories, and novelettes. In 1932 he added another sixty-three titles to his record, but he also made a crucial gesture toward expanding his market by completing the text of his first novel, provisionally entitled *Reasonable Doubt*. He later claimed that the 264-page manuscript had taken half a day to plot and four and a half days to write. The novel was published in March 1933 as *The Case of the Velvet Claws,* and Perry Mason (originally named Ed Stark in the manuscript) began a career that would carry him essentially unaltered through four decades at an average of two "Cases" per year.

Gardner had not intended to inaugurate a series. Before it was accepted by a publisher, however, he had forwarded to his agent a second novel, *Silent Verdict* (published in September 1933 as *The Case of the Sulky Girl*), featuring a second lawyer-protagonist, Sam Keene. Thayer Hobson, president of William Morrow, offered to accept both manuscripts, but suggested that the two heroes be synthesized into one and that Gardner consider extending the series further. Gardner responded with alacrity, submitting three more Mason novels for publication in 1934 (in addition to the one hundred and eight shorter pieces published in 1933 and 1934). His first thought had been to replace the blatant, pulp-style surnames, Sharp and Keene, with the less pointed "Stone." "Stone" suggested solidity, but it also implied inertness, the very antithesis of Gardner's intention. "Perry Mason" did satisfy his sense of the character: "A mason is one who works with stone and, to my mind at least, gives an impression of granite-hard strength."[11]

Consistency was always the hallmark of the Gardner product. The eighty Mason novels that succeeded the first two undertake no significant formal or substantial innovations. Having dashed off in a few days a basic pattern of action and a small repertory cast of characters—and having observed the commercial success of the pattern and the cast—Gardner was content, and was able, to fascinate himself and his audience with endless ingenious, superficial variations. The first two Mason novels established Gardner's contract with his readers. They could expect not only that justice would triumph, but that its victories would pursue a familiar strategy and transpire on a familiar terrain. To adopt Gardner's baseball metaphor, the managers (Mason and the D.A.) would be the same, and though the roster necessarily changed with every game, the uniforms would not; the diamond would always be regulation; the game would always last nine innings and be won by the home team in the ninth on a grand slam.

The Case of the Sulky Girl contributed two new elements to the stereotype: the climactic scene of courtroom confrontation and, as a corollary, Mason's explicit competition with the District Attorney. The rest of the characteristic Mason conventions were conceived full-formed in *The Case of the Velvet Claws*. The central characters are all there; Mason's special virtues—his loyalty to his client and his strengths as a fighter—receive dramatic emphasis; Della Street passes through the only doubts she will ever entertain about her boss; Paul Drake functions efficiently as a ready (and implausible) source of information. *Velvet Claws* also introduces the standard energies which motivate the action of the typical Mason case: the time pressure under which Mason operates and the decisive tensions between Mason and his innocent but imperfect client, between Mason and the devious actual criminal, and between Mason and the established forces of law. Finally, *Velvet Claws* epitomizes the complexity of Gardner's plotting. As the following synopsis suggests, Gardner was perhaps too prodigal of his genius for complicating action.

The Case of the Velvet Claws opens, as do most of Mason's cases, with a client consulting a lawyer concerning a bizarre problem tangentially related to an ensuing murder. The client is, as are most clients, an attractive woman (the usual phrase is "a girl with plenty of curves"). Gardner saw a vulnerable female as the most suitable object for Mason's heroic defense. In *Velvet Claws* she is married and has been threatened with blackmail. The previous night, without the knowledge of her husband, she had attended a party at the Beechwood Inn in the company of an opportunistic politician, Harrison Burke. There was an attempted robbery, and the police took the names of all those present. They have promised not to reveal the names of the client or of Burke, but a scandal sheet, *Spicey Bits,* has obtained Burke's name and intends to publish it along with a demand that his female companion also be identified. The woman, who gives what Della Street instantly recognizes as a false name, hires Mason to negotiate with Frank Locke, the editor of *Spicey Bits.*

Mason visits Locke's office and learns that the magazine has a standard procedure by means of which the victims of its blackmail may purchase its silence. Mason temporizes, and then through a clever strategem discovers that *Spicey Bits* is secretly owned by George Belter, a respectable businessman. He arranges for Paul Drake to investigate Frank Locke's shady background, then drives over to Belter's "mansion." He demands that Belter withdraw this particular "spicey bit." Belter disavows any connection with the magazine and rudely dismisses Mason. As he departs, Mason encounters Belter's wife, recognizing her as his client. She quickly revisits him in his office, admits that she is Eva Belter, and declares that although she wants a divorce from her brutal husband, she will lose her chance for alimony if her dalliance with Burke is revealed. Mason agrees to continue to represent her. He visits Burke and requests and receives a thousand dollars to carry on his fight against the blackmailers.

That night Mason receives a hysterical phone call from Eva Belter. He drives out to meet her and learns that Belter has been fatally shot. Eva professes her innocence and claims to have heard a man arguing with Belter prior to hearing a shot. She identifies the voice as that of Mason. Although irritated by this gratuitous falsehood, Mason persists in her defense and helps her rehearse her story. They drive to the mansion, discover the body, and notify the police. As the police are examining the scene of the crime, Carl Griffin, Belter's nephew, drives up. He is intoxicated, and his car has a flat tire. He admits to being

Belter's principal heir and only friend. While making coffee for Griffin and the police, Mason briefly interrogates Mrs. Veitch, Belter's housekeeper, and her daughter, Norma.

Mason goes to work on the murder case. Announcing himself in a race against the police, he pushes Paul Drake into a predawn inquiry regarding the owner of the murder weapon. This proves to be a man who is a friend of Harrison Burke. Both the friend and Burke have vanished, though Burke does forward to Mason two thousand dollars in traveler's checks. Mason decides to register incognito at a hotel. There he meets Eva, who surprises him with a handwritten will which leaves all of Belter's property to Griffin. The will, as Eva points out, is an obvious forgery (it will turn out that she has forged the will in Griffin's favor in order to discredit the identical, actual will which she has destroyed).

Meanwhile Drake has discovered that Frank Locke, the *Spicey Bits* editor, is being blackmailed by a girl, Esther Linten, as well as by George Belter, who has been using his knowledge to maintain his control over his editor. Locke, it seems, had once gotten a girl pregnant in Georgia, murdered her, and fled the state after his first trial ended in a hung jury. Now he must embezzle money from his *Spicey Bits* accounts in order to pay Esther Linten for her silence. Mason now makes elaborate preparations to frame Locke for the murder of Belter (blackmailing Esther Linten to secure her cooperation in his plot). Locke capitulates and promises not to print the Burke-and-companion item in *Spicey Bits*.

The next morning Mason learns that Eva has confessed to the police that it was Mason's voice she heard arguing with Belter just before his murder. When Eva visits Mason and Della at his hotel, Mason dictates a reconstruction of events which culminates in Eva shooting Belter. He uses a silent Mrs. Veitch to corroborate, apparently, his account. Eva nearly faints at the accuracy of his reconstruction, and confesses her guilt. At that instant the police, informed of

Mason's whereabouts by Eva, burst into the room to arrest Mason. The lawyer hands them Eva's confession and they take her into custody. Della Street, who has all along been urging Mason to abandon his double-crossing client, is now shocked and disappointed by his betrayal of her. Griffin and his lawyer visit Mason in his office and suggest that he is entitled to some compensation for his clever exposure of Eva. Mason throws them out.

Mason now sets Drake on the trail of the Veitches. His hunch proves fruitful. Drake discovers that Norma, who has just announced her engagement to Carl Griffin, was formerly married to a man named Harry Loring. Mason and Drake visit Loring as he is packing to leave town, and they are just in time to intercept a process-server delivering a decree annulling Norma's marriage to Loring. Mason threatens to prosecute Loring for bigamy, and Loring confesses that at Norma's instigation he invented a previous marriage in order to give her the annulment.

Mason calls the police and arranges to meet an officer at Belter's mansion. There he charges that the Veitches overheard Carl Griffin shoot his uncle and that they have since blackmailed him into promising marriage to Norma. Norma, deceived by Mason's bluff, blurts out a confession. Eva Belter had shot at her husband, but had missed. The bullet had fallen harmlessly into the bathwater. Later, while Eva was phoning Mason, Griffin had returned home and, hearing of the incident, had asked his uncle to recreate the scene. Griffin then shot and killed Belter, retrieved Eva's bullet from the tub, and went back into town to prepare an alibi by getting drunk and letting the air out of his tire. Eva is released, but Mason brusquely dismisses her expressions of gratitude. As she departs, he suggests that she blackmail Harrison Burke into paying one half of her five thousand dollar legal fee.

Before examining the implications of this precipitous rush of events, a word or two must be said about its vehicle—Gardner's superselling prose style. Though he seizes upon every opportunity to compound the action of his narrative, Gardner does little to provide a tangible context for that action. Few paragraphs are more than a half dozen lines long. The events of *Velvet Claws,* like those of all the Mason novels, emerge primarily through dialogue. And as a result of the burden placed upon it, the dialogue becomes a formalized instrument designed to convey information rather than a spontaneous expression of personality. In a sense, *all* conversations in the Mason novels imitate the model of courtroom cross-examination. Raymond Chandler, a master at using colloquial speech to reveal character and milieu, makes a relevant observation in a letter to his publisher, Hamish Hamilton: "By the way, do you ever read Erle Gardner's stuff? . . . I know him very well and like him. He is a terrible talker, just wears you out, but he is not a dull talker. He just talks too loud and too much. Years of yapping into a dictaphone machine have destroyed the quality of his voice, which now has all the delicate chiaroscuro of a French taxi horn."[12] The dictaphone destroyed more than Gardner's physical voice. His prose as well has the quality of a taxi horn.

Two examples may be taken from the scene, nine pages long, in Chapter 7 in which Mason first hears of Belter's death. He and Eva are sitting in his car.

> "What's the trouble?" Perry Mason asked.
> She stared at him with her white, wet face, and said, "Drive out to the house, quick!"
> "What's the trouble?" he repeated.
> "My husband's been murdered," she wailed.
> Mason snapped on the dome light in the car.
> "Don't do that!" she said.
> He looked at her face. "Tell me about it," he said, calmly.
> "Will you get this car started?"
> "Not until I know the facts," he replied, almost casually.
> "We've got to get there before the police do."
> "Why have we?"
> "Because we've *got* to."
> Mason shook his head. "No," he said, "we're not going to talk to the police until I know exactly what happened."
> "Oh," she said, "it was terrible!"

"Who killed him?"

"I don't know."

"Well, what *do* you know?"

"Will you turn off that damned light?" she snapped.

"After you've finished telling me what happened," he persisted.

. . . .

"Then what happened?"

"Then I crept up the stairs because I wanted to hear what was being said." She paused, catching her breath.

"All right," pressed Mason, "go on. What happened then?"

"And then," she said, "I heard the shot and the sound of a falling body."

"Just the one shot?"

"Just the one shot, and the sound of the body falling. Oh, it was terrible! It jarred the house."

"All right," said Mason. "Go on from there. Then what did you do?"[13]

Neither excerpt represents naturalistic conversation. The dialogue functions as a mechanism for transmitting a body of data to the reader, not as a likely response to a crisis. By breaking the exposition into staccato exchanges, Gardner avoids the absurd genre convention of having characters deliver improbably coherent summaries of their actions. But his alternative has limitations of its own.

Mason's interjections are frequently pointless: "What's the trouble?" "Then what happened?" "Then what did you do?" (ten repetitions in the first three pages). Mason practices the art of detection in the interrogative mode. This technique may trace its roots to the model of Socrates, and Mason is surely the most Socratic of detectives. He attempts to tease the truth out of his witnesses with an inexhaustible skepticism and curiosity. Of course, where Socrates's inquiries were general and abstract—What is Justice? Courage? Good?—Mason's are particular and concrete—Where did you run? Did anybody see you? Then what did you do? (p. 60). But often Mason's questions merely punctuate an exposition, breaking it into visually digestible portions. Eva does not need to be provoked into reporting her verson of events, nor do Mason's questons deflect her from insisting upon that version. His frequent "All right's" (eight repetitions in Chapter 7) indicate that his contributions to the dialogue are designed to expedite exposition, not to guide it.

Moreover, despite the exclamation points, the italics, and Eva's intermittent expressions of impatience, neither witness nor interlocutor seems genuinely affected by the tragedy which they believe has just occurred (and which, in fact, is occurring as they speak). Both are calculating the odds against a murder charge as they spar with words. Chandler once complained to Gardner that Mason was sometimes unnaturally "pedantic," instancing his use of "Whom do I ask for?"[14] "Why have we?" in the first excerpt may be excellent, concise grammar, but it seems dramatically unsuitable. Eva and Mason speak entirely in short complete sentences, hers declarative, his interrogative. This stichomythia precludes even the possibility of a "delicate chiaroscuro."

But subtlety is not the purpose of a French taxi horn, and Gardner's dialogue does indeed effectively clear up a crowd of details. In the course of the nine pages, the reader learns painlessly of Eva's initial version of the crucial events, first hears of Mrs. Veitch and Norma, and receives a first impression of Carl Griffin. Several pages develop Eva's declaration that it was Mason's voice she heard arguing with her husband, and Mason traps her in an inconsequential lie regarding Harrison Burke. These last two episodes serve to confirm Eva's duplicity and Mason's acuity. Finally, the dialogue reveals in passing significant little facts, such as the time of the evening shower ("It seems to me that he went out to the golf club and played golf this afternoon. When did it start to rain?" "Around six o'clock, I think," said Mason. "Why?" "Yes," she said, "that's the way I remember it. It was pleasant this afternoon, and Carl was playing golf" [pp. 63–64].

The Mason novels, unlike so many famous American contributions to the genre, are narrated in the third person. But Gardner's ubiquitous reliance upon dialogue insures that nearly every incident is presented from an individual point of view. The only completely objective "paragraph" in the two excerpts consists of the line "Mason snapped on the dome light in his car." The crucial event in *Velvet Claws*—the murder of Belter—is never depicted, but it is *narrated* twice by Mason, and each narration has a dramatic context. In the first Mason portrays Eva as the murderer in order to surprise important admissions from her and then to insure that she, not he, be arrested for the crime. The second recreation—the true one—is also designed for a specific audience, Norma, and succeeds in surprising a confession from her.

The necessary settings of these verbal actions—Mason's office, Belter's mansion, Mason's hotel—are minimally realized. They suffice to orient the reader, and little more (e.g., the car dome light). They resemble the supplementary stage directions of the playwright, rather than the incorporated representations of the novelist; they are, indeed, far less precise and concrete than the scenes of George Bernard Shaw. Raymond Chandler's Marlowe novels depend for much of their effect upon the careful evocation of the lifestyles and habitats of southern California in the forties and fifties. Gardner ignores atmosphere entirely. Mason and Frank Locke decide to carry on their negotiations at a neutral site.

> The two men walked into the lobby of the cheap hotel.
> "How about the parlor?" asked Locke.
> "Suits me," said Mason.
> They walked across the lobby, took the elevator to the mezzanine floor, walked past the manicurist's room, and sat down in chairs that faced each other, with a smoking stand in between.
> "All right," said Locke. (p. 19)

The manicurist's room and the smoking stand are the only gratuitous details. Gardner's extreme economy can be clearly seen by contrast with Chandler's treatment of a similar scene. In *Farewell, My Lovely* Philip Marlowe enters a rundown hotel:

> I got out and walked back across the intersection and went into it. Two rows of hard empty chairs stared at each other across a strip of tan fibre carpet. A desk was back in the dimness and behind the desk a bald-headed man had his eyes shut and his soft brown hands clasped peacefully on the desk in front of him. He dozed, or appeared to. He wore an Ascot tie that looked as if it had been tied about the year 1880. The green stone in his stickpin was not quite as large as an apple. His large loose chin was folded down gently on the tie, and his folded hands were peaceful and clean, with manicured nails, and grey half-moons in the purple of the nails.[15]

To Philip Marlowe, a sense of place and time is crucial to the meaning of his investigation. (In the illustration cited, he is pursuing a case which leads back to the time when the hotel and its environs were owned and habituated by affluent whites.) Perry Mason does not need to be sensitive to the nuances of atmosphere. Gardner's preoccupation with the pace of his action prevents him from lingering over its surroundings. Although the contingencies of later cases forced the admission that Mason practices law in Los Angeles, the proper name of the city is never even mentioned in *Velvet Claws*. Just as he conscientiously avoids dating his tales in historical context, so Gardner tries as much as possible to avoid locating them in geographical space.

The external world encountered by Perry Mason and his clients is a deliberately vague one. It exists only insofar as it resists an actor—only insofar as it limits or determines an action. The most real portions of Belter's mansion are the bathtub into which the bullet falls, the coffeepot over which Mason first questions the Veitches, and the umbrella rack which holds a vital clue. The players and the playing are everything; the stage appears only in a supporting role.

And there is a great deal of playing in *Velvet Claws*.

Every chapter contributes new directions in the movement
of the narrative. For Gardner, fiction means action, and
action, quite simply, means motion. His characters are always on the go. Perry Mason, Eva Belter, Frank Locke,
Carl Griffin, Harrison, Norma and Mrs. Veitch, Esther
Linten—all are ambitious go-getters. They are the sort of
middle Americans, full of pep, that had been satirized by
Sinclair Lewis. Gardner presents them without prejudice.
The only division is between the honest (the "square-
shooters") and the dishonest. Restlessness afflicts all of
Gardner's characters. Mason, pacing the floor of his office
or racing to make an appointment with an informant, is a
hero of the type. Gardner's people are creatures of the
automobile age, and are happiest on the road.

They are in this respect typically American. Americans
have always taken to travelers—Johnny Appleseed, Natty
Bumppo, Huckleberry Finn, Jack Kerouac. Mason's
travels are limited to city streets (with occasional excursions into the mountains or flights over to Las Vegas), but
he too finds salvation—spiritual, social, economic—by
keeping on the move. He rebels against the deskbound
confinement of traditional legal practice and finds fulfillment in plunging into the relentless activity of pursuing
his inquiries—questioning witnesses, trailing suspects,
tampering with evidence. And invariably he runs into
other individuals—clients, criminals, bystanders, district
attorneys—engaged in similarly active pursuits; hence the
confusion of intrigues in *Velvet Claws,* the plots and counterplots, motives and countermotives. Gardner's novels
share the usual assumption of detective fiction: that the
world of human action is purposeful, and therefore intelligible, and therefore manageable. This is part of the
basic reassurance Perry Mason offered to his readers at a
time when the American way seemed in crisis.

Velvet Claws, however, suffers from a surfeit of cross-
purposes. An excess of action interferes with the coherence of the narrative. Eva's attempt to invalidate Belter's
will belongs to the category of superfluous complications.

It occupies parts of three chapters (11, 12, 15), and it re-confirms Eva's mendacity and Mason's perspicuity. But these qualities have already been adequately demon-strated. Gardner invents the forged will problem merely to color a vacant corner of his crowded canvas. Were he a painter, he would be a master of the baroque. Instead of pausing for a meditation upon the motives and behavior of a character, he simply inserts a reiteration of a characteris-tic action.

Consequently, Gardner's characters lack depth. They resemble the "humours" characters of the eighteenth cen-tury. Once their ruling passion has been established, it rarely alters. Their only unpredictable actions are dis-tortions forced upon them by the requirements of the plot. Eva is permanently a self-serving liar, Harrison Burke a hypocritical politician, Carl Griffin a callow opportunist. Eva, in fact, is typed even before she speaks a word. When Della announces her arrival at Mason's office, she con-fides, "She looks phony to me" (1). Phony she remains. Again, these simplifications contribute to a reassuring sense that personalities can be deciphered and classified.

Mason makes a revealing comment to Eva on the night of the murder as she offers him a brief sketch of Belter's character:

> "You must know that my husband is a queer man. He doesn't really love any one. He wants to own and possess, to domi-nate and crush, but he can't love. He hasn't any close friends and he's completely self-sufficient."
>
> "Yes," said Mason, "I know all that stuff. It isn't your husband's character that I'm interested in. Tell me some more about this Carl Griffin." (p. 63)

Thus Mason abruptly dismisses the matter of the victim's personality, a topic which might have been thought indis-pensable in a murder investigation. Mason's cavalier atti-tude is, of course, designed to move the conversation effi-ciently on to a new subject, but it epitomizes Gardner's indifference to even routine psychological insight. Belter has ceased to be an actor; he therefore ceases to be a suitable topic for discussion. In general, "character" in Gardner's novels may be defined as "the sufficient excuse for action." Each of the Mason novels introduces a dozen or so of these reductive "characters." Mere quantity makes this a remarkable achievement: the series offers an anatomy of midcentury, middle American, enterprising types.

The device of reiteration works in the plot of *Velvet Claws* as well as in the characterization. It can be most cleary seen in the blackmail situations listed below:

1. Frank Locke blackmails Harrison Burke (and, by implication, Eva Belter) for the indiscretion at the Beechwood Inn. Locke wants money.
2. George Belter blackmails Locke for having killed the girl in Georgia. Belter wants to control his editor.
3. Esther Linten blackmails Locke for the same crime. Esther wants money.
4. Eva Belter blackmails Perry Mason for, as she claims, his argument with Belter just prior to the murder. Eva wants to insure Mason's commitment to her defense.
5. Mason blackmails Esther Linten for having blackmailed Frank Locke and for having committed perjury at his trial in Georgia. Mason wants her cooperation in framing Locke for Belter's murder.
6. Mason blackmails Locke for the Georgia murder. Mason wants him to cease blackmailing Burke and Eva.
7. Mason blackmails Harry Loring for confessing to an imaginary bigamy. It is not clear what Mason gains from this; he holds the annulment papers which prove Norma's prior marriage. Mason does insist that Loring remain in town, but Loring does not reappear in the narrative.
8. Mrs. Veitch and Norma blackmail Carl Griffin for

the murder of his uncle. They want him to marry Norma.

9. Mason suggests that Eva blackmail Burke for his Beechwood Inn indiscretion. Mason suggests that Burke pay half his legal fees.

That Burke is the victim in the first and the last items on the list provides an ironic symmetry to the plot.

Blackmail seems to be the common currency of human exchange in the world of *Velvet Claws*. All relations reduce themselves to bald assertions of power: employer-employee, client-lawyer, lawyer-witness, fiancée-fiancé, lover-lover. Belter, the apparently respectable businessman, secretly derives his fortune from the operation of a professional journalistic blackmail syndicate. And everyone seems fatalistically to accept this state of affairs. Eva and Burke meekly propose to pay off Locke and *Spicey Bits*; Norma assumes that Carl Griffin will make an acceptable husband; Harry Loring easily acquiesces to the annulment of his marriage. Frank Locke is outraged by Mason's conspiracy to frame him for the murder of Belter, but he readily capitulates when Mason blackmails him for murdering the girl in Georgia.

This pervasive expectation of the exercise of power in human relationships accents Mason's extraordinary integrity. Carl Griffin and his lawyer naturally assume that Mason expects a reward for having betrayed his client, and are shocked when he spurns their offer. Eva too believes that Mason's loyalty can be secured only by holding over him the threat of implication in the crime. Finally, and most dramatically, Della Street suspects Mason's trustworthiness. After he demonstrates that his betrayal of Eva was strategic, not cowardly, she renounces all doubts forever:

> "Why didn't you explain?" she asked chokingly.
>
> "It wasn't that," he said slowly, choosing the words, "it was the fact that it needed an explanation that hurt."
>
> "Never, never, never, so long as I live, will I ever doubt you again." (p. 212)

Della, in perfect fairy tale fashion, is as good as her word. She too is a consistent Gardner character.

There is another significance to the blackmail motif. Blackmail implies certain reliable standards of behavior. These may be legal, as in blackmail for murder, or social, as in blackmail for visiting a club with another man's wife. In either case, society imposes clear restrictions upon the activities of the individual—thou shalt not kill, thou shalt not commit adultery. Mason, as a lawyer-detective, is a priori dedicated to a definite system of value judgments and rules of order. Blackmail, the perversion of those values and rules, reaffirms their existence. Detectives in the American tradition are often deprived of such a stable moral background. In the end, Sam Spade has only his loyalty to his dead partner to guide him. Philip Marlowe finds corruption everywhere and withdraws into the lonely integrity of his seedy office and his empty apartment. Perry Mason may manipulate—and even violate—the laws and customs of society (he too engages in blackmail), but they remain in force as a solid external context to all actions. They are fundamentally respected by all characters, especially blackmailers.

There is one final effect of the recurrent blackmail motif. The victim is usually Mason's client. His clients are always innocent of murder, but because the blackmail necessarily has some basis in fact, the client is not purely innocent. Eva Belter *did* go to the Beechwood Inn, she *has* been indiscreet. The reader identifies as much with the vulnerable suspect as with the self-confident rescuer. That the suspect is subject to common frailties encourages this identification: the players in an adult fairy tale cannot be too pure.

Blackmail then, ubiquitous in *Velvet Claws,* functions in many of the Mason novels. Criminals, victims, and lawyers are fully conscious of the firm written and unwritten standards by which the society judges its citizens. Another recurring motif in the series, also present in *Velvet Claws,* is the frame-up. Gardner usually provides his characters with the imagination, the inclination, and the necessity to invent their own fictions. As the plot involves them in awkward entanglements, they resort to plot-making of their own. Not content merely to conceal their misdeeds, they fabricate entire alternative realities. The instinctively mendacious Eva is the paradigm of this type. She tells the truth only under extreme compulsion. Many of Mason's clients, for a variety of motives, follow her pattern. A bit of honesty with their lawyer might have spared them prosecution (and would, of course, have aborted the mystery).

There are other story-tellers in *Velvet Claws*. Carl Griffin, profiting from a fortuitous sequence of events, seeks safety by arranging the evidence to point the guilt toward Eva. The Veitches help Harry Loring invent a prior marriage in order to facilitate an annulment. As part of his plan to control Frank Locke, Mason frames him for Belter's murder. The most dramatic frameup occurs when Mason reconstructs a scenario in which Eva kills her husband. Fiction-making falsifies history, but may also be a device for revealing it. In the end, Mason uses an invention—Carl Griffin's confession—to shock the truth from Norma. Much of the complexity of Gardner's narratives arises from the plot-making facility of his characters.

Velvet Claws introduces two other typical motifs. The most important concerns wills. Last testaments are naturally the province of a lawyer. Many of Mason's clients consult him initially with regard to the provisions of a will. Wills are a familiar enough device in detective fiction, providing a ready motive for murder. But in the Mason series there is a further significance. A will represents yet another exercise of power in human relations, here the power of the dead over the living. Belter's intention to disown his wife after his death is an extension of his brutal treatment of her in their marriage. Other wills—such as those forbidding a marriage or installing an unsympathetic trustee—serve the same purpose. Mason always deploys his ingenuity to frustrate these conditions. Individuals—including heirs—ought to be inherently free.

Bribery also reappears in other novels. It has two general functions, both evident in *Velvet Claws*. First it points to a corruption of values in American life. Gardner embraced this accusation with less enthusiasm than other hard-boiled writers, but the genre almost demanded that he at least acknowledge it. Thus when Mason needs the help of a friendly policeman to identify an unlisted telephone number, he secures the friendship with a twenty-five-dollar inducement. The second function of bribery is to emphasize Mason's own incorruptibility. He righteously expels the solicitous Carl Griffin from his office.

One last aspect of the plot of *Velvet Claws* merits brief discussion, and that concerns Gardner's use of clues. Occasionally clues play a central role in the solution of the mystery. Mason arrives at the truth in *The Case of the Crooked Candle* (1944) by relating the way a candle has burned to the shifting of the tides. Generally however action, not deduction, is Mason's modus operandi. Clues confirm guilt, rather than discover. When Eva and Mason enter the Belter mansion on the night of the murder, he notices a puddle of water underneath the umbrella stand (Chapter 8). During the final revelation scene (Chapter 19), he uses this observation to prove that Carl Griffin did indeed arrive at the house between Eva's flight and her return in Mason's company. Points such as these are a concession to the genre; Gardner's main interest lies elsewhere.

Two typical elements of a Mason plot are absent from *Velvet Claws*. The first and most obvious is the courtroom climax. Mason reveals the actual criminal through a cross-examination of witnesses—the Veitches—but not in the regulated forum of a court of law. The ploy that he adopts —the pretense that Griffin has already confessed— would have been disallowed by any judge. Nearly all the later novels rely ultimately upon the courtroom as the appropriate structure for determining innocence and guilt.

Corresponding to the missing courtroom is the missing district attorney, Mason's otherwise inevitable antagonist. In part his role is filled here by the police. They conclude that Mason himself has been involved in the crime and are

actually prepared to charge him with murder. Hamilton
Burger and his fellow district attorneys never go so far, but
they do regularly threaten Mason with disbarment for various procedural transgressions—influencing witnesses or
tampering with evidence. This subsidiary conflict is not
developed in *Velvet Claws*. The police are easily convinced
by Mason's framing of Eva; later they are even willing to
cooperate in his baiting of Norma Veitch.

Thus the authorities do not become involved in constructing false plots of innocence and guilt. They simply
follow Mason's leads, both false and true. The district attorney is usually more inventive. The apparent guilt of
Mason's client in the later novels results from the accidental or conspired collusion of the criminal who proposes a
false scenario and the district attorney who accepts and
sometimes embroiders it. In *Velvet Claws* the only
counter-plotter is the very lucky Carl Griffin.

The absence of these normal elements allows for a fuller
concentration upon the performance of the three core
players: Perry Mason, Della Street, and Paul Drake. Mason
establishes himself in the first full paragraph of *Velvet
Claws*:

> Perry Mason sat at the big desk. There was about him the
> attitude of one who is waiting. His face in repose was like
> the face of a chess player who is studying the board. That
> face seldom changed expression. He gave the impression of
> being a thinker and a fighter, a man who could work with
> infinite patience to jockey an adversary into just the right
> position, and then finish him with one terrific punch. (p. 1)

The chess player is a traditional image for the detective.
Even Philip Marlowe plays chess. But it seems somewhat
inappropriate for Perry Mason. Gardner rarely portrays
Mason studying the board once a case has begun. Few
detectives are less given to detached analyses of the problems which confront them. The second image—that of the
fighter, the boxer—much more accurately reflects Mason's approach to detection (and is derived from Gardner's

own character and experience). Mason continually dances around the band of circumstances which enclose his client. Provocative movement, not analytic repose, suits his temperament. He does "jockey" for position, forever driving or flying to interview a new witness. And in *Velvet Claws* he does convict Griffin and the Veitches through a sudden thrust, "one terrific punch." In the middle of the novel, Gardner refers back to this initial image:

> Back and forth, back and forth he paced, his hands behind his back, his head thrust forward, and slightly bowed. There was something of the appearance of a caged tiger in his manner. He seemed impatient, and yet it was a controlled impatience. A fighter who was cornered, savage, who didn't dare make a false move. (p. 96)

This is the essential Perry Mason.

Della Street, the ideal confidential secretary, is a thoroughly loyal subordinate. Her virtue is dramatically defined in *Velvet Claws*. She undergoes an evolution from ordinary respect and concern to disillusionment to recovery and growth into unquestioning, transcendent loyalty. Character development of this sort is uncommon in the Mason novels, and Della's metamorphosis, once achieved, is permanent.

A second facet of Della's character is her stout bourgeois heritage. Most of the featured players—Mason, Drake, Burger, Tragg—lack backgrounds; they simply act according to their mature roles. Gardner provides Della with a bit of personal history to validate her middle-class intuitions. Mason tells her: "Your family was rich. Then they lost their money. You went to work. Lots of women wouldn't have done that" (p. 15). These four short sentences—twenty words—comprise a capsule biography of a heroine of the depression. Things were going well for America and for Della's family; there was a crisis; all seemed lost; Della, with true American grit, has had to start over to earn her livelihood. Lots of men wouldn't have either. All of Gardner's fiction repeats this lesson: don't give in to despair. If the system—the economic sys-

tem or the judicial system—knocks you down, pick your-
self up and fight back: work. The sympathetically
portrayed characters in the Mason series are those who are
making or who have made their own way. If they are rich,
it is because they have founded the company, or patented
the invention, or made the wise investment. Mostly they
are ambitious young people who work in offices, pet
shops, cocktail lounges.

A victim of the Depression and a working girl, Della has
literally earned the right to speak for these self-reliant individuals. And from her vantage point, she condemns Eva
Belter:

> "I hate everything she stands for!" said Della Street. "I've
> had to work for everything I got. I never got a thing in life
> that I didn't work for. And lots of times I've worked for
> things and have had nothing in return. That woman is the
> type that has never worked for anything in her life! She
> doesn't give a damned thing in return for what she gets.
> Not even herself." (p. 14)

Thus, at the very outset of the series, Gardner establishes
its class bias. Throughout, the virtues of diligence, industry, earnestness are respected and rewarded. Della will
even decline Mason's proposals of marriage because they
would mean giving up her career as his secretary. She is
frequently called upon to express her reactions—
invariably sensible—to the individuals who enter Mason's
office. Her credentials—her middle-class common sense
and her feminine intuition—guarantee her reliability.

Paul Drake must be one of the least realized characters
ever to occupy so many pages of fiction. He has two personal distinctions: he prefers to sit crosswise in chairs,
draping his legs over one arm, and he frequently complains of having to eat cold, greasy hamburgers while
Perry and Della dine on steak and potatoes. In *Velvet
Claws*, Mason makes a point of informing Eva Belter that
"When I hire a detective, he's hired to get just one fact" (p.
5). But in practice, Drake is permanently on call to perform any task or to obtain any information. He always has

suitable, efficient, anonymous operatives, and he maintains "inside sources" with the police and the press, able to provide him with the proper data at the proper moment. No plausible explanation is given for the peculiar limits to his knowledge. He is merely a plot expediter, supplying enough information at any given time to keep the action moving and the mystery unsolved. He is most often seen reporting to Mason or receiving a report from one of his agents. Gardner never depicts him pursuing the craft of detection. When he appears on the streets, it is in the company of Mason. Occasionally he is asked to pick a lock. Paul Drake is perhaps the most artificial convention in the Mason series. For this reason, he cannot supply Mason with genuine friendship. Drake is a trustworthy accomplice, but not a rounded personality. Mason's only emotional relationship is with Della Street—heterosexual and platonic.

Drake does serve one predictable dramatic function. Three-quarters of the way through every case he declares that Perry's client is "guilty as hell" and advises Mason to admit defeat. The moment comes in Chapter 17 of *Velvet Claws*. Mason has turned Eva over to the police. He returns to his office and announces, "Now I've got to save her." Drake responds: "Forget it. . . . In the first place she isn't worth it, and in the second place, you can't" (p. 178). Della always believes; Drake always doubts: verities such as these make the universe of Perry Mason a secure one.

The Case of the Sulky Girl

The plot of the second Mason novel, *The Case of the Sulky Girl* (1933), is slightly less baroque than that of the first. The constant press of events is somewhat relieved, and a coherence of motive and action is more evident. In part this result is due to the introduction of the courtroom conclusion, which both reduces the space available for extravagant complications (remembering that Gardner engineered his fictions to specified lengths) and in itself represents an extended dramatic analysis of the preceding action. *Velvet Claws* exemplifies one tendency of Gardner's art—toward the sound and fury of constant motion and conflict; *Sulky Girl* exemplifies the other—toward the traditional mystery form involving a single main action with its pertinent corollary deceptions. In *Velvet Claws* every connection between characters was based on self-serving motives; consequently, there were as many plots as characters. *Sulky Girl* does not lack for Gardner's standard diversions: it boasts a controversial will, blackmail, an interrupted phone call, a framed chauffeur, and a false confession. But there is also a sentimental, non-self-serving, love subplot, and only one major conspiracy obstructs justice.

The victim is a wealthy businessman, Edward Norton. Norton has been appointed trustee of his niece's substantial inheritance, and he has threatened to divert it to charities should she proceed with her planned marriage to Rob Gleason. Frances Celane, the niece, originally employs Mason in an attempt to break the provisions of her father's will; later Mason also acts as counsel to Rob Gleason, by then Frances's husband, when both are accused of killing Norton. The actual murderer is Norton's partner, Arthur Crinston. Crinston, abetted by Norton's secretary, Don Graves, has been embezzling money from the firm. Through a carefully orchestrated maneuver, Graves claims to have witnessed the commission of the murder by Rob and Frances. Mason forces a reenactment of the crime in order to discredit Graves's testimony and thus to demonstrate his (and Crinston's) guilt. Two red herrings help to obscure the truth. The first involves Graves's initial, unsuccessful attempt to direct suspicion toward Norton's drunken chauffeur. The second results from the coincidental efforts by Norton's housekeeper to blackmail Frances for secretly having already married Rob Gleason.

The plot of *Sulky Girl* thus corresponds essentially to the traditional form of the detective story. All of the complications, with the exception of the tangential blackmail subplot, proceed logically from the original conspiracy. There is a single source for the death and confusion that disrupts the world of Frances Celane, and once that source has been isolated by Perry Mason, the world is restored to innocence. Frances is happily married to Rob, who has proved his worth by offering to confess to the crime in order to spare Frances. Despite the apparent tragedy of Norton's death, the novel ends with a typically comic resolution. Frances even promises to reform her shrewish temperament.

This conclusion contrasts with that of *Velvet Claws*. Eva Belter (who, as Della Street puts it, ". . . doesn't give a damned thing in return for what she gets. Not even herself . . .") was left quite alone, dismissed by Mason and facing at best an uncertain future with Harrison Burke. There are a number of unpenalized villains in *Velvet Claws*: Eva, after all, did attempt to commit murder; Locke did commit it; Esther Linten committed blackmail; Harry Loring committed perjury. Mason in each instance exposed the truth, but only Carl Griffin and presumably the Veitches, are purged from society. In *Velvet Claws* everyone except the detectives is guilty of some serious crime—the victim, the criminal, the client, the witnesses, even the police. *Sulky Girl* reverts to a more normal pattern; the sins of most individuals are no more than venial. True guilt can be purged.

In many particulars, *Sulky Girl* merely repeats the formula of *Velvet Claws*. Mason is again identified as a fighter, and in much the same language:

> [a news reporter addresses Mason] You've got a reputation among lawyers of being a fast worker, and a two-fisted campaigner. You've got the reputation of jockeying a case around so that you get in a position to give one knock-out punch and then concentrate on that punch.[16]

The shape of *Sulky Girl* may be more traditional, but Mason remains as kinetic a figure as ever. Motion and interaction are his weapons, not contemplation.

Della remains unshakably loyal, a fact emphasized when Drake exercises his unshakable skepticism.

> If you think you're going to be able to save either one of your clients in this case, you've got more optimism than I have. I just bet half of Della Street's salary for this month, that your clients were going to be convicted, and, after talking with you, I'm going out and try and get a bet for the other half. That shows how much confidence I've got. (p. 198)

Just as wicked stepmothers seem never to tire in their abuse of their Snow Whites, so Drake ceaselessly misplaces his confidence and Della endlessly proclaims her faith in her boss.

Mason's client is again a girl with plenty of curves. Though he occasionally defends a male client, and sometimes even an elderly client, the overwhelming proportion of his clientele are female and young. Gardner defended himself against the charge of redundancy:

> It is easy to say the Mason stories are all similar, because they deal with a murder, a woman who is suspected and acquitted, but you can say almost the same thing about every detective story written. . . . Perry Mason deals with the big, masculine, protective element of sex psychology. To bring out his talents it needs a woman who is suspected of crime.[17]

Gardner's modern fables are consciously designed to draw upon a number of reassuring formulas—a generic pattern of action, distinct goods and evils, simplified personalities, the middle-class work ethic. Stereotyped sexual roles— vulnerable female, big, masculine protector—are another of these formulas.

Frances Celane is good-looking and frail. And like most of Gardner's creatures, she too is subject to a single ruling passion. Indeed she becomes an extreme example of Gardner's practice of stenciling in a personality with a few indelible strokes. In the earliest Mason novels, Gardner adopted the device of teasing the reader by ending each book with a hint of the client to come (he had to discontinue the practice when his rate of production led to confused publishing schedules). As a result Della Street defines Frances Celane's character *before* the beginning of the novel in which she appears. At the end of *Velvet Claws,* Della announces the new arrival:

> "It's a girl expensively dressed, good looking. Seems well bred. She's in trouble, but she won't open up."
> "Sulky, eh?"
> "Sulky?—Well, perhaps I'd call her sort of trapped."
> "That's because you like her looks," Mason grinned, "If you didn't you'd call her sulky. What's your hunch, Della? You usually have pretty good hunches on how the cases are going to turn out. Look at the last client."
> Della Street looked at Eva Belter, then looked hurriedly away.
> "This girl," she said slowly, "is angry inside, all torn up. She's a lady, though, almost too much of a lady. She's like . . . well, maybe she is sulky." (p. 215)

Della is of course quite right. When Frances Celane walks into Mason's office on the first page of *Sulky Girl,* she has already been typecast as a trapped, angry, sulky girl.

Remarkably, at the end of the novel, she professes to have been chastened by her experiences and declares herself committed to reformation. In practice however she has been as single-mindedly hot-tempered as Eva Belter was mendacious. Similarly, Norton's housekeeper is simply avaricious; her husband simply slothful; the chauffeur simply drunken; a corroborative witness simply pompous. Crinston and Graves are stereotypical villains who, under pretense of protecting Frances, advance their own self-interested designs. One does not read of abused childhoods or environmental deprivations in Gardner's novels. These abbreviated morality-tale figures prevent him from dramatizing insights into the abnormalities of human psychology, but they do allow him to present economically plots of action that expose typical response to extraordinary situations. His characters may be easily classified, but their classes are many, and the circumstances in which they find themselves various and extreme.

A few other observations on the nature of Gardner's characters may be in order. They are nearly all independent individuals. All have rooms of their own. (The girls occasionally share apartments with roommates.) They are middle-class, or, at most, lower upper-class. There are no vagrants. Most work for a living, including the women. The men are frequently successful entrepreneurs, often inventors or spectulators. Nearly everyone drives an automobile; trains and planes also figure frequently. The murders they commit are normally crimes of calculation, rather than of passion (there are *no* pathological killers). Eva Belter did *not* kill her husband to escape from her marriage; Frances Celane did *not* kill her uncle to enter into marriage. Carl Griffin did kill Belter to gain money; Crinston and Graves did kill Norton to conceal the loss of money.

There are other repetitions in *Sulky Girl* which indicate that already in his second novel Gardner has settled into a routine. Frances pays blackmail money to her uncle's housekeeper; her father's will attempts to regulate her life. The press again plays a role in the problem, though embodied in a more respectable representative than *Spicey Bits*. Mason exploits his acquaintance with a reporter on *The Daily Star* to manipulate the public reception of his case. He arranges for a news photographer to pose Frances showing "plenty of leg." Later he issues statements to reporters which serve to blackmail the recalcitrant district attorney into staging the recreation of the crime. Mason may virtuously crush a scandal sheet or cynically exploit the legitimate press, but the management of publicity remains a primary consideration in Gardner's view of the pursuit of justice in America.

The attempt of the authorities to implicate Mason himself in the crime represents another echo of *Velvet Claws*. There the police threatened to arrest Mason for Belter's murder. In *Sulky Girl* the charge against him is serious, but not capital. Convinced that Frances has paid Mason's fee from money stolen from her uncle on the night of the murder, the district attorney's office threatens to charge

Mason with receiving stolen property. They even ransack his office looking for the incriminating currency. Mason however has cleverly mailed the money to himself, and it eventually appears that the money was given to Frances by her uncle before his death. In later versions of this formula, the prosecution's charges are often justified— Mason has tampered with evidence or witnesses—but Mason always escapes being penalized because his errancies invariably end with bringing the true culprit to justice. At the conclusion of *The Case of the Glamorous Ghost* (1955), after Hamilton Burger has departed in disgust, the trial judge expresses a common sentiment: "A faint smile softened the jurist's face. 'I deplore your procedure, Mason,' he said, 'but I'm damned if I don't admire the effectiveness of your technique.' "[18]. The judge, like Lester Leith's Captain Carmichael, is ultimately compelled to sanction the bold irregularities of the "effective" hero.

Like Drake's persistent pessimism, this convention of having Mason skate on thin ice (the cliché is Gardner's, used ad infinitem) amplifies the suspense by stressing Mason's personal peril, but it also crystallizes one of the fundamental antagonisms that underlie the series. Gardner draws upon the traditional conflicts between the guilty and the innocent, and between the guilty and the detective. Mason, however, is also locked in a struggle with the authorities who administer the system of justice. Sherlock Holmes, Philo Vance, Nero Wolfe—all express a degree of contempt for the competence of the regular police, but none of them doubts the efficiency or the good intentions of the judicial system itself. Mason's battle, professional and personal, is more radical. The adversary relationship between defense counsel and district attorney represents the basic mechanism of the Anglo-Saxon concept of justice, and it provides Gardner with an inexhaustible premise for dramatic action. It supplies him with a ready-made structure and a useful myth.

The outlines of the structure are simple. The first section of each novel portrays the preliminary actions leading to the decisive act of murder. The exposition of this portion usually takes one of two forms. The first is that employed in *Velvet Claws* and *Sulky Girl*: a client approaches Mason with a legal problem—often related to blackmail or a will—and then is suddenly entangled in a murder case. These office introductions are reminiscent of the 221B Baker Street scenes that open so many Sherlock Holmes tales. The imagined furnishings of Mason's office are far less substantial than those of Holmes's lodgings, but Gardner did take his cue from Conan Doyle in attempting to make these stereotyped prologues as original and provocative as possible. The second, less common type of introductory exposition involves a narrative of the remarkable experiences of the eventual client, with Mason being consulted just prior to the murder. Whichever preliminary strategy Gardner adopts, there follows a middle section of frenetic action as Mason, Della, and Drake rush about the city and the countryside, discovering and altering evidence, interviewing witnesses, and anticipating the conclusions of the police. This section ends with the arraignment of Mason's client on the charge of first degree murder.

This leads to the famous third stage of the Mason structure: the courtroom confrontation between Mason and the district attorney (Hamilton Burger being the most famous, but by no means the only prosecutor to lose to Mason). In *Sulky Girl*, the forum is actually the jury trial. More commonly, Mason presses his defense in a preliminary hearing, appointed only to determine whether the prosecution has sufficient evidence to bind the defendant over for a trial. Thus normally the arguments, examinations, cross-examinations, and objections are aimed at convincing the single, legally trained mind of a judge. His task is *not* to decide the innocence or guilt of the defendant, but to insure proper observance of the required procedures and to determine whether there is probable cause to bind him or her over for trial. He acts as a referee, not as a judge. And even on those rare occasions when, for variety, Gardner faces Mason with a jury trial, the jury never actually considers the crucial question. As he does in *Sulky Girl,* Mason takes the case out of their hands by identifying irrefutably the true culprit before the jury is called upon to render judgment.

This invariable rule of Mason's courtroom practice has important implications for the meaning of the series formula. Gardner is not, as one might suppose, celebrating the virtual infallibility of the Anglo-Saxon adversary system of justice. He uses its institutions and its procedures as the familiar skeleton for his narrative, and at intervals he has Mason proclaim his faith in its efficacy:

> It's the function of the lawyer for the defense to see that the facts in favor of the defendant are presented to the jury in the strongest possible light. That's all he's supposed to do. It's the function of the district attorney to see that the facts in favor of the prosecution are presented to the jury in the most favorable light. It's the function of the judge to see that the rights of the parties are properly safeguarded, that the evidence is introduced in a proper and orderly manner; and it's the function of the jury to determine who is entitled to a verdict. . . .
>
> The lawyer for the defense has to counteract the vigor of the prosecution by putting up as shrewd and plausible a defense as he can. That's the theory under which our constitutional rights are given to the people. (*The Case of the Howling Dog,* 1934)[19]

But this dialectical approach to the discovery of moral truth proves largely illusory in the dramatic unfolding of the novels.

The prosecution actually contributes very little toward the establishment of real innocence and guilt. Although officially dedicated to that end, in fact it operates only to obstruct revelation. It is, in the precise sense of the word, prejudiced: committed for a variety of extraneous reasons—politics, vanity, obstinacy—to a version of events based on preliminary indications. It remains inflexible in this commitment. Mason often scores his points by expos-

Hollywood confirmed the mass appeal of the supersellers. In 1934 Warren William starred as Perry Mason in the first of several film adaptions of Gardner novels. Here he is shown in a lobby card for *The Case of the Howling Dog*, a Warner Brothers movie.

ing new evidence or new interpretations of evidence which force the flustered district attorney into hurried consultations with his associates and panicked calls for continuances. All of the district attorneys in the Mason novels have two characteristics: they feel an antipathy for Mason, either for his reputation or for his person; and once they have subscribed to an interpretation of a sequence of events, they seem unable to alter it to accommodate new circumstances.

Professionalism and open-mindedness are precisely Mason's greatest virtues. He never blinds himself with personal animosities, and so is never embarrassed into comic displays of confusion or frustration; he never locks himself irrevocably into a certain understanding of the links between events. Mason does not, as the prosecution does, seek to confirm his knowledge of who is guilty. He admits that he doesn't know who is guilty. *The Case of the Shapely Shadow* (1960) illustrates this feature of Mason's approach to the inquiry. Midway through one of his unusual jury trials, Mason complains to Della: "Hang it, Della, I feel I have that jury interested. I think that they would like to go along with my theory of the case—only I haven't got any theory of the case, I don't dare to get one until the prosecution has put on all its evidence."[20] These agonies of uncertainty enhance the suspense of the conflict, but Mason's circumspection and his responsiveness to the contingencies of evidence reflect his essentially unprejudiced outlook. His only presumption concerns the innocence of his client.

Ultimately, then, the important underlying truths are revealed not by judges, who merely referee, nor by juries, who need not deliberate, nor by prosecutors, who adhere fanatically to their orthodoxy, but to the defense attorney, who dares to assemble the evidence. The crucial dialectic occurs between Perry Mason and the witnesses, a dialectic which occupies three stages, only the last of which transpires in the courtroom. Mason questions his client in his office; he travels around the city and the country to interview various individuals; and finally he cross-examines experts and eyewitnesses in court. The last institutional setting, with its oaths, its relics (Exhibit A), and its arcane vocabulary, provides a ritualistic formality to the conclusion of the dialectic. There is an incantatory magic in Gardner's comforting fairy tale. The unvarying geometry of the courtroom, the defined roles of judge, prosecutor, and defense attorney, the familiar refrains—"I object on the grounds that it is incompetent, irrelevant, and immaterial"—evoke a quasi-religious sanctity to the proceedings, but the efficient cause of the final discovery remains Mason himself.

Despite the significant legal paraphernalia, the Perry Mason series conforms to the essential message of the traditional detective story. Truth—moral truth—cannot be disclosed by systems or institutions. Neither the police nor the courts are capable of discerning the twists of criminality or the rectitude of innocence. Only individuals are capable of such perceptions—gifted individuals in the classical form, committed individuals in the hard-boiled form. Mason, the fighter, belongs to the second category. He is distinguished by his total loyalty to his client and by his active pursuit of all leads which might vindicate him or her. Character—quintessential Middle American self-reliant character, not aristocratic intelligence—secures justice in the world of Perry Mason: this reassuring theme has a permanent appeal, but seemed especially relevant at a time when large institutions—commercial and governmental—were proving themselves manifestly unequal to the task of running the nation.

The competition between defense and prosecution has two noteworthy effects. The first is to reinforce the importance of the counterplot. Corresponding to the actual plot of motivations and actions is an equally plausible— often more plausible—plot of false connections. The truth is opposed not only by untruth, but by anti-truth. The framing of the innocent is a staple of the detective story tradition, but the structure of the Mason novels demands a false accusation as a premise of the action. And the chief architect of the anti-truth is the district attorney. With procrustean rigor, he suppresses inconsistent indications, forcing Mason to use clever cross-examinations to expose inconvenient information.

Sulky Girl offers a prototypical example of this construction. When questioned by police at the scene of the crime, Don Graves—still acting according to the original plan which called for casting suspicion upon the chauffeur— testifies to seeing a lone man assault Norton. Later developments cause him to shift his testimony and to claim to have seen two figures in Norton's room—a man, whom he now positively identifies as Rob Gleason, and a woman, presumably Frances Celane. Mason however cannot exploit this inconsistency in court because the record of the original statement has been "lost." A newspaper reporter leaves no doubt as to the nature of the "loss": "Don't let Claude Drumm [the trial deputy in charge of the prosecution] fool you with any of that bushwa about being fair. He's the one that ditched the notes that contained the first statement Don Graves made to the police—the one in which he said he recognized Devoe [the chauffeur] as the murderer, and didn't say anything about there being some other person in the room" (p. 186). The prosecution—the government—may be as ruthlessly self-interested as the criminal conspirators, Graves and Crinston.

Mason avoids bias through self-imposed naivete. His dialectical relationship with those he encounters is a Socratic one, with Mason drawing inferences from the answers he receives in his continual questionings. Cross-examining the prosecution's witness, Mason frequently analyzes their analyses. Like Socrates, he demonstrates that experts often presume too much upon their expertise; and like Socrates, by professing his own ignorance, he proves himself the wiser man.

A second effect of the competition between defense and prosecution is the remarkable pace of the Mason novels. If any aspect of Gardner's craft of fiction has been admired, it has been his success at maintaining narrative momentum. The reader who concedes him a chapter concedes him the novel. Gardner was aware of the importance of sustaining relentless action. Regarding *Velvet Claws*, he wrote to his publisher: "I want to establish a style of swift motion. I want to have characters who start from scratch and sprint the whole darned way to a goal line." In the same letter he admitted that this ideal was "far in advance of such technical skill as I have acquired from my writing."[21] But the ambition and the self-criticism indicate the consciousness with which Gardner set about mastering this aspect of the art of very popular fiction. Only Mickey Spillane rivals him as champion of the two-hundred-page sprint.

Velvet Claws, Gardner's first attempt to extend his pulp training to novel length, does suggest immature "technical skill": the ramifying plots resemble more a half-dozen sprints in different directions. *Sulky Girl* is more disciplined in this regard, and the development is due at least in part to the introduction of the defense-prosecution dichotomy. In *Velvet Claws*, Mason avoids the formality of a trial. In *Sulky Girl*, he adopts the opposite strategy: "I'm going to force them to bring that case to immediate trial" (p. 141). By instituting a trial or a preliminary hearing as a definite "goal line," Gardner managed to pilot his plotting into a steady course.

As a result, Mason is placed in an explicit race with the district attorney. He often mentions the pressure upon him to obtain the latest information, and he demands (and receives) from Paul Drake nearly instantaneous results: " 'I think,' said Mason, 'that this is another case where I'm going to be working against time. I don't think there's any information that your operatives will get that the police won't get sooner or later. I want to have it sooner, and want the police to get it later" (*Sulky Girl*, p. 100). Having it sooner seems to have no practical advantage in *Sulky Girl*, but in later novels Mason frequently disconcerts the district attorney with surprise testimony.

More importantly, by defining his competition with his antagonists—police, prosecutors, other lawyers—as a race, Mason offers some justification for the improbable speed with which he rushes about gathering data. Even before the murder in *Sulky Girl*, when his object is only to secure the liberty and the rights of Frances Celane, Mason operates on an astonishing schedule. The first twenty-four hours of *Sulky Girl* (which technically begin the moment after Mason dismisses Eva Belter from *Velvet Claws*) comprise a sequence of actions which, when tabulated, is clearly incredible. Frances Celane's initial interview with Mason occurs in the morning (Chapter 1). She insists upon returning that afternoon at four to hear his judgment regarding her father's will (2). She then arranges for Mason to meet with Arthur Crinston at 4:45 (3) and for him to visit her uncle at his home at 8:30 (4). Mason then returns to his office to ponder the problem until Frances calls him at 1:15 A.M. to announce the murder (5). Mason drives back out to the house and conducts a series of interviews (6–8), leaving after dawn of the second day (9). Chapter 10—devoted to the red herring of the chauffeur—takes place in Mason's office on an undetermined date, quite possibly the same (second) day. When Gardner specifies time lapses, they are very brief, usually a portion of a day; unspecified time lapses *may* be very brief. Rarely are weeks mentioned; months never.

Thus the action seems to flow from episode to episode in a sort of timeless present, moving from morning to afternoon to evening to night to morning. Close attention to details of chronology is not encouraged, but, if undertaken, reveals that the sequence of action is not only improbable, but often impossible. Yet such violations of temporal verisimilitude are the product of design, not carelessness. Critic Charles Norton reports the following exchange between Gardner and one of his New York editors:

> "Uncle Erle," we'll say, "it has to be later than that for Perry Mason to have discovered the body, run into Tragg, inter-

viewed two suspects, and flown to Las Vegas and back. It'd take him that long to get to the airport."

"Dammit," thunders Uncle Erle, "you people back there will ruin my story. One thing Perry Mason has is *pace*, and if you go on having him crawl from one thing to another, there won't be any more Perry Masons because nobody will read them."[22]

Mason has to remind his own staff of this key to his success. In *The Case of the Empty Tin* (1941), he tells Della, "Speed, in case you haven't noticed it, is our middle name."[23] At the end of *The Case of the Duplicate Daughter* (1960), Mason summarizes the lesson of his career—a lesson which his readers evidently found encouraging:

Perry Mason at the scene of the crime. This time it is Ricardo Cortez portraying the lawyer-sleuth in the 1936 Warner Brothers film *The Case of the Black Cat*. The title was somewhat altered from the Gardner novel.

" 'There was only one way to go,' he said. 'If I had stopped I'd have been engulfed, and if I'd gone any other way I'd have fallen over a precipice. . . . In fact, that's the only technique to use . . . when you get in a fight, *keep moving*' " (Gardner's ellipses and emphases).[23] Mason is the archetypal American fighter, and "*keep moving*" is an injunction he follows faithfully. And his reward was that through eighty-two cases, his audience kept reading.

The Case of the Eighty Encores

The succeeding eighty Mason novels undertake no significant revisions of the precedents established in *Velvet Claws* and *Sulky Girl*. Characters, scenes, and plot situations remain essentially unaltered; only incidental details—a nickel phone call, automobile running boards, seamed silk stockings—distinguish the earlier novels from the later. This timeless quality gives the series a peculiar resonance: Gardner's craft of fiction resembles the musical art of the fugue, with its recapitulations and variations of a theme, its premium on ingenuity. Particular identities change in each of the eighty-two movements, but the outlines always remain the same. In addition to the normal cast of entrepreneurs and aspiring secretaries, Mason sometimes encounters Middle America's non-pathological lunatic fringe—crusty old miners (*Drowsy Mosquito*, 1943), sleepwalkers (*Sleepwalker's Niece*, 1936), bizarre scientists (*Grinning Gorilla*, 1952). But all assume responsibility for their own actions and the personality of each strikes a single typical note.

The uniformity of the underlying pattern of action (i.e., crisis, confusion, resolution) is emphasized by the repetition of superficial conventions of scene and plot—office, courtroom, races, loyalty, skepticism, cross-examination, blackmail, inheritance, manipulated evidence. The reader may find reassurance in being always able to identify (and identify with) the unambiguous characters and to recognize the definite stages of the action.

There are however a few minor trends visible over the forty years of Perry Mason's practice. Sidney Drumm, the cooperative, bribe-taking policeman who appears in *Velvet Claws*, is succeeded by the belligerent, even brutal Sgt. Holcomb. Holcomb, a stereotype from the hard-boiled school of detective fiction, continues to represent the police force throughout the thirties. In *The Case of the Silent Partner* (1940) he is replaced by Lt. Tragg, a far more suave and sophisticated officer of the law. Gardner shifted stereotypes deliberately, in an effort to portray the police more sympathetically. Tragg and Mason continue to oppose one another as the investigations proceed, but without the personal animosity and high-handedness that characterized Holcomb's attitude toward the law and lawyers. Gardner transferred the burden of emotional antagonism to the relationship between Mason and the district attorney, usually the apoplectic Hamilton Burger.

Gardner also acted to eliminate all traces of religious or racial prejudice that slipped into his fiction. In *The Case of the Caretaker's Cat* (1935) Mason finds himself opposed by another lawyer, Nathaniel Shuster, "a damned jury-briber—a pettifogger." Shuster, a caricatured Jew, has deformed teeth that cause Mason to indulge in some unattractive wit: "If there's anything in reincarnation, he must have been a Chinese laundryman in a prior existence. Every time he snickers, he sprays his audience, like a Chinese laundryman sprinkling his clothes."[25] Shuster never reappears, and the rest of Mason's cases confine themselves to the society of white, Anglo-Saxon Protestants.

Only once does Mason defend a black client—"a young Negro lad who had been accused of robbing a pawnshop." He obtains an acquittal in a brief, incidental episode in *The Case of the Fabulous Fake* (1969, chapter three), the last of the Mason novels written by Gardner. When blacks appear elsewhere, they are usually cleaning rooms or operating elevators. In a late non-fiction book—*Cops on Campus and Crime in the Streets* (1970)—Gardner professes himself a solid supporter of black civil rights, and, considering his uncondescending friendships with Chinese-Americans, Mexicans, and Mexican-Americans, there seems no reason to doubt his sincerity. But the early novels do contain such thoughtless clichés as "That's awfully white of you, Mr. Mason" (*Haunted Husband,* 1941).[26] Because Gardner was *not* engaged in a sensitive exploration of the ways in which colloquial language expresses character, he eventually terminated their use.

In 1945 Gardner dedicated a Mason novel, *The Case of the Golddigger's Purse,* to "To the Friends I Have Found 'South of the Border.' " In succeeding years he took to prefacing every novel with a similar one- or two-page dedication. The objects of these encomiums were the various criminal justice professionals—forensic scientists, district attorneys, educators, prison wardens—whom he encountered in his own long involvement in the field, particularly during his service on The Court of Last Resort (1948–58). These dedications stand as testimony to Gardner's serious interest in judicial inquiry in America and to the national and international friendships he derived from that interest.

The only other "development" in the Mason series occurred when, at the end of *The Case of the Lame Canary* (1937), Della Street finally persuaded Mason to take a vacation voyage to China. Gardner and his wife had made a similar trip in 1931 (throughout which Gardner kept himself to a schedule of eight novelettes per month). He used this device at a time when he was considering abandonment of the Mason format altogether. Conan Doyle waited nearly a decade before resurrecting Sherlock Holmes after his debacle at Reichenbach Falls; only seven months passed before Gardner published Mason's return in *The Case of the Substitute Face* (1938).

There is some truth to Julian Symons's observation that "upon the whole the early Mason stories are the best."[27] This is not the result of any change in the series's formula. The underlying structure remains constant: guilt is definitely assigned, and to someone other than Mason's client.

The characters continue to be one-dimensional and to belong to the same class. Even the elements of the superficial formula are the same. The problem occurs when these elements are no longer coherently related to one another. The familiar parts are forced together: Gardner seems almost desperately determined to sound every one of his notes, however discordant in its context. This fault becomes most visible when the famous courtroom climax serves no apparent function. Mason and a prosecutor run through the motions of their combative direct and cross-examinations to no end. Mason wins the race through an entirely extrajudicial intuition.

The resulting cacophony can be illustrated through a partial summary of the fantastic sequence of events in *The Case of the Horrified Heirs* (1964). A rich spinster is the victim of a conspiracy to forge a page of her will and then

Donald Woods took over as Perry Mason in the last of the Hollywood movies to feature the Gardner superhero. Here he does a little investigating in *The Case of the Stuttering Bishop* (1937).

to kill her. To commit the forgery, the conspirators—
including a nurse, a drone brother-in-law, a chauffeur, and
the chauffeur's seedy brother—arrange to have a legal
secretary framed on a charge of drug smuggling in order
to have secure access to the stationery and typewriter used
to compose the original will. They then attempt three times
to poison the old lady with arsenic. Failing in this, they
arrange to steal the secretary's car and use it to force the
spinster's limousine (driven by the accomplice-chauffeur)
off the road into the ocean, thus once again framing the
secretary. The chauffeur escapes from the car, but is
knocked unconscious; the body of the spinster is not recovered. Mason comes to the rescue in what thus far seems a
normal case—a victimized working girl, a will, forgery, a
frame-up.

The problem lies in the resolution. The courtroom
scene, occupying only part of one chapter (the eighteenth
of twenty-three), is distinctly inconsequential. In the chapter following, as Mason and Della dine on steaks, Mason
asks *himself* a formal series of questions. Inspiration strikes
at the end of the meal and Mason and Della, along with
Paul Drake, dash over to the tenement apartment of a
police informer. When the man won't open his door,
Mason calls up Lt. Tragg, who rushes over and uses his
authority to force an entrance. Mason immediately recognizes the man as the chauffeur's brother and, to force him
to speak, announces that two mob "torpedoes" are waiting
in the stairwell to execute him. The man immediately col-
lapses, confesses the entire conspiracy, and pleads for
police protection. Mason and Della leave Tragg to wrap up
the loose ends and return to their office. They find a little
old lady in the waiting room (it is now very late evening).
Mason guesses correctly that she is the spinster. She was
thrown free when the car went over the cliff, and after
ascertaining that the chauffeur was merely unconscious,
she decided to conceal herself until her murderers were
brought to justice. Coincidentally, she has chosen this
moment to reveal her existence to Mason, the attorney
who has been defending the woman accused of murdering

her. She offers him a check for twenty-five thousand dollars, and writes another for fifty thousand to compensate his client for her entirely unnecessary trouble.

Such serendipity betrays the meaning of Mason's competitive spirit. He does not stick to the prescribed course, and everyone—including the victim—seems to win the race. In *The Case of the Moth-Eaten Mink* (1952), Mason tells Drake, "There's a reason for everything."[28] The literal truth of this proposition is a fundamental article of faith in any detective story. Judged by this standard, many of the late Mason novels are tainted with heresy. The connections between events are not reasonable or, even temporarily, credible. The earlier novels then are usually the better ones. The last Mason case to sell more than two million copies was *The Case of the Cautious Coquette* (1949). But though the decline in quality is measurable, it is slight. Ultimately the reader's choice is not for this or that case of Perry Mason, but for (or against) the cases of Perry Mason. Even the slipshod members of the series—those novels with what Jacques Barzun and Wendell Taylor aptly call "huddled" endings (and which Gardner referred to as "thimblerigged")—will not disappoint too greatly anyone who has accepted the basic formula of Mason's world.

In *The Case of the Howling Dog* (1934) Mason defends his style of action:

> "We're a dramatic people," Perry Mason said slowly. "We're not like the English. The English want dignity and order. We want the dramatic and the spectacular. It's a national craving. We're geared to a rapid rate of thought. We want to have things move in a spectacular manner."[29]

Mason's adventures in adversary law fully satisfied this "national craving." His career is an argument that conflict—dramatic and spectacular conflict—is the means to the end of justice. Order in America is a dynamic principle, achieved by a community of self-reliant individuals pushing for their rights. Each of Mason's cases records a triumph of the competitive spirit.

The D.A. and the Hard-Boiled Op(ess)

On December 12, 1935, the editor of *Country Gentleman* offered Gardner ten thousand dollars to produce for the magazine an acceptable hero for a new novel-length serial. Three days later Gardner sent off a tentative outline, and on January 13 he submitted the final installment of *The Thread of Murder*. The narrative was then published in book form under the title *The D.A. Calls It Murder* (1937), and thus Gardner began his second major series. The ninth and final volume, *The D.A. Breaks an Egg*, appeared in 1949.

In quality as in quantity, the D.A. series is the least of Gardner's three principal novel series. The D.A. concept is even more tightly constricted by formulas than that of Perry Mason. A few stereotyped relationships form the predictable core of every Mason novel: Mason-female client, Mason-district attorney, Mason-Della Street. These necessary tensions are infinitely repeatable because they are inherent in the institutional premises: a lawyer must have a client and a secretary; he must confront a district attorney. The conventions which prescribe the essential relationships in the D.A. series are both too many and too accidental.

As the inaugural volume opens, young Doug Selby has just been elected to the office of district attorney on a reform platform. His position remains precarious throughout the nine novels: the old establishment which ran the small county seat of Madison prior to Selby's election appears ever-ready to exploit Selby's slightest miscue as an excuse for turning him out. The establishment newspaper, *The Blade*, constantly editorializes against Selby, and usually publishes its own hasty conclusions in a vain attempt to upstage him. An unreformed chief of police regularly assists in the effort to undermine Selby's authority. Unlike Mason, Selby cannot be readily threatened with disbarment. Gardner therefore contrives this implausibly persistent political/publicity threat to Selby's professional security.

On Selby's side—elected on the same ticket—is County Sheriff Rex Brandon. Brandon is actually an improvement over Paul Drake. He is a more complete individual, an older man, more experienced and less volatile than Selby. Something of a father figure, Brandon and his wife embody the practical wisdom and homey virtues of small-town America. Selby's Della Street is Sylvia Martin, star reporter for *The Clarion,* the reform newspaper. The emotional relationship between Doug and Sylvia seems more spontaneous and potentially fruitful than that between Mason and Della, but against this pleasant innovation stands the consequent disagreeable matter of Selby's journalistic favoritism. His integrity seems a bit compromised when he issues public statements selectively to an editorially sympathetic newspaper, or when he includes a reporter from that paper in his intimate counsels. Sylvia is not his confidential secretary, and Gardner strains propriety to include her in his plots.

Each of the D.A. novels follows a definite pattern. Someone commits a murder. *The Blade* blames Selby for acting too slowly to apprehend the perpetrator (or, in the several cases where Selby's office initially misidentifies the corpse, for acting too precipitously). *The Blade* outlines its own theory of the crime (imitating the district attorney's counterplot in the Mason series). Selby, Brandon, and Sylvia rush around the countryside interviewing witnesses until they uncover the real culprit. *The Clarion* celebrates Selby's triumph.

As the series continued, Gardner inserted two other recurring conventions. One involves the introduction of Selby's old flame, Inez Stapleton, a dark beauty who has decided to earn his respect by becoming a lawyer herself. Inez offers Selby one predictable legal adversary; Alphonse Baker Carr offers another, more important one. "Old A.B.C." is what Perry Mason would recognize as a most competent jury-bribing pettifogger. Carr is in some ways Gardner's revenge on Mason; he is a Mason with an unlocked id. Mason exercises his exciting lack of scruples on behalf of innocent clients; Carr merely extends his unscrupulousness to include his choice of clients. Though he always comes up just short in his struggle with Selby, Carr's witty self-possession makes an attractive contribution to the series.

Ultimately the action of the D.A. novels is too forced; the motivations too contrived. The symmetries are not subtle: *Blade/Clarion*, police chief/sheriff, Inez/Sylvia, Carr/Selby. There is simply no reason for *The Blade* to keep insisting upon its naive counterplots; and the abundance of misidentified corpses suggests that Gardner was hard-pressed to invent temporary advantages for Selby's opponents. The characters in short are too obviously puppets, and the action is too clearly programmed by external considerations. After completing a volume or two, the reader returns to the series not to wonder at Selby's ingenuity, but at Gardner's. He ceases to identify at all with the actors in the fable.

Nonetheless Gardner's ingenuity is sufficiently wonderful to be enjoyed as such. And the small-town environment he evokes has its pleasant aspects. His portraits of the comfortable Brandon kitchen or, in *The D.A. Calls A Turn* (1943), of solidarity of the large Freelman family, suggest a nostalgia for domestic values largely missing from his other two more cosmopolitan series.

If the D.A. books were too convention-bound to have the superselling appeal of the Perry Mason cases, Gardner's third novel series seems to have suffered from the opposite defect. The "Donald Lam—Bertha Cool Mysteries" comply with the normal requirements of the detective story genre—crisis-confusion-resolution—and they were by no means unpopular—the success of the series justified twenty-nine titles, the last of which, *All Grass Isn't Green*, was published posthumously. And, because their superficial form was a bit more liberated, they are generally better written than the Mason cases. But none of them became supersellers, and none of them are currently in print.

Gardner began the series in 1939 in part as a challenge to his publisher. He submitted the original manuscript through his agent under a pseudonym. Only after it was accepted for publication did Gardner acknowledge authorship, and he continued to maintain the imposture publicly for a number of years. Eventually he allowed the book covers to read "Erle Stanley Gardner writing under the name of A. A. Fair."

In the first Lam-Cool mystery, *The Bigger They Come* (1939), Donald Lam, a twenty-eight year old, one hundred twenty-eight pound disbarred lawyer, applies for a position at the B. Cool Detective Agency, a one-woman outfit dealing primarily with routine divorce cases. Bertha Cool, "somewhere in her sixties" and weighing two hundred twenty pounds (later reduced to a still substantial one sixty-five), is a hard-boiled, tough-mouthed, penny-pinching private eye. After hiring Donald, she instructs him to buy himself an 85¢ shirt, a 25–35¢ necktie, and a 20¢ breakfast. ("Now listen, Donald, don't you go blowing that money. Twenty-five cents is absolutely tops on breakfast.")[30] Avarice is her humor; caution is her practice: Bertha frequently complains about the dramatic complications Donald involves the firm in. At least once a novel she exclaims, "Fry me for an oyster!"

Gardner clearly intended the Lam-Cool mysteries as a sport upon the contemporary fashion in detective stories. In Bertha he proposed a hard-boiled female; in Donald he proposed a detective viewed by everyone, including himself, as "a little runt." Whenever he encounters physical aggression, Donald puts up a good, but invariably losing fight. As he informs Bertha at their initial interview, he has learned to compensate with his wit. Lam often mentions that his disbarment resulted from his discovery of a perfectly legal way to commit murder and to escape conviction. (He actually employs the maneuver in *The Bigger They Come,* and Gardner always maintained that the procedure was valid under existing law.) Lam always provides the driving intelligence of the series. Bertha may be the senior partner, but Donald is the traditional masculine risk-taker who stuns everyone with his ingenious solutions to the questions of the crime. Gardner's sport is not really that subversive.

Like Perry Mason and Doug Selby, Donald Lam conducts his investigations more through action than ratiocination. He too is a highly mobile detective who prefers to confront individuals rather than examine evidence. And he too races toward his conclusions—the police are always threatening to lift his license or even to arrest him for the crime. An endangered and attractive working girl is usually implicated in some aspect of the murder, and the characters all come from the same middle classes that populated the Mason and Selby novels. But there are no prescribed antagonisms—no Hamilton Burger, no *Blade*.

There is, however, a further significant feature of the series. Like nearly all fictional detectives, Bertha and Donald do not age visibly during their thirty-two-year career. Agelessness seems to be a corollary prerequisite of the genre, and especially of its superselling examples. Readers want first to be reassured that the world is intelligible at least to some extraordinary mortals; then they demand that these extraordinary individuals be virtually immortal. Perry Mason never acknowledges the passage of time. All of his characteristics and his relationships are permanent. His dramas transpire in a simultaneous present which admits of neither historical past or future. Imperviousness to time need not, however, be so absolute. Donald Lam and Bertha Cool do not age, but they do progress.

They have pasts. Bertha's weight is a response to the discovery of the unfaithfulness of her ex-husband. At the beginning of *Spill the Jackpot* (1941) her doctor registers her in a sanitarium, where she loses some sixty pounds. In the same year, through a neat bit of extortion, Donald becomes a full partner in the firm (*Double or Quits*). Donald then appropriates Elsie Brand, the hard-worked secretary, as his personal Della Street. Donald, having debuted as a penniless embodiment of the depression job-seeker, responds to World War II by enlisting in the Navy (*Owls*

Raymond Burr *was* Perry Mason to millions of television viewers who followed the CBS series from 1957 to 1966. He never lost a case through all the hundreds of broadcasts. CBS tried to rekindle the appeal with a new series in 1973 starring another actor as Mason, but with only moderate success.

Don't Blink [1942]). During the next two adventures (*Bats Fly At Dusk* [1942] and *Cats Prowl At Night* [1943]), he remains largely offstage. He returns in *Give 'Em the Ax* (1944), having been invalided out of the service after contracting "bugs—tropical bugs." These are, perhaps, slight concessions to thirty-odd years of history; but for forty years Perry Mason was utterly intransigent.

Two other features of the Lam-Cool mysteries distinguish them from Gardner's other novels. The first of these concerns point of view. All the adventures except the two which occur during Lam's hitch in the navy are narrated by Donald. Although his voice is not a subtle interpretive instrument, neither is it quite as efficiently flat as the neutral voice which sets the scenes in Mason's cases. Lam's asides are not strongly colored by his character, but the presence of the "I" at least serves as a reminder that reality depends upon perspective. Lam's prose has much the same flavor of the French taxi horn, but the reader does have some sense of where the taxi is coming from.

If institutionalization justifies the emotional relationships in the Mason series, it also strictly limits them. It explains Mason's loyalty to his clients, his trust in Della, his antagonism toward the district attorney. But it also limits them: Mason, as a professional, dares not love his clients (or Della) and dares not hate the district attorney. Lam is more liberated; he can express sympathy for other people, he can even experience sexual attraction. His evolving relationship with Elsie Brand grows to be more intimate than Mason's routine affection for Della. Lam's responsiveness can even involve him in peculiar, non-formulaic predicaments.

Spill the Jackpot, one of Gardner's better novels, illustrates the advantage of unconventionality. In the course of an investigation, Lam encounters two Las Vegas characters—Louie, a casino bouncer, and Helen Framley, an attractively disreputable girl who has been systematically robbing the slot machines. Louie, a punch-drunk ex-boxer, becomes a devoted admirer of Donald. The two develop a friendship that, though obviously imitative of that between George and Lenny in Steinbeck's *Of Mice and Men,* is still far more intensely personal than any enjoyed by Perry Mason. Louie gives Donald exacting lessons in the art of boxing and explicit instructions in the techniques of bilking the slot machines. Louie's detailed dissertations relate to another source of the appeal of the detective story: the protagonist's mastery of more than moral insight. He knows (or learns) how the world works. With his unsurpassed courtroom finesse, Mason is a specialist in this regard, but he never seems to be uninformed in any field of knowledge. In *Spill the Jackpot,* Donald Lam and the reader are together initiated into an esoteric field of practical knowledge.

Lam discovers the body of Helen Framley's male accomplice in her Las Vegas room, and, as his client is under suspicion, Lam takes Helen and Louie out of the city. A bittersweet romance develops as the jaded Helen rediscovers the value of living in the company of the brainy detective and his brawny admirer. But before Lam can determine whodunit, he returns to the hideout cabin and finds Helen and Louie gone. She has left a letter confessing to the murder, pleading self-defense. She says that she and Louie will always love Donald, but that they have decided to form a new team, apparently with the intention of continuing to use their expertise in slot machines.

The sentimental unhappy ending is finely done. Donald's reactions are understated; he quietly returns to Las Vegas. And then he does a bizarre thing. He proceeds deliberately to frame an innocent man for the murder not as a means (as Mason framed Eva Belter) but as an end. His victim, an embezzler whose defalcations precipitated the action of the novel and who thus—very indirectly— might be considered responsible for the crime, has absconded, and the narrative ends with him missing but marked for murder one. This unusual shift from the standards of legal justice to emotional (poetic) justice is possible only because the novel's narrator has a dramatic emotional and moral identity that may excuse his actions.

The use of a first person point of view also permits

Gardner to insert more evocative passages of description
into the novels. This is the other distinctive feature of the
Lam-Cool mysteries. Again, the reader cannot expect a
symphony from a taxi horn, but Lam is allowed some sensitivity to his environment. *Spill the Jackpot* offers a good
illustration of scene-setting at its most articulate. On their
flight from Las Vegas, Lam, Helen, and Louie spend a
night in the desert. Gardner devotes a full chapter to the
episode. The following scene is representative:

> "How about a campfire?" Louie asked.
> I said, "Someone might be looking for us along the road."
> "Yes. I suppose so. How about a little music?"
> "Got a radio?" I asked.
> "Somethin' better," Louie said.
> He pulled a harmonica from his pocket, tenderly
> wrapped his warped fingers and battered knuckles around
> the instrument, and raised it to his mouth.

Louie plays tunes which blend in with the quiet of the
desert night, and Helen leans against Lam's shoulder as
the music becomes "a part of the darkness, the stretch of
silent sand, and the steady stars."

> I could feel her steady, regular breathing, the warmth of
> her cheek, could smell the fragrance of her hair. Her hand
> stole into mine, slender and soft. I felt her shoulders heave
> as she took in a deep breath, then gave a long sigh.

Twice the "distant snarl of approaching automobile" grows
to a "whine," and headlights "danced vaguely up and
down the main highway, casting weird shadows" in the
"still warm" night as Louie continues playing. His music

> had the majesty of organ music. It was, of course, due in
> part to the environment, the desert, and the steady stars, in
> a sky which looked as though it had been freshly washed
> and polished by some cosmic housekeeper. Louie played by
> ear, but he was an artist, and he made that harmonica
> accomplish things one would have thought impossible.

When he stops, the desert returns to its "eternal silence."
Helen speaks to Lam: "It's close to heaven out here."

I could feel the warmth of her body through her clothes and mine, and feel the weight of her head settling down against my shoulder. Once or twice her muscles gave involuntary little twitches, as the nerve tension relaxed, and her body surrendered itself to drowsiness.[31]

Lulls in the action such as this are rare in Gardner's fiction. This scene, which extends for several pages, represents the extreme of his attention to the physical and psychological nuances of imagined reality. And as a result the limitations of his mimetic art are most visible. The predominance of dialogue—of information-laden conversation—normally overshadows the poverty of the perceived or felt context (e.g., the insubstantial dome light which illuminates the dialogue in *Velvet Claws*). Here Gardner devotes an entire chapter to recreating an environment and a mood, and thus displays to the fullest his craft of fiction.

Its most noteworthy feature is its utter simplicity. Donald Lam's diction in his exchanges with other characters has been plausibly commonplace: Gardner was not, as Chandler was, a scientist of slang, but he could readily reproduce an efficient version of direct everyday speech. But although Donald's account of his night in the desert is recollected in tranquility, not spoken in haste, it too relies upon an exceedingly simple vocabulary. The adjectives are both short and obvious: the sand is "silent," a sigh is "long," shadows are "weird." The fighter's fingers and knuckles are "warped" and "battered"; the girl's hand is "slender and soft." Often the impressions are vague: Louie's "majestic" music is anonymous; the "fragrance" of Helen's hair is unspecified. And, even in this brief excerpt, some descriptions consist of repeated tags: the stars are twice identified as "steady" (Helen's breathing is also "steady"). Similarly, "warm" accounts successively for (1) Helen's cheek, (2) the night, and (3) Helen's body. The two "snarling," "whining" cars with their "dancing" headlights are hardly an original device. Gardner employs the most reductive sensory language to convey his scene.

And yet the passage does perform its function. Only the critic lingers over these details which are designed to be literally beneath notice. Gardner simply achieves his intentions: he reveals that the lummox, Louie, has a poetic facet to his personality; he dramatizes in stereotypical terms to which every Middle American can relate the growing intimacy between Helen and Donald; and he suggests that there is something awesome about the desert at night, something which can be felt by the common man, if not articulated in his common language. His repetitions—of "steady," of "warm," of "silence"—suggest exactly this pervasive, unspeakable awareness. Gardner does not push language to define such experiences; his practice even reassures the reader that some things may indeed be decently left undefined. What cannot be said with a Hallmark card, need not be said. Louie, Helen, Donald, and the desert are joined in an *un*imaginative sympathy. Louie's music symbolizes this sympathy, and for this reason it should be nameless. The desert scene is an epiphany of the banal. Appropriately, the most original image in the passage occurs in the surprisingly domestic simile of the sky "which looked as though it had been freshly washed and polished by some cosmic housekeeper." Gardner's intimation of the grandeur of the Creator expresses itself not as God the Poet or God the Painter, but as God the Good Housekeeper.

Donald Lam's night in the desert, then, works. By way of reassurance it provides an unoriginal, inoffensive evocation of the mystery of existence. Perry Mason's unusual lecture of consolation on the meaning of death in Chapter 17 of *The Case of the Haunted Husband* (1941) serves a similar purpose. These occasional comforting observations regarding the unfathomable, benevolent divinity which shapes our ends extend to cosmic proportions the reassuring message of the immediate plot of moral action. More directly, Donald's night is the necessary and sufficient prelude to the tenor of the emotional crisis that follows—his discovery that Helen is the murderer and that she and Louie have run off together, each professing perpetual fidelity to Donald.

In connection with this episode, one last matter claims attention: sex, the staple of the standard superseller. Spillane and Fleming exploited their reputations for sensational treatments of sexual matters; Gardner remained loyal to the inhibitions imposed upon him early in his career. In his pulp period, Gardner once had a row with an editor when he presumed to have a half-dressed wife iron a skirt in the presence of her husband. Gardner responded to the editor's objections to this salacious incident by killing the wife off in the next adventure. In his novel series Gardner remained steadily circumspect, continuing to observe the proprieties even in the sixties. Mason, Selby, Lam, and Cool are clearly heterosexual, but never actively so.

But neither could Gardner entirely ignore the attraction of sex. *Spill the Jackpot* illustrates his typical handling of the subject. After enjoying the desert silence, Helen, Louie, and Donald settle down to sleep.

> "Bedtime," Helen announced. "Mine's the end bed. Donald, you sleep in the center."
> She moved over to her blankets, slipped out of her outer clothes. It was too dark for details, but the starlight showed the general contours of her figure as her outer garments slipped down her smooth limbs. I watched her without curiosity and without self-consciousness. It was as though one were seeing a beautiful piece of statuary by starlight.
> She slid under the covers, twisted and turned for a moment, slipping out of her underclothes, then sat up in bed to pull pajamas on and button them around her neck.[32]

Louie is "slightly embarrassed" by all this; so probably is the reader. Donald's "without curiosity and without self-consciousness" protests too much. The excessive delicacy of "limbs" and of the high-buttoned pajamas seems a bit silly.

A similar episode of very soft pornography which opens *The Case of the Dubious Bridegroom* (1949) provoked a comment from Raymond Chandler: "Gardner is well aware that an appeal to the French postcard type of aficionado is not without a certain commercial value (a matter of which he is not apt to lose sight), and he tries to get in a little leg here and there without disturbing the suburban hypocrisy of the *Ladies Home Journal.* The result has all the naughty charm—for me at any rate—of an elderly pervert surprised while masturbating in a public toilet. The poor old dear is just a bloody Victorian at heart."[33] Chandler is being rather hard on his friend, and his own later handling of Philip Marlowe's affairs in *Playback* (1959) is no less embarrassing than any of Gardner's incidental pruriencies. Chandler is correct to observe Gardner's committed subservience to "commercial values." What is remarkable is that regarding sex he pursued these values with such diffidence. Both Spillane and Fleming were to profit enormously by capitalizing on an appetite for vicarious sex. Gardner, "the poor old dear," continued to confine himself to matters of more definite morality. While Spillane and Fleming emerged as the Dionysiacs of the atomic age, Gardner, heir to the depression, persisted in an Apollonian devotion to good (good enough) form and suppressed the unruly energies of sex (and, as well, other unruly energies, such as those of unqualified patriotism).

Happy, Healthy and . . . Rich

Despite the puerility of his incidental treatment of sex, Gardner was doubtless the most mature of the three supersellers. The world of Perry Mason may be simplistic and optimistic—these qualities are the desiderata of the fairy tale, but it is recognizably adult. His characters are typical, but they are typical of the commonplace bourgeois world for which he was writing. Gardner was himself apparently a healthy and happy man, generous and open-minded, and his fiction reflects this spirit. Spillane and Fleming may be more complex personalities; certainly their fiction seems more pathological in its content. There are no maniacs in Gardner's fiction; mania abounds in the novels of Spillane and Fleming.

In place of Gardner's self-reliant, working middle class, Spillane and Fleming focus upon the social extremes— the urban dispossessed (Spillane) and the idle or megalomaniac rich (Spillane and Fleming). Gardner's people inhabit the daylight—business hours; Spillane's and Fleming's belong to the night—to nightmares, and especially to the nightmares of children. They represent a child's fears—of gunplay in dark apartments, of malignant doctors, of seductive-destructive women (and homosexuals), of ogrelike men with fat faces and claws instead of hands, even, most obviously, of dragons—villains in both Spillane and Fleming adopt the very name of this archetypal beast. And the affirmative daydreams in the fiction of Spillane and Fleming seem as well to embody particularly childish forms of ego-gratification. There is, to be sure, a sense of moral responsibility in the novels of both Spillane and Fleming, but Gardner alone acknowledges the more mundane responsibilities of adult life. Crime is a dramatic interruption in the life of Mason's clients; they never forget that routine gainful employment must be their normal condition. In the worlds of Spillane and Fleming, on the contrary, melodramatic violence is accepted as part of the standard lifestyle. Maturity does not make Gardner a better writer, but it does distinguish him from his fellow supersellers.

2

Mickey Spillane

Erle Stanley Gardner was in a sense the novelist laureate of the New Deal. Franklin D. Roosevelt's message to the nation was that the system—slightly modified and directed by a benevolent Democratic leadership—could work, that a new spirit of enterprise might yet redeem the land of opportunity. Gardner engaged himself to dramatize the same argument, taking the judicial system as his paradigm and demonstrating that for all its defects it did still promote justice—at least when the defense attorney was a two-fisted, all-American fighter like Perry Mason. The law and the courts might be imperfect, but ultimately they did protect the innocent. This unrevolutionary proposition obviously appealed to a disquieted audience, and it corresponded nicely to the reassuring unrevolutionary rhetoric of FDR.

Harry Truman and Ike Eisenhower found a rather unlikely laureate in Mickey Spillane. The frenzied emotions and actions of his fictions would seem almost antipathetic to an apparently anesthetic period of American history. The nation had won the world's war; the GIs had returned to a prosperous economy, inspired the first Levittown, and set about booming babies as the sign of the recovered promise. America was the envy of the world, and the old reassurances seemed superfluous. Not coincidentally the period marks the decline in both the quality and the appeal of Perry Mason. Developments in jurisprudence made the heroic fighter-lawyer less of a necessity. Gardner's novels continued to sell well, but "well" now meant one million copies rather than two (*The Case of the Long-*

Legged Models [1958], was the last Mason novel to sell over a million copies). The American system had proven itself economically, militarily, judicially. A secure population could surely wean itself from fairy tales.

Then in 1947 *I, the Jury* exploded upon the literary marketplace. Its popularity was unprecedented, and it was followed in the next five years by six more superselling novels, the least of which sold a million and a half more copies than Gardner's biggest bestseller. If Gardner was careful to dress his self-reliant hero in a suit of legal restraints, Spillane took equal care to strip his hero of all restraints. Perry Mason bends to his superego; Mike Hammer indulges his id. Through artful dialectics Mason forces the villain to expose himself before the convened representatives of the community; Hammer corners the villain in a back room and kicks his teeth in. Perry Mason wears a vest into the armholes of which he can hook his thumbs as he paces back and forth in his office working the angles of his case; Mike Hammer wears a speed rig for his army issue .45. These antitheses could be continued, but the point is clear. Perry Mason reassured his readers that a man might make an endangered system work; Mike Hammer assures his readers that a triumphant system need not necessarily overwhelm a man. In the first instance, the reader felt threatened by a system that didn't work; in the second, by a system that did. The specter of the Organization Man haunts the world of Mike Hammer.

Perry Mason, no less than Mike Hammer, avowed the virtue of individualism, but Hammer embraces the creed with revivalist fervor. He asserts himself vigorously in every situation Spillane can contrive for him. He defines his world through a series of me-vs.-them conflicts. Self-reliance is pushed to the border of paranoia. Hammer makes a fetish of admitting no one to authority over him—neither police nor politicians, psychiatrists nor fiancées. He is a complete anti-organization man, and invariably he beats the organization—a blackmail ring, the Mafia, the Communist Party, the district attorney's office. Perry Mason acted out the fantasy of readers who felt vulnerable to the incomprehensible disintegration of the existing social structures; Mike Hammer enacts the fantasies of those who, securely programmed into the postwar prosperity, resented the conditions of their security. Hammer lives dangerously and he takes orders from no one.

Hammer's character may be examined more closely in the context of his adventures. The character of his author remains less accessible. Still alive and active, Spillane has not been the subject of a biography, and though he is reported to be working on an autobiography, he has retained a degree of privacy with regard to his personal life. The following sketch derives from standard reference sources.

Frank Morrison Spillane was born in Brooklyn on March 9, 1918 and was raised in Elizabeth, New Jersey. He attended Kansas State College. He began his writing career by contributing to slick magazines, shifted to the pulp market, then in its decline, and finally moved into the new field of the comic book. He made contributions to Captain Marvell, Captain America, Plastic Man, and Prince Namor. During World War II he served in the U.S. Army Air Force, flying combat missions and training pilots. He worked as a trampoline artist for Ringling Brothers, Barnum, and Bailey and he cooperated with a federal government investigation into narcotics. In 1952 he converted to Jehovah's Witnesses, and perhaps coincidentally failed to publish a novel for the next nine years. In 1961 he resumed his writing career, producing sixteen books, only one of which—the first—qualifies as a superseller. Spillane's last thriller was published in 1973; in 1981 he published what he called an "adventure-detective" novel for children, *The Day the Sea Rolled Back,* the first in a planned series of six.

Spillane's first novel was neither as hard-earned as Gardner's nor as sudden as Fleming's. The most distinctive feature of his training was his participation in the engendering of the comic book. His novels transpose into literary form several aspects of the art of the comic book. Spillane's characters are designed for immediate recognition. Their outlines are simple; their colors are primary. His men are muscular; his women voluptuous. His landscapes—usually cityscapes—are generalized and are often rendered with ominous angles and dark shadows. Spillane's plots are far more complicated than those employed by the comics, but they progress in much the same manner: a Spillane novel consists of a set of discrete scenes—panels of action. Each panel is fixed against a certain background—an office, an apartment, a bar, a street—and usually contains only two characters—Hammer and an ally or an adversary. There are brief transitional panels in which Hammer drives from one confrontation to another, and there are thought panels in which the reader can almost see a cloud of ideas bubble from Hammer's head. And of course Spillane always gratifies the appetite for cartoon violence—Biff! Zowie! Smash!!

But where the comic book is an objective medium, Spillane's novels are intensely subjective. Nearly all are narrated in the first person, and the character of the narrator supplies the crucial tone of the action. In this respect Spillane is most indebted to the hard-boiled tradition. The point can be made by noting that although Spillane's stories have been adapted for cinema and for television, the adaptations have never enjoyed the phenomenal success of the books. Even the device of the voice-over fails to convey the necessary narrative tone. By contrast, visualizations of Perry Mason (on television) and James Bond (in cinema) equaled or exceeded the popularity of the original prose. Gardner and Fleming relied upon third-person narration.

The Plot Thins: *I, the Jury*

Enter Mike Hammer:

I shook the rain from my hat and walked into the room.

Nobody said a word. They stepped back politely and I could feel their eyes on me. Pat Chambers was standing by the door to the bedroom trying to steady Myrna. The girl's body was racking with dry sobs. I walked over and put my arms around her.[1]

Several of the permanent themes of the Hammer series can be detected in this opening paragraph of *I, the Jury* (1947). The first of these appears in the first word—the first letter—of the novel (and of the novel's title): I. Spillane's fiction takes as its normal voice what might be called the imperative first person. "I am" is the fundamental proposition of each novel; all other values are relative. Everything else exists as it is perceived by the narrator, Hammer. It is a felt world rather than an actual one, and Hammer's feelings are strong. In this solipsistic universe other characters tend to be realized in so far as they resist Hammer's power. None resists very long.

In this initial paragraph Hammer takes immediate possession of the scene: "Nobody said a word. They stepped back politely and I could feel their eyes on me." Hammer inevitably acts as a cynosure. Here a roomful of policemen investigating the murder of a fallen comrade and comforting his hysterical girlfriend freeze instinctively at Hammer's entrance. He will with equal ease dominate the office of an angry district attorney, a gathering of mobsters, or a United Nations cocktail party. Where Mike Hammer is (he doesn't need to talk), everyone listens.

The rain mentioned in the first sentence strikes a minor chord. It always rains in Hammer's New York City. Precipitation is an essential part of the psychological as well as of the real atmosphere. It turns the cityscape into something gray and looming, something alien and uninhabited. The rain beats against windows, splashes up from gutters, and drives everyone but Hammer and his antagonists from the streets. Sometimes it also provides an explicit metaphor for Hammer's vocation: to purge the city of filth.

Mike Hammer's very first action is also significant: he tries to console the weeping Myrna. The primary emotional force which drives the "I" of *I, the Jury* is hatred,

hatred for the murderer of his friend. But Hammer is not solely a bloodthirsty avenger. In every novel he commits himself to two types of affirmative relationship. One is egotistical—lust (sometimes, as in *I, the Jury,* expressing itself as love). The other, often neglected by Spillane's critics, is compassion. Hammer always finds at least one object of disinterested concern. Here it is Myrna, the bereaved former drug addict. In other novels it may be a reformed prostitute or stripper, or a young boy or girl, or a vulnerable old man. Hammer's sympathies are not often aroused, but in *I, the Jury* they are aroused first.

Still, the remainder of the first chapter concentrates upon the more violent motive of revenge. The scene of this first panel of action is the apartment of Jack, Myrna's fiancé and Hammer's wartime buddy. The room itself is barely sketched:

> A trail of blood led from the table beside the bed to where Jack's artificial arm lay. Under him the throw rug was ruffled and twisted. He had tried to drag himself along with his one arm, but never reached what he was after. (p. 6)

A trail of blood, a table, a bed: these are the minimal props that establish the scene. They—and a chair over which Jack's holster is looped—are the only details Spillane provides, and each of them contributes to Hammer's reconstruction of Jack's death:

> That chair was over there by the bed. . . . After the killer shot Jack, he pulled himself toward the chair. But the killer didn't leave after the shooting. He stood here and watched him grovel on the floor in agony. Jack was after that gun, but he never reached it. . . . The trigger-happy bastard must have stood by the door laughing while Jack tried to make his last play. (p. 6)

Inert evidence reveals to the discerning eye of the detective the torture of Jack's final minutes. But the point of the passage is not merely the traditional reassurance that the pattern of a man's life (and death) is in some sense permanent. Through rational analysis, Hammer recovers a crucial portion of Jack's existence, but the tone of his reconstruction indicates that recovery is only part of his task. He must also "get" that "trigger-happy bastard." The chasm that divides Mike Hammer from the traditional detective lies in that addition.

Hammer defines his responsibility in his apostrophe to Jack's corpse.

> Jack, you're dead now. You can't hear me any more. Maybe you can. I hope so. I want you to hear what I'm about to say. You've known me a long time, Jack. My word is good just as long as I live. I'm going to get the louse that killed you. He won't sit in the chair. He won't hang. He will die exactly as you died, with a .45 slug in the gut, just a little below the belly button. No matter who it is, Jack, I'll get the one. Remember, no matter who it is, I promise. (p. 8)

The traditional detective was content to discover truth. He allowed society—the police and the courts—to act upon the truth. Hammer, the anti-organization man, takes both obligations upon himself. Revelation and retribution are indivisible: the passion which drives him to seek the killer also compels him to kill the killer.

The ultimate embodiment of social organization in the world of the detective is the jury. The jury represents the Anglo-Saxon conviction that twenty-four eyes see more clearly than two. Perry Mason is something of an organization man manqué. He regularly affirms the clear-sightedness of the jury, but he always avoids resting his client's fate upon the jury's vision. Mike Hammer begins his career by stating his simple and absolute rejection of the principle of achieving justice through the jury system:

> A jury is cold and impartial like they're supposed to be, while some snotty lawyer makes them pour tears as he tells them how his client was insane at the moment or had to shoot in self-defense. Swell. The law is fine. But this time I'm the law and I'm not going to be cold and impartial. I'm going to remember all those things. (p. 7)

The passionate individual speaks against the dispassionate organization.

Spillane has been mocked for the apparent contradiction of the emotional weeping of a cold, impartial jury. In his rushes of emotion, Hammer is quite capable of chopping logic and acting on unfounded associations rather than proceeding according to irrefutable arguments. But his meaning here makes sense. A jury responds sympathetically to the present sufferings of the defendant; it remains emotionally ignorant of the past sufferings of the decedent. Hammer—or a prosecutor—can reconstruct the events of Jack's death, but they cannot convey the pain implied in those events. "Nobody in the box would know how it felt to be dying or have your killer laugh in your face." (p. 7) Hammer is a precocious advocate of "victim's rights."

I, the Jury is in many ways a homage to Dashiell Hammett's *The Maltese Falcon.* In both novels the detective loses a friend and then discovers that the woman he loves is the killer. But although in the end Sam Spade remains loyal to the memory of his partner, his relationship with Miles Archer—that "louse"—differs radically from that of Hammer and Jack. Spade, a much more complex character, can adopt a pose of cynical detachment; Hammer's outburst in Chapter 1 inaugurates a career of unswerving emotional engagements. "I'm going to remember all those things." "Those things" are the pains suffered by Jack (or by one of a succession of friends or objects of pity). Hammer kills because he, unlike a jury, knows what it feels like to die.

The last important element introduced in the first chapter of *I, the Jury* is Hammer's relationship with Pat Chambers, the police captain. Chambers epitomizes the organization man, and Hammer forcefully distinguishes the two approaches to criminal investigation:

> You're a cop, Pat. You're tied down by rules and regulations. There's someone over you. I'm alone. I can slap someone in the puss and they can't do a damn thing. No one can kick me out of my job. Maybe there's nobody to put up a fuss if I get gunned down, but then I still have a

private cop's license with the privilege to pack a rod, and they're afaid of me. I hate hard, Pat. (p. 8)

The private individual thus has two advantages: he is free from organizational restraints ("You have to follow the book because you're a Captain of Homicide," [p. 8]) and his motivation is entirely personal ("I hate hard"). Nonetheless, even the most defiantly individualistic of detectives needs access to official information. Pat Chambers, a personal friend and a police captain, mediates between Hammer and the organization.

But Chambers is more than a friend and a source of information; he is also a competitor. Hammer announces, "From now on it's a race," and Pat accepts the challenge (p. 6). He wants the killer too: "I'll be trying to beat you to him. We have every scientific facility at our disposal and a lot of men to do the leg work. We're not short in brains, either" (p. 11). The individual vs. the organization: Spillane sets up for Hammer the same situation in which Gardner placed Mason. Both protagonists view themselves as contestants in a race. If Sherlock Holmes arrived at the solution of a problem before Inspector Lestrade, it was because he saw things more clearly than the representative of Scotland Yard, not because he had outrun the inspector. The metaphor of a race would not have occurred to him. Hammer and Mason view themselves as sprinters. Getting the answers first is for them a priority, and they are not always scrupulous about how they get them. This premise of the race helps to justify the improbably fast pace of the action in the novels of both Spillane and Gardner.

Spillane apparently composed as rapidly as Hammer investigated. (He boasts of requiring between three days and two weeks to complete a novel.) His solecisms are often held against him, but they rarely obstruct the momentum of his prose. He may use "duplicity" when he means "complicity," but such errors should give pause to few readers, and they need not be dwelt upon. A single, amusing example of Spillane's carelessness appears in the first chapter of *I, the Jury*, and it may serve to epitomize this aspect of his art. Hammer asks about the time of Jack's death. Pat Chambers replies: "The coroner places it about five hours before I got here. That would make it about three fifteen. When I get an autopsy report we may be able to narrow it down even further" (p. 10).

Chapter 1 is devoted to establishing the race and the runners; Chapter 2 outlines the course—the cast of suspects that Hammer and Chambers must cover. The scene is Hammer's office in the Hackard Building—"my sanctum sanctorum"—and it introduces Hammer's tough, voluptuous, virginal secretary, Velda. Velda, who holds her own P.I. license, is at once more independent and more dependent than Della Street. She frequently participates in the violent actions of the narratives, but she is also sexually spellbound by her boss. Although Della was a devoted accomplice, rarely acting in Mason's absence or without his instructions, she also preserved a sense of her integrity as a working woman. Velda does more, but would eagerly marry Mike and do nothing. In *I, the Jury* her hair is "coal-black" ("titian" in *The Body Lovers* [1967] and "auburn" in *Survival: Zero* [1970]) and "long in a page-boy cut." This cut, combined with her toughness and her training, is the first slight sign of sexual ambiguity in the Hammer novels. Mike Hammer's women always have prominent busts, but they are often—in one instance incredibly—masculine in their other attributes.

Though the office scene presumably takes place little more than five hours after the early morning murder, Velda has already managed to assemble dossiers on the principal suspects. The previous night Jack had held a party for "a group of old friends he knew before the army" (p. 9). Despite his claim that "Jack was about the best friend I ever had" (p. 7), Hammer needs Velda to brief him on Jack's strange collection of friends: Myrna, Jack's fiancée; Hal Kines, a medical student; the Bellemy twins, Mary and Esther, wealthy heiresses; George Kalecki, a reformed bootlegger; and Charlotte Manning, a gorgeous blonde psychiatrist with "breasts that jutted out," a muscu-

lar stomach, and a suggestive last name. Velda expresses some jealousy at Hammer's reaction to Charlotte's photograph.

In Jack's apartment Hammer had concentrated upon his personal desire for revenge. In his office he expands his warrant for action.

> After the war I've been almost anxious to get some of the rats that make up the section of humanity that prey on people. People. How incredibly stupid they could be sometimes. A trial by law for a killer. A loophole in the phrasing that lets a killer crawl out. But in the end the people have their justice. They get it through guys like me once in a while. (p. 16)

Hammer is contemptuous of "the people," but it is in their name that he undertakes his bloody purges. Perry Mason viewed the law as the ultimate protector of the innocent; Mike Hammer sees it as the last refuge of the guilty: the difference between these two perspectives defines the essential difference between the two protagonists and the messages they carried to their audiences.

Hammer also emphasizes a secondary aspect of his personal motivation. He has made a promise to Jack's corpse (already published in the morning newspaper). Keeping his word thus supplements a desire for revenge. The chapter ends with a transitional panel in which Hammer bets Velda ("a sandwich against a marriage license") that the police will be following them when they leave the office. He consumes his sandwich in an automat.

The third chapter opens at George Kalecki's country house in Westchester county. Hammer questions Kalecki about the time that he and Hal Kines returned to the house after leaving Jack's party. He then issues a blanket threat: "Before I'm done I may shoot up a lot of snotty punks like you, but you can bet that one of them will have been the one I was after, and as for the rest, tough luck. They got their noses a little too dirty" (p. 20). Hal Kines enters and attempts to ambush Hammer; Hammer knocks him unconscious. Pat Chambers arrives and ignores

Kalecki's demand that Hammer be arrested for assault. Hammer then delivers a sucker punch that leaves Kalecki "vomiting his lungs out" and departs with his pal Chambers. Kalecki had forgotten that Jack was former cop.

Hammer and Chambers drive back into the city and meet in Chamber's office to discuss the case over bourbon. Chambers recounts Myrna's past as an addict and Jack's unsuccessful endeavor to break the drug ring which had supplied her. Hammer speculates on the possible classifications of murder: "There are only a few. War, Passion, Self-Protection, Insanity, Profit and Mercy Killings. There are some others, but these are enough." He somehow intuits that only profit and self-protection are admissible in the present case, and then logically excludes profit. "The killer knew that Jack had some poop which would mean exposure or worse. To protect himself, the killer knocked Jack off." Hammer's self-confidence is breathtaking. Even if his classification of murder were exhaustive, he could not possibly eliminate insanity or passion. Similarly there is no justification for his assumption that the killer must have been a party-goer. Arbitrary (and correct) exclusions of this sort recur frequently in the "logic" of the novel. Hammer is a hero of the will, not of the intellect. He seems often to will the solution of his immediate problem. That his assertions are sometimes disguised as argument or dialogue cannot conceal their basically irrational character.

Chapter 4 belongs to Charlotte Manning. The first part involves an interview at her office. Charlotte's receptionist finds Hammer's unshaven, wrinkled appearance repulsive; Charlotte responds more favorably. She has read Hammer's "promise" to Jack, and despite the probable disapproval of her former professors, she endorses it. " 'I understand,' she remarked. 'To a man friendship is a much greater thing than to a woamn'" (p. 34). She "sincerely" hopes that Hammer catches the man who killed Jack. The remainder of the chapter carries Hammer to Charlotte's apartment, where he and Chambers corroborate her alibi and obtain the information about her door-

bell that will eventually enable them to invalidate that alibi.

The fifth chapter begins with Mike and Chambers sharing a beer in a deli. Chambers reports that George Kalecki was shot at "late last night." The time scheme becomes a bit confused here, because this is still apparently the afternoon of the day on which Jack was shot. Like Gardner, Spillane maintains the pace of his narrative at the cost of exact chronology. Hammer proceeds to break into Kalecki's Manhattan apartment to search for evidence. Kalecki and Kines find him there and, though outraged, submit to further questioning. Hammer then visits the Bellemy apartment in the same building.

The athletic Mary Bellemy invites him in, answers his questions, excuses herself to take a bath, and returns in "a sheer pink negligee." She too has a noteworthy abdomen: "What I could see of her stomach was smooth parallel rows of light muscles, almost like a man's" (p. 47). Hammer kisses her, then flips open the negligee. In doing so, he makes an unusually aggressive sexual gesture. Normally Hammer's women strip themselves entirely for his benefit while he observes from a distance. Even here, Mary has invited the gesture, and to her obvious dismay Hammer does nothing more than look.

Hammer returns to his office and reviews the case (Chapter 6). He reiterates his commitment to the race. All his suspects remain viable. He decides to investigate Kalecki's underworld connections, and this leads to a typical Spillane scene at the Hi-Ho Club, a black bar run by Big Sam. Hammer learns from Big Sam that Kalecki is still active in the numbers racket. He then goes into a back room to talk to Bobo Hopper, a mentally retarded youth and sometime numbers runner. Bobo provides Hammer with another object of compassion. Hammer explains Bobo's condition as "an example of what environment can do to a man" (p. 53), but he never extends this unexpected sociological observation to the case of criminals. Environment explains; it cannot excuse.

Directly juxtaposed to Hammer's gentle treatment of

Bobo Hopper is his reaction to the two knife-wielding thugs who break into the back room. The scene is touched by the casual racism endemic in the tough-guy fiction of the thirties and forties. One of the attackers is "coal black," the other "high yellow." Hammer refers to "dinges" and "bogies," but neither here nor elsewhere is racial animus a primary consideration. Hammer is never one to mince his prejudices (e.g., against homosexuals or communists); his relative indifference to race seems almost decent.

The main purpose of the scene in the back room of the Hi-Ho Club is to provide Hammer with a justifiable opportunity to commit mayhem. One passage may be cited at length to illustrate Spillane's infamous attention to the details of physical mutilation:

> The knife came out again and this time I got the hand in a wristlock and twisted. The tendons stretched, and the bones snapped sickeningly. The high yellow let out a scream and dropped the knife. I was on my feet in a flash. The big black buck was up and came charging into me, his head down.
>
> There was no sense to busting my hand on his skull, so I lashed out with my foot and the toe of my shoe caught the guy right in the face. He toppled over sideways, still running, and collapsed against the wall. His lower teeth were protruding through his lip. Two of his incisors were lying beside his nose, plastered there with blood.
>
> The high yellow was holding his broken wrist in one hand, trying to get to his feet. I helped him. My hand hooked in his collar and dragged him up. I took the side of my free hand and smashed it across his nose. The bone shattered and blood poured out. (pp. 56–7)

That final blow is completely gratuitous, but the broken teeth and the smashed nose are Spillane trademarks. Spillane's heroes do much of their fighting with their shoes and their knees. Their targets are invariably the faces and the groins of their opponents: their aim seems always to extinguish the identity and/or the manhood of the enemy. Hammer deliberately destroys the character of the "high yellow": "That guy probably was a lady killer in Harlem, but them days were gone forever" (p. 57).

Hammer's victory is complete, but it is also utterly pointless. The two blacks are never implicated in any aspect of the investigation into Jack's death. Their attack on Hammer is merely a bit of the random brutality that pervades his world. Hammer follows his triumph with a brief stop at his apartment for a shower and a shave, then he returns to Charlotte's apartment. It is 6:00 P.M., presumably of the first day.

Charlotte and Hammer engage in a long exchange that serves two purposes. The first is to establish solidly the romantic relationship between them. In order to distinguish the love he shares with Charlotte from the sexual liaisons he enjoys with women like Mary Bellemy, Hammer insists upon keeping the relationship pure. He declines Charlotte's explicit invitations and promises her fulfillment on their wedding night. That Charlotte eventually reveals herself to be a murderous man-hater doubtless explains Hammer's instinctive refusal to taint himself with her flesh.

The second purpose of the episode is to amplify Hammer's heroism further. Bobo and Big Sam have both been impressed by Hammer's physical power ("Gee, Mike, you're pretty tough. Wish I was like that" [p. 57]); Charlotte, the psychiatrist, now expresses awe at his mental power. After studying his record she has concluded: "I saw a man who was used to living and could make life obey the rules he set down. Your body is huge, your mind is the same. No repressions" (p. 61). This is the basis of his attraction for her. She has seen professionally too many pitiful, weak, repressed non-men. These of course are the neutered organization men who do "obey the rules." Hammer by contrast is the "real man" who makes his own rules. Charlotte tries to help Mike by reviewing with him the list of suspects, but she admits that "The discovery of murderers and motives belongs to more astute minds than mine" (p. 63).

The next chapter advances the plot. After a night of sleep (at last), Hammer breaks into Jack's sealed apartment and discovers his hidden notebook. He and Velda decipher a reference to a brothel, and to Velda's horror, Hammer proposes to investigate.

The business of the brothel—Chapter 8—is a complicated one. Jack had apparently discovered that a young prostitute, Eileen Vickers (now going under the alias of Mary Wright), had been seduced into the trade by a nefarious scheme operated by Hal Kines. Kines is not the young collegian he seems to be, as Hammer proves by following a trail of yearbooks from Jack's apartment to Times Square to the Public Library. In fact, Kines has made a career of attending colleges, getting beautiful coeds pregnant, and turning them over to a prostitution ring. By the time Hammer understands the operation and returns to the brothel with Pat Chambers, both Eileen Vickers and Hal Kines have been murdered in Eileen's room. The variety of the brothel's patrons allows Hammer to denounce the hypocrites: celebrities, politicians, "rich jokers," "fat greasy people from out of town." The case of Eileen Vickers, abandoned by her puritanical father, gives Hammer yet another object for compassion. And finally the occasion also provokes a brief homily on the dangers of venereal disease.

As the action accelerates, the chapters begin to divide into more panels. Chapter 8 requires six: the brothel (questioning Eileen), Hammer's automobile (meditation), Jack's apartment, a Times Square bookstore, the Public Library, and the brothel again. Chapter 9 employs comparable units. It opens with the results of the raid on the brothel. The murderer has escaped. Hammer returns to his apartment for another night's sleep (panel 2). The following morning, after stopping by Kalecki's empty apartment (panel 3), Hammer meets Charlotte in Central Park (panel 4). Kalecki fires a gun at them from a passing car, but Hammer's reflexes save them. He escorts Charlotte back to her apartment (panel 5). He enters her bedroom, discovers her naked, and embraces her. The embrace hurts her, but she doesn't pull away. He refuses another invitation ("No, darling, it's too beautiful to spoil. Not now. Our time will come, but it must be right" (p. 103)— Hammer is speaking). Hammer drives her to her office; then, on his way to meet Pat, runs briefly into Bobo Hopper (panel 6).

The scene in Charlotte's apartment gives Hammer yet another opportunity to review his case. These recapitulations are necessary in part because there is so little obvious direction to his "investigation." Not only are his strategies generally ad hoc, they frequently result in action that is violent but inconsequential. Hammer's reviews provide the illusion of coherence, an illusion that is sometimes weak. Charlotte asks Hammer how Jack could have known that Hal Kines would visit Eileen that night. And how could he have known that the killer (of Hal and Eileen) would be there? "Sounds sort of scrambled, doesn't it?" comments Charlotte. "You're not kidding," replies Hammer. "But as the plot thickens it thins out, too" (p. 106). It thins out because the suspects, one by one, beginning with Hal Kines, are killed off. The rationale of Hammer's investigation seems almost to parody the traditional "process of elimination." The answers Hammer finally provides to Charlotte's questions are barely credible. After killing Jack, Charlotte realized that she had to kill Hal Kines because Eileen might expose Kines who would then expose Charlotte. So she sent Kines to kill Eileen, killed both Kines and Eileen, and escaped fortuitously by following the brothel madam through a hidden exit.

Chapter 10 opens with Hammer and Chambers questioning the madam. She describes the hidden exit, but denies that she was accompanied in her escape. (Charlotte evidently happened upon the door a moment before it automatically closed behind the madam. "The killer had a little luck," observes Mike [p. 114]). After revisiting the brothel, Hammer returns to his apartment to fix himself dinner. He then calls again at the Bellemy apartment, receives an invitation to a party to be held at their country club, and submits to being seduced by Mary. Just as the Hi-Ho Club incident typifies Spillane violence, so Hammer's encounter with Mary typifies Spillane sex. Charlotte diagnoses Mary as a pathological nymphomaniac, but her sexual appetite is shared by most Spillane women. She flaunts her body—especially her breasts; she puts her arms around Hammer; she pulls his mouth close to hers.

> Her mouth met mine, her arms getting tighter behind me. I leaned on her heavily, letting my body caress hers. She rubbed her face against mine, breathing hotly on my neck. Whenever I touched her she trembled. She worked a hand free and I heard snaps on her dress opening. I kissed her shoulders, the tremble turned into a shudder. Once she bit me, her teeth sinking into my neck. I held her tighter and her breathing turned into a gasp. She was squirming against me, trying to release the passion that was inside her.
>
> My hand found the pull cord on the lamp beside the divan and the place was in darkness. Just the two of us. Little sounds. No words. There wasn't need of any. A groan once or twice. The rustle of the cushions and the rasping sound of fingernails on broadcloth. The rattle of a belt buckle and the thump of a shoe kicked to the floor. Just the breathing, the wetness of a kiss.
>
> Then silence. (pp. 118–19)

Hammer is the passive object of passion. He leans, lets, touches, hears. She meets, rubs, trembles, works, bites, squirms. In part his passivity serves to elevate Hammer. Women instinctively desire him. In part, his ability to conquer without action or design relieves him of moral responsibility for the consequences of his conquest. He owes Mary Bellemy no more than a night of pleasure.

Spillane treats the actual lovemaking rather coyly. Hammer and Mary exchange pain—bites and squeezes— and then turn off the lamp. Such exchanges usually accompany sex in Spillane's fiction. Pain seems to be one proof of passion. And such discretion usually characterizes the treatment of the act of love itself. Spillane reports the soft pornography of foreplay, but leaves unspecified the details of climax. A discreet curtain of darkness and silence preserves the decencies.

Hammer leaves the Bellemy apartment and returns to his own. Again he reviews his diminished list of suspects. His attention focuses upon George Kalecki. In the middle of the night he decides to race upstate to Parksdale, the location of the college where Hal Kines had most recently been enrolled. He intimidates a dean of men ("His face had gone pasty white and he looked ready to faint" [p. 122]), rushes over to Kines's dormitory, fires through his window, and kills Kalecki. The plot grows thinner.

As easily as he had overwhelmed the dean, Hammer commands the obedience of the students and of the irate chief of the county police ("after a demonstration of arm waving, shouting and bulldozing of which I did not think myself capable, he retreated hastily and just as promptly unarrested me" [p. 126]). Organization men of all sorts collapse before Hammer's manifest personal authority. Hammer discovers that Kalecki had been burning papers. A scrap reveals that in addition to working his prostitution scam, Hal Kines had also operated a blackmailing syndicate and that Kalecki had been one of his victims (Chapter 11). Hammer drives back to the city, meets briefly with Pat Chambers, then visits Charlotte. After giving her a report on his activities, he falls asleep. He awakens at 4:00 P.M. (fourth day), eats breakfast, skims a book on hypnotism from Charlotte's shelf, and visits a barber for a trim. He hears police sirens; on a "hunch" he follows them to a street where the body of Bobo Hopper lies. Bobo had been gunned down while carrying a prescription box containing heroin. Pat Chambers informs Hammer that a number of prominent citizens currently undergoing drug rehabilitation had received their supplies from "a half-witted little guy"—Bobo. Hammer reminds Chambers that they are still in a race to get the killer, then he returns to Charlotte's apartment to retrieve the wallet he had left behind.

Chapter 12 is devoted primarily to the party at the Bellemy estate, but it begins with a series of transitional panels that sustain the impression of continuous activity. Hammer visits his tailor, returns home for a meal and a shower, escorts Charlotte to a movie ("a fantastic murder mystery that had more holes in it than a piece of swiss cheese," [p. 140]) and then to a bar. There, after declaring that no wife of his will have a profession outside the house, he formally proposes marriage and Charlotte accepts. Hammer knocks unconscious two "wise guys" who presume to leer at his fiancée as he escorts her home. He resists another offer for a preview of the wedding night and returns to his apartment to sleep.

The next day (the fifth) he wakes up, showers, and fries himself some potatoes because a mouse has chewed its way into his only box of cereal. Spillane regularly inserts these domestic interludes—meals and showers particularly—in order to anchor the frenzy of his plots in the routines of ordinary life. Dealing with animal functions—they never record his reading, for example—they serve to make Hammer's physical presence more concrete.

Hammer drives Myrna up to the Bellemy estate. He reveals further elements of his character: he refuses to undress in front of Mary Bellemy in the daylight; he literally pours out his contempt on a pair of "pansies"; he allows Mary to seduce him again by leading him into the woods and taking off her clothes. The important action occurs when Hammer returns from the seduction to find that Myrna has been murdered in a cloakroom. The plot is now about as thin as it can get. Jack, Hal Kines, Eileen, George Kalecki, and Myrna (and Bobo Hopper) have all been murdered. Of the potential suspects, only Charlotte and Mary survive (Esther Bellemy has never really been a factor), and Mary was with Hammer at the time of Myrna's death. Pat Chambers arrives with the homicide squad. The police collect everyone's alibi. Hammer notices some white powder beside Myrna's body. He and Chambers agree that the case is hopeless. He drives Charlotte back to her apartment and then returns to his own.

The next day—Sunday, the sixth day of the case—Hammer spends alone, meditating upon the case (Chapter

13). It rains. On Monday he consults a druggist and learns that the white powder he found beside Myrna is heroin. Suddenly he realizes the truth. He breaks into "the killer's" apartment and waits, working himself into a righteous wrath. "Remember what I promised you? I'd shoot the killer, Jack, right in the gut where you got it. Right where everyone could see what he had for dinner. . . . Yes, Jack, it's almost finished. I'm waiting. I'm waiting" (p. 165). Charlotte enters, and there follows one of the most famous scenes in detective fiction. As Hammer holds his .45 on her and reconstructs the sequence of events leading to six murders, Charlotte performs a provocative striptease. Italicized paragraphs describing the stages of her disrobing counterpoint Hammer's step-by-step account of her homicidal conspiracies. Physical attraction and moral repulsion build to a simultaneous climax as Charlotte finally stretches our her arms to embrace Hammer and, obeying the higher call of his promise to Jack, he shoots her once in the belly.

The parallels between *I, the Jury* and *The Maltese Falcon* have already been noted. The figures of the dead comrade and the deadly female are central to both, but the reductive character of Spillane's version can most clearly be seen in a comparison of the two conclusions. Sam Spade finally realizes that only Brigid O'Shaughnessy could have killed his partner, Miles Archer. In a monologue addressed to Brigid, Spade reviews the evidence of her guilt and describes the options available to him. He lists seven reasons for turning her over to the police, among them his duty to his partner and to his profession, the necessity of relieving suspicions that he himself killed Archer, the impossibility of ever trusting her, and the fear that she might have been relying upon his mercy. "Now on the other side we've got what? All we've got is the fact that maybe you love me and maybe I love you."[2] The police arrive; Spade hands Brigid over and returns to his office alone.

Spade ultimately defers to the judicial system; this most obviously distinguishes him from Mike Hammer. But a series of minor contrasts emphasizes Spillane's invariable resort to the most melodramatic construction. Spade "maybe" loves the woman he must abandon; Hammer loves and even proposes marriage to Charlotte. Brigid kills Archer; Charlotte kills Jack and Hal and Eileen and George and Bobo and Myrna, and she runs a drug ring. Brigid tries to seduce Spade's emotions; Charlotte appeals directly to Hammer's libido. Brigid *might* betray Spade; Charlotte *would* betray Hammer: he discovers a gun hidden on a table next to where she planned to embrace him. Spade's is a tentative monologue in which he probes his own motives; Hammer's is a virulent tirade against Charlotte that suggests no awareness of his own role in the drama. Spade's final decision reveals the high cost of living in a hard-boiled world. Hammer's loneliness at the end of *I, the Jury* is not sad, but self-satisfied. The last words of the novel put a seal upon his uncompromised, superhuman integrity:

> "How c-could you?" she gasped.
> I only had a moment before talking to a corpse, but I got it in.
> "It was easy," I said. (p. 174)

To this acme of sublime self-righteousness the narrative has raced. Hammer's driven personality and driving prose culminate in this conclusive act of the will. The reader is never allowed to withdraw and exercise his critical faculties. Were he to do so, he would find Hammer's long indictment of Charlotte to be singularly unconvincing.

Although he had promised "to make the killer sweat— and tell me how it happened, to see if I hit it right" (p. 165), he does not in fact allow Charlotte to speak. Instead he moves unanswered from count to count of his indictment.

> 1. Everything begins with Charlotte's deformed character. She wanted wealth and power, and her profession hardened her in her contempt for

men. "You no longer had the social instinct of a woman—that of being dependent upon a man" (p. 167).

2. She began to distribute heroin to her patients.
3. She met Hal Kines in his pose as a medical student. She hypnotized him ("He was a fool to do it, but he had no choice if he wanted to play his role" [p. 168]!), and discovered his villainies.
4. But Kines was an adult, not a student; therefore, stalemate. (!)
5. Jack had come to suspect Hal, and through Eileen had learned that he would be visiting the brothel.
6. Charlotte feared that if Jack arrested Kines, Kines might implicate her; therefore, Charlotte shot Jack. (Not Kines!) Then she performed the clinical experiment of tantalizing Jack with the gun on his chair. ("No, you don't have to answer me because there could be no other way" (p. 169).
7. Charlotte sent Kines to the brothel to threaten Eileen, followed him, and shot them both in her room. (Why then? Why there? Why Eileen?)
8. Kalecki had found out about Charlotte ("Hal must have gotten drunk and spilled the works, [p. 170]). Kines told Charlotte that Kalecki knew, and therefore Charlotte took an unsuccessful early shot at Kalecki (Chapter 5).
9. Kalecki tried to shoot Charlotte in Central Park.
10. Hammer kills Kalecki; Charlotte is "lucky."
11. Bobo Hopper dropped a drug delivery and foolishly tried to have it refilled by a suspicious pharmacist. Charlotte's client phoned her to report the missing delivery and she rushed out to shoot Bobo. ("Even then I didn't get it. But I started narrowing it down" (p. 172).
12. Myrna tried on Charlotte's coat in the Bellemy cloakroom and discovered a packet of heroin in the pocket. Charlotte shot her and escaped along a window ledge ("like a human fly").

This then is the true plot of the action, the concealed coherence which the detective discloses.

But not one of Hammer's charges has much objective validity. Some—such as his account of Charlotte's motive for killing Jack—are ridiculous. And yet the improbabilities are easily overlooked. No reader can doubt Charlotte's guilt. The measure of reality in Hammer's world is not sense, but sensibility—Hammer's own aggressive sensibility. His unquestionable perceptions and interpretations *are* reality. At the end of the novel he slashes through appearances to assert the truth. His assertions are verified neither rationally nor empirically, but merely through the reader's unavoidable acquiescence to the forcefulness of his rhetoric. Perry Mason is no less infallible than Mike Hammer, but Mason always presents his conclusions as arguments, inviting refutation from the district attorney (and from the reader). Hammer delivers his final harangue in the presence only of the condemned man or woman, and he inevitably punctuates his indictments with a bullet that admits of no rely.

I, the Jury raises one last issue. Hammer accuses Charlotte of becoming a criminal because she has lost her proper sense of her dependence upon men. She lusts unnaturally after money and power. The question arises, isn't Hammer himself, a bloodthirsty apostle of power, equally culpable? He is not. The lust for power comes naturally to men. Moreover power means something quite different to Hammer. Power, for Charlotte, consists in wealth, and the pursuit of wealth leads her into large-scale, long-term criminal conspiracies. She constructs networks of vice—drugs, blackmail, murder; corruption becomes a way of life. Hammer's antagonists are usually of this sort; crime and subterfuge pervade their lives. They are systematic criminals, organization men and women who have slipped into the habit of killing.

Hammer is thus their anti-type. Power for him is an immediate physical reality, imposed by a fist or a gun. Each confrontation is complete in itself; he never expects to sustain his control, he never considers repercussions. Kalecki insults him, he punches Kalecki; Kalecki shoots at him (as it seems), he shoots at (and kills) Kalecki. Hammer regards these exercises as normal. It does not occur to him to gain permanent ascendency by blackmailing Kalecki. His demonstrations of his power are always spontaneous; it is not in his nature to plan retributions carefully or to indulge in slow torture of an adversay. Charlotte's revolting experiment with the dying Jack is altogether beyond him. Despite their shared homicidal tendencies, Mike Hammer and Charlotte Manning are genuine antitheses.

My Typewriter Is Quick

Like Gardner, Spillane chose not to alter his successful set of formulas. He followed *I, the Jury* with five Hammer novels published between 1950 and 1952, and then, after his return to publication in the sixties, with five more. In all of them the basic conventions are observed: the driving, driven personality of Hammer; the shadowy, rainy New York City background; the standardized scenes of violence and sex; Chambers, the reliable friend; Velda, the devoted secretary; and the variety of Hammer's low-life acquaintances. Always there is the trademark surprise ending in which Hammer confronts and extinguishes the psychologically deformed murderer.

My Gun Is Quick (1950), Hammer's second adventure, is equipped with all the standard features. Hammer befriends a vulnerable redheaded prostitute. Shaken by his generosity, she decides to abandon her immoral way of life, but is abruptly killed in an apparent hit-and-run accident. Hammer instinctively rejects the police conclusion, and his further investigation into her life and death leads him to a cheap hood, another former prostitute, a pimp, a nightclub hostess, a racketeer, and a wealthy philanthropist. Hammer is equally at ease with all these citizens: he has sex with the women, beats up some of the men, is beaten up by others, shoots some of the men, is shot by others, and finally manages to incinerate the instigator of all the mayhem.

Three street-wise women succumb to Hammer's forceful personality. All three are murdered. His kindness to the prostitute, "Red," inspires her to mend her ways and to compose an emotional letter expressing her gratitude to him. Though his encounter with her in a cheap restaurant is very brief, Hammer later refers to her as his "buddy." Ann Minor, a hostess in a club operated by the racketeer, Murray Candid, decides to sell her boss out to Hammer and to go somewhere else to make a new start. She arranges to meet Hammer in her apartment in order to give him the information he has requested. While he studies the material, she removes her clothing and seduces him. When soon thereafter her body is found floating in the river, Hammer supplies the coroner with the hint that makes him change the cause of death from suicide to murder.

Lola Bergan is the main sexual attraction. She is a former prostitute who has given up the profession after a stay in the hospital taking the cure for venereal disease. At their first meeting, she and Hammer go for a sentimental walk on the beach at night. Though Hammer again confesses himself in love, he no longer insists upon keeping the relationship "pure." Nonetheless, he declares that she has "a mind and body cleansed of any impurities,"[3] and she actually assumes a symbolic virginity by dressing herself in a special sheer silk gown that can be removed only by being ripped off of her. She assists Hammer in the investigation, making inquiries which in later novels will be assigned to Velda.

There is more violence in *My Gun Is Quick* as well as more sex. Hammer passed unharmed through *I, the Jury*, but beginning in *My Gun Is Quick* he too is beaten and shot at. His recoveries, however, are rapid and complete, and he repays his attackers with interest: "I rolled on top of him and took that head like a sodden rag and smashed and smashed and smashed and there was no satisfying, solid thump, but a sickening squashing sound that splashed all over me." Thus ends a hood who threatened Red and drew a knife on Hammer. Hammer is no longer invulnerable, but he remains invincible. His resilience merely adds another dimension to his strength.

Mary Bellemy's wealth permitted her to indulge in carefree nymphomania; Arthur Berin-Grotin, philanthropist and scion of a distinguished family, is a genuine plutocrat. If *I, the Jury* echoed *The Maltese Falcon*, *My Gun Is Quick* recalls Chandler's *The Big Sleep*. Mr. Berin, like General Sternwood, is old and near death. His Long Island estate makes an impression upon Hammer comparable to that which the Sternwood mansion made upon Philip Marlowe. Berin employs Hammer, and Berin's wayward daughter and his chauffeur figure prominently in the plot. All these elements are manipulated by Spillane to serve his melodramatic ends.

Hammer feels no awkwardness in the presence of the very rich. He even recognizes Wagner as the composer of a recording played for him by Mr. Berin. (In *The Snake*, he ostentatiously recognizes Franck's Symphony in D Minor.) But Hammer's natural environment is populated by the marginal classes of society—janitors, dockworkers, "newsies," pimps, bartenders. Big Sam and Bobo Hopper represented this underworld in *I, the Jury*. The rogue's gallery of *My Gun Is Quick* is considerably larger. Feeney Last, the "greaseball" chauffeur; Cobbie Bennett, the frightened pimp; Nat, the jeweller; Shorty, the short order cook; the tough bartender in a homosexual bar; Martha Porter, Red's frowzy landlady: these are the urban flotsam with whom Hammer identifies himself. He describes them in *Survival: Zero*: "To a uniform or a badge they were deaf, dumb and blind, but I wasn't department material and they could read it in my face. I was one of them, living on the perimeter of normalcy."[4] They are the tough, alienated, unorganized men and women massed at the bottom of society. They are largely ignored by respectable citizens, and they are usually exploited by organized crime figures like George Kalecki (gambling) or, in *My Gun Is Quick,* the nightclub owner, Murray Candid (prostitution). There were a number of respectable bourgeois citizens in *I, the Jury*—the college dean, the owner of the Times Square bookstore, Jack's neighbor—all of whom obsequiously submit to Hammer's direction. They tend to disappear in the later novels, which are populated almost exclusively by the rich, the poor, and the criminal.

Spillane deliberately removes his fiction from the "realistic" world of the middle class. His New York City is not the white-collar grid of offices, theaters, and two-bedroom apartments. Mike Hammer's Manhattan consists of a few luxurious penthouses and a lot of tenements, neighborhood bars, and back alleys. The topography of his city is as essentially emotional as the plots of his investigations are essentially irrational. Incidental imagery contributes to the impression of an Unreal City. Hammer drives to his apartment: "I cut across town, then headed north to my own private cave in the massive cliff I called home"(*My Gun Is Quick*, p. 6). High-rise buildings loom like prehistoric mountains. And the streets become a jungle: "The rain had laid a pall over the city, keeping the spectators indoors. Only the tigers were roaming the streets this night" (p. 137). Hammer and his kind are the tigers who dare to roam the darkened landscape in a fierce struggle for survival.

Or the city is an arena: "There isn't a Coliseum any more, but the city is a bigger bowl, and it seats more people. The razor-sharp claws aren't those of wild animals but man's can be just as sharp and twice as vicious" (p. 5). Hammer develops this image at length in the first paragraph of *My Gun Is Quick*, and he returns to it toward the end: "They talk about the Romans. They only threw human beings into a pit with lions. At least then the lions had a wall around them so they couldn't get out. Here they hang out in bars and on the street corners looking for a meal" (p. 143).

The detective novel is usually scrupulously mimetic. At the very least, the validity of clues and deductions depends upon a common sense of everyday reality shared by the reader and the detective. Sherlock Holmes inhabits a verifiable late Victorian London; Philip Marlowe and Lew Archer occupy a recognizable southern California. Both Gardner and Spillane avoid such verisimilitude, though for different reasons. Gardner constructs the minimal stage necessary to bear the actors of his drama. The background in Spillane's fiction is an ever-present, crucial ingredient in the narrative. It provides the heightened, almost operatic setting for the heightened, almost operatic characters and events that constitute his melodramas. Spillane's novels are in a sense popular proletarian operas, and the spectacular proportions of his stage sets, like those of the Met or Covent Garden, are scaled to the grand emotions of the singers (or of the detective) rather than to the normal experience of the audience. Thus though it is rendered less concretely than are the environments of Conan Doyle, Chandler, or Macdonald, Spillane's city is far more important to the meaning of his narrative than was Gardner's.

Vengeance Is Mine! (1950), the third Hammer novel, ends with Spillane's second most notorious surprise. There are additionally a few minor innovations, but the action basically follows the familiar pattern.

The narrative once again opens with the death of a comrade. Jack had been Hammer's "best friend," Red was his "buddy," Chester Wheeler is an old GI pal who has come to New York from the Midwest on a business trip and after a night of celebration is found dead in Hammer's bed, having been shot with Hammer's .45. Hammer awakens, hungover, unable to recall the events of the night. Pat Chambers attributes Hammer's drinking to his sorrow at the loss of Lola in *My Gun Is Quick*. The police conclude that Wheeler committed suicide, but the district attorney nonetheless insists upon stripping Hammer of his private investigator's license—his "ticket."

The backward reference to Lola and later to Red and Charlotte marks an attempt to establish a chronological continuity in the series. Such efforts are usually slight (except in the special instances of *The Girl Hunters* and *The Snake*), but they place Spillane's practice midway between Gardner's thoroughly autonomous productions and Fleming's careful attention to sequence.

The loss of his P.I. license (and consequently of his right to carry his .45) emphasizes his alienation from normal society and elicits further evidence of his resourcefulness. He transfers his agency to the still-licensed Velda and proceeds to dominate the mean streets with only his reputation and his fists. This transfer signals the expansion of Velda's role. She plays a significant part in the investigation and in the process becomes the object of Hammer's anxious concern. He rescues her moments before a gangster can consummate a rape. Velda shoots and kills the would-be rapist.

The loss of his license also sets up a typical confrontation between Hammer and the bureaucratic district attorney. The D.A. does not conceal his delight at Hammer's misfortune, and Hammer responds by charging the D.A. with incompetence. In a second encounter, Hammer's rhetoric grows more violent. He calls the D.A. a "yellow-bellied little bastard" and a "crummy turd" and he refers to his staff as "political behind-kissers with the guts of a bug and that's not a lot of guts." These rather childish insults manage to reduce the D.A. to a state of imbecility: "His legs, his knees, his whole body shook with coarse tremors. I'd never seen a guy as mad as he was," and his aides must carry him out of Hammer's presence.[5] Parallel to the main plot of Hammer's destruction of a blackmail organization runs this subsidiary drama of his castigation of an official bureaucratic organization.

The plot involves two principal sets of characters. One group belongs to the world of high fashion. The Anton Lipsek Agency had supplied the models at an affair attended by Chester Wheeler shortly before his death. Lipsek, a fashion photographer, and three of his models play important roles in the action, and all are dead by its conclusion. Connie Wales, one of the models, serves as Hammer's new helpmate/bedmate. Her unusually full figure occasions Hammer's sneer at the flat-chestedness of most models. Connie takes Hammer to her apartment, slams her fist into his jaw, rips off her dress, and demands that he "make" her. Hammer slaps her face as hard as he can, *then* he makes her.

The most striking member on the staff of the Lipsek Agency is its presiding genius, Juno Reeves.

> Her face had a supernatural loveliness as if some master artist had improved on nature itself. She had her hair cut short in the latest fashion, light tawny hair that glistened like a halo. Even her skin had a creamy texture, flowing down the smooth line of her neck into firm wide shoulders. She had the breasts of youth—high, exciting, pushing against the high neckline of the white jersey blouse, revolting at the need for restraint. (p. 28)

Hammer frequently refers to Juno as an Olympian, "the queen of the gods and goddesses." As a successful professional woman, she begs comparison with Charlotte Manning, and as with Charlotte, Hammer refuses to consummate his affair with her. But his reluctance this time is based not upon the anticipation of marriage, but upon an instinctive aversion that conflicts with his desire. "She's the best-looking thing I ever saw," Hammer admits to Connie. "I get steamed up watching her from fifty feet away. Whatever a dame's supposed to have on the ball, she's got it. . . . But here's something you can tuck away if it means anything to you. I don't like her and I don't know why I don't" (p. 42). In moments of intimacy with Juno, he gets a "creepy feeling" in his gut. This tense relationship builds until it explodes at the novel's climax.

The second important set of characters belong to the underworld. It is headed by a gangster named Dinky Williams, aka Clyde. Clyde operates a chic nightclub in the Bowery, frequented by fashion models and wealthy tourists thrilled by the prospect of slumming. In a back room, guarded by his thugs, Clyde also maintains an illegal casino. The other principal hood, Rainy, is a "tough punk" who runs a boxing arena and is available as an intimidator. Both Clyde and Rainy are killed in Hammer's purge.

But the primary object of Hammer's wrath in *Vengeance Is Mine!*—the people responsible for the death of Chester Wheeler—turns out to be a blackmail syndicate attached to the Lipsek Agency. With the models as bait and Lipsek as the photographer, it has been a profitable racket. At its center Hammer again discovers a woman, Juno. The echo of *I, the Jury* is confirmed when Hammer, holding a gun on Juno and recalling Charlotte, decides that he cannot again shoot a woman. Juno seizes upon his hesitation to launch an assault against him. In the struggle that follows, Hammer tears off her dress and makes a discovery that enables him not only to shoot Juno, but also to spit upon her corpse: *"Juno was a man!"*

These, the last words of the novel, are the reductio ad absurdum of the traditional detective-story "surprise" ending. True, there have been hints—Juno's high-necked blouses, Hammer's discomfort in her presence, a scene in a homosexual bar. But the imposture remains incredible. Juno turns out to be a very muscular man, yet Hammer has admired her smooth throat and round thighs, and the movement of her breasts and the swing of her hips; he has even danced with her. Hammer's amazement at his own gullibility—"Me, a guy that likes women, a guy who knows every one of their stunts . . . and I fall for this"—is exceeded only by the reader's. Hammer's misreading of Juno's gender—added to his virgin fetishism, his fascination with muscular stomachs, his ostentatious revulsion against homosexuals, his association of sex with pain—suggests that despite his machismo, he is not entirely at his ease in matters of sex.

One Lonely Night (1951) introduces a new political element into the Hammer formula. (Spillane did not fully exploit this element until the novels of the sixties, but its intrusion here serves as a reminder of the McCarthy influence on the world of Mike Hammer.) The novel opens with a remarkable scene on the George Washington Bridge. Hammer has just emerged from a trial in which, after being acquitted by the jury, he must submit to a stern rebuke from the judge.

> Goddamn, he wouldn't let me alone. He went on and on cutting me down until I was nothing but scum in the gutter, his fists slamming against the bench as he prophesied a rain of purity that was going to wash me into the sewer with the other scum leaving only the good and the meek to walk in the cleanliness of law and justice.[6]

Hammer, who has usually been the deliverer of wrathful monologues, has had to accept the "lash" of the judge's loathing—"every empty second seemed another stroke of the steel-tipped whip" (flagellation becomes a leitmotif in the novel). The judge concluded his harangue with a crucial question: "One day I would die and the world would be benefited by my death. And to the good there was only the perplexing question: Why did I live and breathe now . . . what could possibly be the reason for existence when there was no good in me?" (p. 7). As he left the courtroom, Pat Chambers had waved his tacit support, but it was Velda who stood most solidly behind him.

Though it is raining, Hammer decides that he needs solitude, "So I followed the hard concrete footpaths of the city through the towering canyons of the buildings and never noticed when the sheer cliffs of brick and masonry diminished and disappeared altogether, and the footpath led into a ramp then on to the spidery steel skeleton that was the bridge linking two states" (p. 5). While he stands on the empty bridge, it begins to snow. A frightened girl rushes up, pursued by a gunman. Hammer shoots the face off the gunman, but when he turns to help the girl, she takes one look at his face ("a mask of kill-lust") and leaps over the railing to her death.

Neither the courtroom scene nor the bridge scene shows Hammer to great advantage. His uncomprehending defiance of the judge's condemnation seems only to verify the indictment; and were further verification required, the black comedy of the girl's suicide would supply it. But Hammer does eventually discover the answer to the judge's question about his reason for existence. *One Lonely Night* is Mike Hammer's apologia pro vita sua. And the girl and her attacker inaugurate the plot: from a coat pocket he tore from the former in his rescue attempt and from the wallet he took from the corpse of the latter, Hammer retrieves peculiar green cards that prove to be passkeys to a Communist Party cell. Moreover, the man and the girl embody the central political message of the novel. The coarse, self-confident killer—actually a Soviet assassin—stands for the brutal threat posed by the Stalinist Communists. And the girl—a nurse from the Midwest who came to New York City "and got tied up with a lot of crappy propaganda the Commies handed out" (p. 171)— stands for a soft, hoodwinked American public, unable to accept the measures necessary to counter the Communist threat. Hammer's mission is to save America from its foolish tolerance of its enemy.

There are again two sets of characters, a small group of patriots and a larger group of Russian and American Communists. Lee Deamer heads the patriots. Deamer is running for the Senate, and Hammer's friends—a reporter, Pat Chambers, and Velda—all strongly endorse him as a decent man, supported by "the people," one who will "smoke out the rats that live on the public and give this country back some of the strength it had before we were undermined by a lot of pretty talk and pretty faces" (p. 26). But Deamer's career is threatened by an inexplicable occurrence: while he was delivering a political speech to an audience that included Pat Chambers, three solid eyewitnesses a mile away saw him commit a murder. The police and the press—all of whom support Deamer—conspire to conceal this "impossible" murder. Only Pat knows that Lee

Deamer has an insane twin brother, Oscar, who evidently committed the crime in a bizarre attempt to blackmail Lee. Hammer agrees to work for Lee in the pursuit of Oscar.

The Communist cell partially diverts his attention. Shortly after learning the meaning of the green cards, Hammer happens to pass by a Communist orator lecturing to a small crowd. Controlling with difficulty his indignation, he follows the speaker to his headquarters. There he flashes one of his green cards and is admitted. The cell members take him for an MVD assassin and treat him with awed respect. "They're supposed to be clever, bright as hell. They were dumb as horse manure as far as I was concerned. They were a pack of bugs thinking they could outsmart a world" (p. 38). Hammer's impromptu impersonation fools not only the American leaders of the cell, Henry Gladow and Martin Romberg, but also a top Russian spy attached to the Washington embassy, General Osilov. When the General presumes to speak to him in Russian, Hammer saves the situation by snarling, "English. You know better than that" (p. 80). General Osilov turns pale and stutters his agreement. These Communists *are* as dumb as horse manure.

Two of the important cell members are women. Linda Holbright has a voluptuous figure, but a horsy face. She comes to Hammer's apartment, kisses him, confesses that it was her first kiss, takes off her clothes, and "asked nothing except to be shown how to be a woman" (p. 89). Hammer takes a night to show her. Afterwards he feels guilty until he realizes that he may have helped to redirect her life. Ethel Brighton, the spoiled daughter of a millionaire, also has confused motives for joining the Party. She takes Hammer to her upstate cottage and offers herself to him. He accepts. Finally he decides that the only way to cure her of her misguided political convictions is to administer a good spanking. This corrective measure is interrupted by a bullet, but he eventually has the pleasure of seeing her reconciled to her father.

Hammer can salvage the female Communists through

his forceful personality. The males however must be exterminated. Velda kills one; Hammer kills the others. In the climactic scene General Osilov has taken Velda captive, carried her to an abandoned warehouse, stripped her and hung her by her wrists from the ceiling. He leers as one of his henchmen whips her naked body. A second watches, "slobbering all over his chin, puking a little without noticing it, his hands pressed against his belly while his face was a study in obscene fascination" (p. 164). Hammer intervenes with a machine gun, slaughters all the villains, rescues Velda, and burns down the warehouse.

The two plot lines—the murder-blackmail mystery that surrounds Lee Deamer and the Communist conspiracy headed by General Osilov—ultimately converge in the surprise ending which returns the action to the George Washington Bridge. Spillane's best endings contrive to be ironic as well as surprising. Charlotte Manning, the beloved psychiatrist, turns out to be a man-hating drug dealer; Juno, queen of the gods and goddesses, turns out to be "a real, live queen." *One Lonely Night* ends with another fine irony that seals the fates of both Lee Deamer and of the Communist Party in America. But more important is the thematic connection between the two plots that is sounded throughout the novel.

This theme concerns "the people." Lee Deamer is the people's choice: "Everybody is after his hide except the people" (p. 25). The Communists perversely make a similar appeal to the populace. The Union Square orator explains "why anybody who tolerated the foreign policy of this country was a Fascist, why anybody who didn't devote his soul and money to the enlightenment of the masses was a traitor to the people" (p. 29). The only unpopular person seems to be Mike Hammer, ostracized by the judge as one who has "no earthly reason for existing in a decent, normal society" (p. 8). Yet events prove that only Hammer truly acts on the people's behalf.

Hammer rejects the label of patriot. He never votes, and admits that he knows nothing about Deamer's political platform. He accepts the commission to help Deamer, but he explains to Chambers, "I'm not doing this because I'm a patriot, see? I'm doing it because I'm curious . . ." (p. 45). His motive for acting remains essentially a private one; he refuses to subordinate himself even to the banner of a political reformer. "Frankly, I don't know a hoot about politics except that it's a dirty game from any angle" (p. 68). (Events throughout his career justify his cynicism; personal integrity is the only certain standard in Hammer's world.) But if his experience among the Communist conspirators fails to make him conform to a political party, it does awaken him to his role as populist hero. A subplot in the novel involves the theft of the secret plans of an unspecified US weapon ("the latest development in the process for the annihilation of man." [p. 101]). The nation is outraged. Hammer listens to a broadcast:

> The music I had on the radio was interrupted every five minutes now with special newscasts that said the people were getting control of the situation at last.
> Of the people, for the people, by the people. We weren't so soft after all. We got pushed too far once too often and the backs were up and teeth bared. (p. 150)

Hammer's vocation emerges in this rhapsody: his back up and his teeth bared, he is the epitome of the people.

And thus he arrives at his answer to the judge's censure. In the moment before he machine-guns the Communists who are torturing Velda (and subverting the judge's "decent, normal society"), he enjoys his epiphany.

> And in that moment of eternity I heard the problem asked and knew the answer! I knew why I was allowed to live while others died! I knew why my rottenness was tolerated and kept alive. . . .
> *I lived only to kill the scum and the lice that wanted to kill themselves. I lived to kill so that others could live. . . . I was the evil that opposed other evil, leaving the good and the meek in the middle to live and inherit the earth!* (p. 165)

Hammer wraps himself in the self-righteous rapture of an Old Testament scourge. As always, emotion rather than reason sanctions his appetite for violence.

The Big Kill (1951) satisfies all the expectations aroused by the first four Hammer novels. There is an emotional opening, violence (several beatings and nearly a dozen violent deaths), sex (two voluptuous women), high life (a movie star), low life (Hammer's sort of people), racketeers, blackmail, a confrontation between Hammer and the D.A., and a neat, ironic ending. One of the unusual features is the role played by an infant. The action begins with Hammer spending a rainy evening in a bar. William Decker enters, weeping. He places his child down on a chair, then walks back out into the rain and almost immediately is shot to death from a passing car. Hammer takes custody of the baby and vows revenge on its behalf. As he tells the movie star, passion is a necessary motive: "I gotta be mad. Goddamn, you can't go at a thing like this unless you are mad."[7]

Hammer's investigation leads him into conflicts with a series of gangsters: Ed Teen, the new head of Charlie Fallon's gang; Lou Grindle, a boxing promoter; and Toady Link, a grotesque, Dick Tracy style villain. Velda, to whom Hammer became engaged in *One Lonely Night*, is absent on assignment in Florida. Pat Chambers stands by as Hammer's loyal friend. Ellen Scobie, "Texas Gal," an assistant to the D.A., discovers in Hammer a true "Texas Man." Total sales of *The Big Kill* are second only to those of *I, the Jury*. Hammer's audience evidently preferred this straightforward renewal of the familiar formulas.

Kiss Me, Deadly (1952), the last Spillane novel to be published in the 1950s, is also probably the least interesting. Its one distinction is its exploitation of the Mafia as the cancerous enemy of American society. "The Mafia. The stinking, slimy Mafia. An oversize mob of ignorant, lunkheaded jerks who ruled with fear and got away with it because they had money to back themselves up."[8] The Mafia is an ideal adversary for Hammer: criminal and organized. And in Spillane's version, it is indeed as lunkheaded as was the Communist Party. Mike Hammer's precocious crusade against the Mafia marks him as a godfather of such popular contemporary pulp series as Don Pendleton's *The*

Executioner (begun in 1969 and now nearing its sixtieth volume). Spillane's notion of organized crime is more naive than that of his heirs, but the melodramas he arranges around the concept are considerably more effective than the antiseptic paramilitary operations of Mack Bolan, "The Executioner." Spillane's mobsters—Carl Evello, Billy Mist, Al Affia—are only slightly more polished editions of the bullies who organized crime in the earlier novels. The word "Mafia" is whispered with awe, but its representatives are ordinary hoods, not cunning, sophisticated Dons.

The action begins when a girl, wearing only a raincoat, hitches a ride with Hammer. His car is run off the road; he and the girl are taken captive; she is tortured and killed; and he barely escapes death when they are placed back in the car and it is pushed over a cliff. Hammer recuperates quickly in a hospital. He learns that the girl was a federal witness against the Mafia. The FBI takes away his license.

Ralph Meeker in action as Mike Hammer in the 1955 movie *Kiss Me Deadly* (United Artists), one of four film versions of the Hammer books.

Hammer resolves to get even: "Maybe I have too much pride, but I don't let anybody get away with that kind of stuff. I'm going to knock the crap out of somebody for all that and if it gets up to Evello it's okay with me" (p. 26). A private motive is necessary to launch Hammer into action, even against the mob. Although he has been defrocked, his pal Pat Chambers continues to share with him the latest police intelligence.

Hammer encounters two beautiful women. One, Lily Carver, moves into his apartment for protection; the other, Michael Friday, is the half sister of the Mafia chieftain, Evello. He also confronts a number of tough enforcers—Mousie Basso, Charlie Max, Sugar Smallhouse. They beat him up; he beats them up. Velda conducts a parallel investigation, is captured, and is rescued at the last minute by Hammer. He also manages to recover a missing drug shipment that has figured prominently but vaguely in the plot. Finally Hammer destroys the two hidden adversaries who have conspired against him.

Though full of typical Spillane action, the narrative is marred by an excess of loose ends. The drug-smuggling subplot is not clearly drawn. Michael Friday, after offering herself to Hammer, simply vanishes from sight. There are undeveloped allusions to the Mafia associations of a Congressman and a lobbyist. Velda speaks mysteriously of waiting seven years for Mike, and when Hammer joins forces with Pat Chambers, he notes "It was six years ago and not now any longer" (p. 40). There is no apparent explanation for this six- or seven-year landmark. Finally, and most importantly, the characters and the motives of the two ultimate villains are never adequately established. One of them has been hardly more than a bystander. The ultimate villain has been a series trademark. Hammer disposes of miscellaneous bad guys in the course of each narrative—"thinning out" the plot, as he phrases it in *I, the Jury*—but the momentum of the narrative drives toward that final, one-on-one confrontation between Hammer and the current embodiment of evil. The ending of *Kiss*

Me, Deadly manages to be startling, but it is too arbitrary to be fully effective.

Whatever its defects, *Kiss Me, Deadly* sold over five million copies. It was not failure that caused Spillane to cease publishing for nearly a decade. Mike Hammer's return to print came in an unusual pair of novels. In the first of these, Hammer searches for his lost Velda. *The Girl Hunters* (1962) ends with the discovery of her location; *The Snake* (1964) opens with their actual reunion, then moves on to recount a new adventure. The resurrected Mike Hammer has changed very little, apparently less than his audience. Though popular, none of the five later Hammer novels qualifies as a superseller.

Spillane felt obligated to render an accounting for Hammer's hiatus. Seven years prior to the beginning of *The Girl Hunters*, Hammer had assigned Velda to a routine job of protecting the jewels of a rich client. Both Velda and the client had disappeared and were presumed dead. The news affected Hammer to the extent that he lost his lust for life and became a drunken bum. As the novel opens, the police pick him up from a gutter and carry him to hear a message from a dying government agent, Ricky Coles. Coles refuses to speak to his agency superior, Art Rickerby, the man who has treated him like a son. Instead he insists upon whispering a message to Hammer: Velda is alive, but her life is threatened by "The Dragon." To the astonishment of the doctor observing him, Hammer instantly sheds his addiction to alcohol and sets off on his mission to rescue Velda.

The resurrected Hammer makes repeated references to earlier times—to *I, the Jury* and *One Lonely Night*. He even mentions his very first case, an assignment from Aliet Insurance. And *The Girl Hunters* is equipped with many of the standard Spillane features: sex and violence; political intrigue; bars and flophouses; low-life characters with names like Old Dewey and Duck-Duck Jones. But Hammer claims too much when he insists that things will be "Like in the old days," that "Now it was just like old

times."[9] There are changes. These range from minor innovations like the addition of "shit" to Hammer's vocabulary or the introduction of newspaper columnist Hy Gardner to the cast of continuing characters to more major
changes like a new definition of the relationships between
Hammer, Chambers, and Velda or the intervention of Art
Rickerby.

Pat Chambers displays a violent contempt for the alcoholic Hammer. Hammer learns to his surprise that Chambers also loved Velda and that he holds Hammer responsible for her death. Chambers's emotions astonish the
reader as much as they do Hammer. By the middle of the
novel, the two men have uneasily overcome their emnity.
Even more surprising than this discovery however is
Hammer's announcement that he knows absolutely nothing about Velda's history prior to her entry into his
employment. He is amazed to discover that she had a Life
Before Hammer: during World War II she served in
Europe at a high level in several intelligence agencies
(OSS, OSI). Her unexpected past is a necessary condition
for the action of the novel, but it does disrupt the continuity of the series.

Art Rickerby adds another new dimension to the series.
Rickerby, a mild-mannered, tough FBI agent, occupies the
same emotional ground that Mike Hammer did in *I, the
Jury*. He seeks to avenge the death of his comrade and
protegé, Rickey Coles, by capturing the notorious Soviet
assassin known as The Dragon. But as Rickerby makes
clear to Hammer, his notion of revenge is different. "A
quick kill would be too good, Mike. . . . But the law—this
supposedly just, merciful provision—this is the most cruel
of all. It lets you rot in a death cell for months and de-
teriorate slowly until you're only an accumulation of living
cells with the consciousness of knowing you are about to
die" (p. 130). Hammer refuses to communicate Coles's
dying message to Rickerby, instead extorting from Rickerby a federal license to carry a gun. This marks a radical
alteration in Hammer's status: he joins an organization.
He acquires official credentials to back up his personal

authority. And his new license is a liberal one. In *The Snake* Rickerby informs him: "You've never been a total un-known and now that you're back, stay back. When we need you, we'll yell. Meanwhile nobody's going to pick up your ticket as long as you stay clean enough. I didn't say legal . . . I said clean."[10]

Governmental approval ill-suits Hammer's character. He tries not to be a good soldier, engaging in a series of petty rebellions against Chambers, Rickerby, and, in *The Snake*, even against his old nemesis, the D.A. The latter incident illustrates the difficulty with the new formula. As in earlier confrontations, Hammer asserts himself bluntly against the D.A., but now he faces down the bureaucrats not merely through the force of his personality but with the authority of his license from his "obscure" but power-ful Federal agency. The D.A. cannot touch him. By gain-ing power as an agent, Hammer has lost something of his power as an individual. And in fact Hammer goes to great lengths to distance himself from his agency. To his pri-mary personal motive in *The Girl Hunters*—the rescue of Velda—he adds the old-fashioned obligation to avenge the death of his friend, Old Dewey. Then, as though these were not enough to demonstrate his lack of altruism, he calls Rickey Coles "a friend of mine," thus appropriating Art Rickerby's revenge motive. Of course Hammer first met Coles minutes before he expired and could hardly even claim him as an acquaintance.

The plots of *The Girl Hunters* and *The Snake* both look backward into the past for their origins. *The Girl Hunters* looks back three years to the death of Senator Knapp, "a man initially responsible for military progress and missile production in spite of opposition from the knotheaded liberals and 'better-Red-than-dead' slobs" (p. 138); back seven years to the "death" of Velda; back twenty years to Velda's first knowledge of a "world conquest scheme." This scheme, outlined by Rickerby in Chapter 7, has been in operation since the First World War. The schemers used the Nazis and are now being used by the Soviets. Velda's disappearance was a voluntary maneuver against the scheme. It led her underground to Russia, through Europe, and now back to New York City. Ricky Coles, who aided her escape to America, reports that The Dragon has been assigned to liquidate her. Hammer, referring to himself as St. George, must slay The Dragon for girl and country—mostly for girl. A major subplot leads him to the widow of Senator Knapp. Laura Knapp serves as Hammer's romantic interest for the duration of the novel.

For the source of its plot *The Snake* looks backward to a 1932 armored car robbery. The head of the gang that attempted the robbery was Sonny Motley, who has served a thirty-year sentence and now polishes shoes. The second-in-command, Blackie Conley, disappeared with three million dollars. Sim Torrence, the young district attorney who prosecuted Sonny Motley, is now a candidate for governor. Hammer must resolve mysteries associated with this old case; he must also protect Torrence's young daughter, Sue. She has coincidentally tried to hide herself in the same building in which Velda was hidden. As he regains his secretary, Hammer acquires a new object of compassion.

The action of *The Snake* is somewhat more coherent than that of *The Girl Hunters*. In Hammer's expository monologue toward the end of the earlier novel, he invoked "fate" several times to explain the true plot of events:

> Now here the long arm of fate struck a second time. Not coincidence—but fate, pure unblemished fate. (p. 149)

> Fate struck for sure when she saw him. (p. 150)

> Coincidence here. Or Fate. Either will do. (p. 150)

As an account of the true history of the world or of Velda—the two histories coincide—Hammer's exposition lacks credibility, even in the context of melodrama. Further, the expansion of the criminal conspiracy to include the major cataclysms of the twentieth century alters its metaphysical status. Hammer's adversaries have hitherto symbolized larger evils; in *The Girl Hunters* they

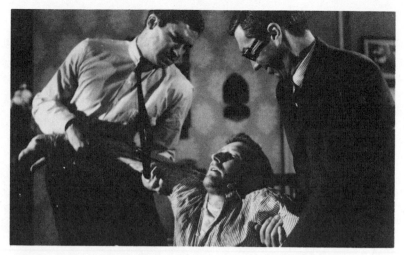

Mickey Spillane himself (center) played Mike Hammer in the
1963 Colorama release *The Girl Hunters.* Very few authors could
do the same for their own heroes.

Television too found Mike Hammer in 1958, with an NBC series
starring Darren McGavin. CBS brought the P.I. back in 1984, in
the person of Stacy Keach, shown here in Hammer's office.
Mickey Spillane's own television appearances no doubt contributed to a revived interest in Mike Hammer.

are a larger evil, nearly the largest. Hammer's paranoia takes on unmanageable international proportions. *The Snake* begins to return him to his former scale of operations. The enemies are archetypal—robbers and politicians—not apocalyptic. An old armored car heist, new gang activities, an endangered girl, an ambitious D.A.—these are matters which Hammer can plausibly investigate, characters which he can plausibly dominate. The conclusion of *The Snake* is almost perfect in its irony and its impossibility. Incidentally, it requires Velda to perform a version of Charlotte's gunpoint striptease. Velda survives.

Velda's return is remarkable. The secrets she brings back from Europe have devastating effects.

> In Moscow thirty men died and in the East Zone of Berlin five more disappeared and in South America there was a series of accidents and several untimely deaths and across the face of the globe the living went to the dead in unaccountable numbers and codes and files were rearranged and meetings hastily brought about and summit conferences planned and in the U.N. buildings whole new philosophies were adopted and . . . (*The Snake*, [p. 19])

Having thus affected global politics, Velda complaisantly resumes her role as Hammer's secretary. One of her first concerns on being reunited with her boss is to assure him that she is still a virgin—this from a woman in her mid-forties, who spent several years as an intelligence officer in London, over a decade as a private investigator in New York, and seven years undercover in Europe! Hammer expects no less. At the end of *The Snake* she apparently loses at last her mark of distinction.

Velda does not appear at all in the next Hammer novel, *The Twisted Thing* (1966), a reworking of a much earlier, unpublished work titled *Whom the Gods Would Destroy*. *The Twisted Thing* is unusual in its setting: it is the only Hammer novel to take place almost entirely outside New York City. The scene is Sidon, a small town evidently near Long Island Sound. The case involves a wealthy scientist, Rudolph York, whose experimental research on his son,

Ruston, has turned the boy into a prodigy. Other important characters include Rudolph's lesbian lab assistant; Ruston's nurse, a former stripper; and a brutal local cop. The action begins with a kidnapping and expands to encompass blackmail, extortion, gambling, and murder.

The restricted locale imposes a degree of unity upon the action—the setting is not far from that of the traditional English country house. The title implies a further principle of thematic coherence. A number of the main actors qualify as "twisted things": Dilwick, the corrupt, sadistic cop; Rita Cambell, the lesbian assistant; Rudolph York, the mad scientist who distorts a boy's personality with his experiments; and Ruston, the frustrated boy-genius. There is a complicated but not too improbable plot of false identities. Spillane supplies an extraordinary clue to the true relationships. Hammer affectionately dubs Ruston "Sir Lancelot." Ruston's true father proves to be a gangster named Mallory (cf. Sir Thomas Malory, *Le Morte D'Arthur*). Moreover, Ruston, like Lancelot, indulges in forbidden love.

The strengths of *The Twisted Thing* do not survive in the next novel, *The Body Lovers* (1967), which tries to synthesize the old Hammer *(Vengeance Is Mine!)* and the new *(The Girl Hunters)*. The case involves a series of bizarre sex crimes. Hammer's investigation leads him to a Junoesque figure, Dulcie McInnes, "Executive Fashion Editor" for the Proctor Group. Hammer, once again merely a private investigator, is threatened (once again) with the loss of his license. The international complications that coincide with these familiar formulas center on Bela Ris, a U.N. delegate from an unspecified third-world country. The Cold War politics of *One Lonely Night* and *The Girl Hunters,* however simple-minded, were at least intelligible. Ris's character and politics are both vaguely corrupt. He is an organizational villain, but neither his organization nor his motives are clearly defined.

Motivations are generally deficient in *The Body Lovers.* A girl cooperates in a series of deceptions, suffers sexual abuse, and endangers her life in order to earn fifty thou-

sand dollars, which she intends to use to support her
brother when he is released from prison. In order to gain
"greater social acceptance," one of the major villains pan-
ders to the sexual sadists who abuse such girls. Even the
weapons used in *The Body Killers* are peculiar; the killers
actually resort to a rare poison "used by certain savage
tribes in South America." The novel is not without some
rewards. Hammer makes a brief foray into the world of
Greenwich Village, and even consents to pose nude for an
artist named Cleo. A pair of elegant parties, one of them
held at the U.N., allow Hammer to demonstrate his natural authority as he bluntly cuts through the pretenses. But
overall the novel is probably Hammer's weakest effort.

    Survival: Zero (1970), Hammer's latest if not his last ad-
venture, is more interesting. It too attempts a synthesis—
of *I, the Jury* and *The Girl Hunters*—and is more successful
than *The Body Hunters.* The action opens with Hammer
observing the death of his old friend, Lippy Sullivan, and
vowing vengeance. Once more, "the ax I was grinding was
a personal one." The pursuit of Lippy's killers leads
Hammer to a cast of familiar characters: Woodring
(Woody) Ballinger, the gangster; Heidi Anders, a Broad-
way actress addicted to heroin (and cured of her addiction
by Hammer's admonitions): William Dorn, wealthy chairman of the board of Anco Electronics; Renee Talmage,
Dorn's head of accounting. Renee, a typical Spillane professional woman, serves as Hammer's sexual companion,
performing the normal striptease in Chapter 6. Much of
the murder investigation takes place in the Beggar's Opera
environment that constitutes Mike Hammer's native
ground.

    A second background plot in *Survival: Zero* concerns a
set of Soviet germ warfare canisters so lethal that it
threatens the entire globe. (Government experts inform
Hammer that a few men in Antarctica might survive until
their supplies run out.) The new Soviet regime wants to
withdraw the threat, but even the Russians don't know the
location of the canisters. Hammer is one of the civilians
who knows of the impending catastrophe, yet he single-

mindedly pursues his effort to make sense of the apparently meaningless death of Lippy Sullivan. In the end the two plots converge. Hammer simultaneously avenges Lippy and saves the world. The conclusion, not one of Spillane's most surprising, is one of his neatest.

But Mike Hammer never recovered his preeminence. All six of the 1947–1952 novels were supersellers; none of the five 1962–1970 novels were. There were some changes in the Hammer formulas—a background of national crisis in four; a withdrawal from the city in the fifth—but the more likely explanation for the diminution of his appeal lies in a change in his audience. Through Mike Hammer, the reader could stand up to the psychiatrists, the cops, the gangsters, the liberals, the Communists—and to all the city halls that seemed to oppress him in the aftermath of the New Deal and the war. With their M-1s, the GIs had conquered the definite evils of the world. When they returned to Levittown and the routines of civilian life, they eagerly identified with the tough, ugly GI who returned to a jungle of a city and with his .45 continued to conquer definite evils. But by 1960 the technocrats had won. In an age of U2s, Sputniks, and missile crises, Mike Hammer seemed something of a misplaced cowboy. Fighting city hall still had its appeal (by 1965 *The Girl Hunters* had sold over 1,800,000 copies and *The Snake* over 1,200,000), but saving the city was the paramount issue. An effective, technological, organizational hero—a James Bond—was required.

Tough Guys and Spies

Two of Spillane's non-Hammer novels achieved superseller status. *The Long Wait* (1951), the only non-Hammer book before the hiatus, sold over five million copies; *The Deep* (1961), the novel which ended the hiatus, sold over two million. Neither diverges greatly from the Hammer mold. The narrators are Hammer tough, speak Hammer talk, and move Hammer-like from violent encounter to violent encounter. As non-series novels, they have the advantage of being designed as self-sufficient units. The later Hammer novels had suffered from two special burdens. Spillane had to keep contriving personal motivations for his hero; hence, for example, the high mortality rate among Hammer's buddies—Jack, Red, Chester, Ricky, Lippy. He also had to dispose of Velda while Hammer enjoyed the favors of other women—sending her on a mission to Miami, turning her into a secret agent, simply omitting her. The non-Hammer novels escape these necessities; they are complete in themselves.

The coherence of *The Long Wait* and *The Deep* derives from a common structure: in both novels the hero returns home after a long absence to claim forcefully what is his. In *The Long Wait,* John McBride returns to the midwestern town of Lyncastle to recover his good name and to revenge himself upon those who five years previously had ruined it by framing him for embezzlement and murder. (In a bizarre complication, McBride believes that he is someone called George Wilson, a fingerprintless man who was McBride's look-alike and best friend and who suffers from amnesia.) Lyncastle is a town corrupted by gambling and other rackets. McBride encounters a variety of Spillane stereotypes: an honest cop who believes that he is guilty of the crimes he was charged with; a corrupt, brutal cop; tough gangsters; a torch singer; a newspaper reporter; a brothel madam; a loyal old man; a voluptuous receptionist. McBride is beaten unconscious a half dozen times (Hammer averaged once or twice a novel), is offered sex by four gorgeous women (Hammer by one or two), and finally, after eliminating the gangsters and the corrupt cop, fulfills his promise by shooting the one who framed him five years ago. A completely happy ending is achieved through the startling revelations of the last page.

Lyncastle, a town of fifty thousand, provides a compact arena for the action. For the first time in Spillane's fiction, characters occupy single-family dwellings. (The conclusion even suggests that John McBride will raise a family in one of them.) This confined setting means that in the course of his crusade, McBride can virtually purge the community of its social cancers. In this respect his achievement differs from that of Hammer, whose vast city can never be more than partially cleansed. McBride's purge recalls the Continental Op's undertaking in Personville (in Hammett's *The Red Harvest*), but McBride's passionate, private motives and his emotional rhetoric distinguish him from the Op. Spillane's heroes act with relentless enthusiasm. From the moment he gets off the bus in Lyncastle, the entire town seems to revolve around John McBride's energetic personality.

The title character of *The Deep* (known by no other

Several of Spillane's non-Hammer novels were filmed in Hollywood. Here Anthony Quinn (center), as a man seeking revenge against those who framed him, receives some threatening attention in the 1954 production *The Long Wait* (United Artists).

name) has the same success dominating the world to which
he returns, here a tough New York City neighborhood.
Twenty-five years previously Deep and his buddy, Bennett, were the leaders of the Knight Owls, a street gang.
During Deep's absence, Bennett built the gang into a
major underworld organization; now, following Bennett's
murder, Deep has returned to avenge the death of his old
friend and to claim the underworld empire as his inheritance. He relives his delinquent youth as he walks the
streets, encountering old friends and enemies—Cat, an
old comrade, now dying of tuberculosis; Augie; Bennie-
from-Brooklyn, a rival claimant to the empire; Mr. Sullivan, the beat cop; Wilson Batten, lawyer and former fence;
Roscoe Tate, the good boy, who has become a prominent
newspaper columnist but who has never left the neighborhood. He also rediscovers Helen Tate—"Irish"—now a
beautiful actress. The power struggle for control of the
gang, Deep's investigation into Bennett's death, and his
ambiguous relationship with the police provide occasions
for numerous violent incidents in the familiar Spillane
vein. Deep finally exposes and kills Bennett's murderer,
then neatly resolves his tense relations with Irish and with
the law.

The most interesting feature of both *The Long Wait* and
The Deep is the motif of return and reformation. The protagonists are regulation invincible tough guys, but the imperative which drives them to revisit their origins—their
hometown or their old neighborhood—is new. Both are
intent upon redeeming their own pasts, and they succeed
by destroying old villains and marrying old girl friends.
Mike Hammer's adventures are located in the present;
they look forward to the solution of an immediate problem. Hammer's motives drive him outward; the motives of
John McBride and Deep drive them backward and inward.
They circle back to their beginnings in order to renew
themselves and their community. The symbol of the renewal is the embrace which concludes both books: each
hero ends in the arms of a good woman. The nuptial bond,

inaccessible to a series hero like Hammer, promises that the time to kill has passed.

A relevant image is developed at the end of *The Deep*. Roscoe Tate, full of hate for Deep as for all the neighborhood gangsters, gloats over Deep's imminent demise:

> You're on a trolley, Deep. You got on when you were a kid. You picked your direction, paid your fare and now you're stuck with the ride. It's all downhill, the trolley's lost its brakes and at the end is a big steel bumper that wipes you right out of existence.[11]

Deep replies that there is a flaw in Roscoe's simile—"A guy could get off the trolley any place he wanted, couldn't he?" (p. 120). Roscoe insists that escape is impossible. At the climax of the novel, Deep returns to the simile of the trolley car: he does have the strength of will to get off wherever he pleases; it is the killer who, in his insanity, is stuck with the ride. Spillane's return novels propose a fairy-tale version of getting off the trolley: get out, get tough, get back. It is the dream of the victimized child and of the tenure-tracked bureaucrat.

The return-reform motif reappears in other works published during Spillane's period of activity in the sixties. "Killer Mine" (in *Killer Mine*, [1968]), "The Bastard Bannerman" (in *The Tough Guys*, [1969]), and *The Erection Set* [1972]) are all based on this structure. Recovery replaces revenge as a primary motive of the non-Hammer novels.

Lt. Joe Scanlon, in "Killer Mine," is a tough city cop who agrees to return to the old neighborhood to investigate four recent murders. His excuse for returning will be to visit Marta Borlig, a neighborhood girl now serving as an undercover policewoman. Although technically an organization man, Scanlon quickly establishes his credentials as a rebel in an exchange with the police commissioner. He succeeds in tracking the killer through the remembered terrain and, in a contrived climax reminiscent of *The Picture of Dorian Gray*, destroys the villain and saves himself, Marta, and the neighborhood.

In *The Long Wait,* the hero returns to a town; in *The Deep* and "Killer Mine," he returns to a neighborhood; in "The Bastard Bannerman," he returns to a family. Cat Cay Bannerman, illegitimate scion of the wealthy Bannermans, returns to the family estate twenty-five years after being run off it. He finds his uncle and two male cousins implicated in a blackmail scheme operated by a local gangster. Cat Cay humiliates his relatives (revenge for injustices suffered as a child easily supplements the return motif), investigates the conspiracy against them, and with typical forcefulness resolves the situation. He also regains a childhood sweetheart and, days before a deadline, learns from the old family lawyer that he will inherit two million dollars if he has never been found guilty of a criminal charge. Despite his forcefulness, he satisfies the provision.

The Erection Set is a replay of "The Bastard Bannerman" at a higher volume. Dogeron Kelly, the illegitimate scion of the wealthy Barrins, stops at the family estate twenty-five years after being run off it. He finds his two male cousins in charge of a nearly bankrupt Barrin Industries. An old family lawyer informs Dogeron that in order to obtain his inheritance he must either prove himself innocent of any criminal charges, or prove his cousins guilty. He succeeds in fulfilling the second stipulation and manages—through this and through other financial manipulations—to gain complete control of Barrin Industries. He promises job security for the loyal members of the company's work force and economic prosperity for the community (both to be based on the rediscovery of a company process for manufacturing anti-gravity devices). There are two important subplots. In the first, Kelly intercepts a Mafia drug shipment; in the second, Kelly recovers his old girlfriend, now a prominent movie executive.

The Erection Set presents in the most extravagant form a boy's fantasy of remaking his world. Like Cat Bannerman, Dog Kelly was the scapegoat of his legitimate relatives. Now he returns with a suitcase full of millions of mysterious dollars and an overwhelming physical presence to confront the weak minds and pasty bodies of his former tormentors. They have wasted away the family fortune and the family name; he will restore them. Kelly fulfills a number of juvenile wishes. An old friend greets him on his return from abroad, promises to support him and to get him a job, then opens his battered suitcase to discover his millions. He humiliates his snobbish middle-aged female cousins by compelling them to remove all their clothes and then calling for the butler. He obtains concrete evidence that one of his male cousins is a sadist and the other is a homosexual. His sexual magnetism thaws the notorious frigidity of the wife of a business competitor (earning the competitor's gratitude). He quietly purchases his sweetheart's old house, has it entirely restored and refurnished, and consummates his affair with her in her old bedroom. Kelly claims to be "Just a guy who wants to come home" (p. 126), but he devotes his energies to reinventing "home" to suit his own requirements.

The Erection Set contains Spillane's most graphic depictions of violence and sex. Mike Hammer (in *The Big Kill*, Chapter 3) and Dog Kelly (in *The Erection Set*, Chapter 9) both encounter a pair of hoods in a men's room. Kelly's account of the gory details is by far the more revolting. The sexual explicitness of *The Erection Set*, new in Spillane, emerged in direct response to the enormous popularity of Jacqueline Susann's novels. Sheila MacMillan, the frigid wife, successfully begs Dog to make her "a three-way woman." Sharon Cass, the movie producer's assistant, professes to have enjoyed all sorts of sex, excepting only "the primary circumstance"—violation of the virginity that she has preserved thirty-two years for her missing sweetheart. The vocabulary of sex in *The Erection Set* tends to be blunt rather than erotic. But Spillane's uncensored imagination had a definite appeal: over a million and a half copies of the book were printed.

The Erection Set is the first of Spillane's novels not to be narrated exclusively in the first person. The voice of Dog Kelly dominates the narrative, but Spillane inserts parenthetically italicized commentaries by other characters, and even relates one chapter (6) in the third person. The device enables the reader to see the hero briefly through the eyes of a whore, a World War II buddy, the old family lawyer, and Sharon Cass.

Two other stereotypical structures emerge in Spillane's later fiction. One is that of the framed man. In "Man Alone" (*Killer Mine* [1968]), Patrick Regan is a policeman accused of having accepted payoffs and of having killed the man who was paying him off. A jury acquits him, but the judge and the public condemn him. To restore his reputation, Regan must break up a syndicate drug racket and expose and kill a corrupt cop. In the process, he meets an old neighborhood girl, formerly a prostitute and a brothel madam, now the operator of a modeling agency and a call-girl ring. Spillane's set of stereotypes remains very narrow. His women range from *V* to *W*, with the whores outnumbering the virgins.

"The Seven Year Kill" (in *The Tough Guys*, [1969]) combines the framed man with the return-reform motif. The protagonist, Phil Rocca, is an investigative reporter who has served a seven-year sentence for a crime he did not commit. On his release from prison, he becomes an alcoholic. Then he accidentally runs into the terrified daughter of the mobster who framed him. Rocca renews his investigations, redeems his reputation, rescues the girl, and destroys the mobster. The frame, the alcoholism (*The Girl Hunters*), the terrified daughter (*The Snake*), the mobster, the redemption, the rescue, and the destruction have all appeared elsewhere in Spillane's fiction.

The second stereotypical structure Spillane experimented with was that of the legitimatized villain; the rogue whose special talents cause him to be conscripted into the service of the community. In the two stories of *Me, Hood!* (1969)—"Me, Hood!" and "Return of the Hood"—the city police need the toughness and the street smarts of the self-proclaimed hood, Ryan. In *The Delta Factor* (1967) the U.S. government needs the toughness of the superhood, Morgan. The action of the *Me, Hood!* stories is standard urban Spillane; that of *The Delta Factor* is unusual in that it transpires on an imaginary Caribbean island. Morgan, a contemporary swashbuckler, slashes his way through casinos, shanties, and castles to destroy the enemies of America. Spillane's imagination typically prefers a Dirty One to a Dirty Dozen; heroism is singular. Neither Ryan nor Morgan is distinguishable in manners or morals from Spillane's presumably more legitimate heroes.

"Kick It or Kill!" (in *The Tough Guys* [1969]) is the only other short story Spillane has published in book form in the U.S. (Two other tales, "The Flier" and "The Affair with the Dragon Lady," have been published in England.) The hero, a stranger, enters a small town, discovers a villainous plot involving sex and drugs, meets an attractive girl, rescues the girl and annihilates the plotters (including a U.S. senator).

The Last Cop Out (1973), the last thus far of Spillane's adult fictions, is to the novels of Mario Puzo what *The Erection Set* was to those of Jacqueline Susann. In neither instance is Spillane composing a pastiche. The plot, characters, and diction of *The Last Cop Out* are definitely those of Spillane, not Puzo. The hero is a tough former cop who quit the force after being framed and suspended "because he was too much cop for the politicians to live with."[12] The novel describes Gill Burke's official and unofficial war against the Mafia. The syndicate is headed by a cunning old don, Papa Menes, and his ambitious lieutenants. In order to exploit fully his Mafia material, Spillane, after twenty-five years of relying exclusively upon first-person narration, shifts to the third person. The result is to reduce the overwhelming presence of the hero and to provide a much more detailed account of the machinations of the mobsters. The sexual preferences and conditions of the Mafia chieftains receive special attention—impotence, sadism, belly-button fetishism, and sodomy, a preoccupation of the later Spillane.

Puzo and Susann were not the only other supersellers to stimulate emulation. By 1964 the James Bond phenomenon had demonstrated its spectacular appeal. As early as

1962 Spillane had nudged Mike Hammer in Bond's direction (*The Girl Hunters*); the apocalyptic subplot of *Survival: Zero* (1970) clearly derives from the Bond formula. But it is in the four-novel Tiger Mann series that Spillane defines his version of the secret agent.

The character of Tiger Mann is essentially identical to that of Mike Hammer (and of all other Spillane heroes). The differences are only superficial. Mann is a tough former GI who carries his .45 in a speed rig and who narrates his violent adventures with absolute self-confidence. In *The Day of the Guns* (1964), Mann seals a security leak at the United Nations and kills a clever Soviet spy and a top Soviet assassin (Vidor Churis). In *Bloody Sunrise* (1965), he protects an important Soviet defector and kills a clever Soviet spy and a top Soviet assassin (Spaad Helo). In *The Death Dealers* (1965), he protects an Arab potentate, prevents the explosion of a nuclear device in Washington, D.C., and kills a top Soviet assassin (Malcolm Turos). In *The By-Pass Control* (1967), he saves America from nuclear holocaust and kills a clever Soviet spy and two top Soviet assassins (Vito Salvi and Niger Hoppes).

As these synopses suggest, Spillane did not overtax his invention. Having proven his formula—both *The Day of the Guns* and *Bloody Sunrise* had sold over 1,200,000 copies by the end of 1965—he was content to repeat it. Even the details tend to be uniform. All three of the clever Soviet spies are female. All three are destroyed on the last page by the special device with which his research and development department has equipped Mann (explosive pellet, poison pen, poisoned benzedrine inhaler). Mann is sexually active in every novel; twice he entertains his partner at a sex show at a private Middle Eastern club (the Casbah and the Turkish Gardens). Mann has encountered two of the top Soviet assassins earlier in his career: he has shot two fingers off the hand of one; he has shot the other in the larynx.

Perhaps the most obvious sign of Spillane's aversion to

novelty is the character of Rondine, Tiger Mann's Velda.
Rondine appears as a major character in *The Day of the
Guns*. Under the name of Edith Caine, she is a beautiful
British translator at the U.N. Mann confidently identifies
her as Rondine Lund, a Nazi spy with whom he had once
been infatuated and who had escaped from him by shooting him in the stomach after making love. Throughout the
novel Mann threatens Rondine with imminent retribution,
despite her protestations of innocence and her obvious
youth. In the end, Edith Caine proves that she is not Rondine by proving that she is a virgin. Rondine was actually
Edith Caine's elder sister, the unmentionable black sheep
of the Caine family. Mann's obsession with Rondine and its
happy refutation comprise an interesting psychological
phenomenon. But in the next novel in the series, Rondine
(as Mann insists upon calling her) subsides into a conventional character—the girl who wants to marry the hero,
who occasionally assists him in his assignments, and who
sometimes requires him to rush to her rescue.

Spillane faced one important difficulty inherent in the
Tiger Mann concept: the necessity that the hero be affiliated with an organization. He tried to overcome the
problem by making Mann's organization the renegade operation of a patriotic multi-millionaire, Martin Grady, and
by making Tiger Mann an isolated individual within the
renegade operation. Instead of confronting the D.A. and
his bureaucratic cohorts, Mann confronts and stares down
the bureaucrats of the intelligence establishment, embodied in Hal Randolph, head of the IATS (Spillane's
pseudo-CIA). Indeed, Mann's most dramatic ideological
conflicts are with the IATS; the Soviet system is by comparison a rather nebulous threat. Nonetheless, Tiger
Mann's assignment depends upon an organized support
system. He calls in to "Newark Control" to obtain information, and he relies upon Martin Grady's limitless wealth to
equip and reinforce him. He employs all the standard spy
paraphenalia—scramblers, passwords, dossiers, electronic
bugs. But he does keep asserting his independence. Like

all Spillane protagonists, and unlike Perry Mason or James Bond, Tiger Mann abhors the idea of any restraints upon his freedom to act as he will.

One Lonely Knight

Spillane was twenty-nine when he published his first superselling novel; Gardner had been forty-four, Fleming would be forty-five. In other, more important ways, Spillane stands apart from his fellow supersellers. Once Gardner and Fleming began to produce their novels, they produced them continuously until their deaths. Gardner maintained a steady rate of three or four a year; Fleming, more modestly but no less consistently, held himself to one a year. Spillane's career proceeded in discontinuous bursts: seven novels in five years, a decade of silence, sixteen books in twelve years, another decade of silence. Spillane has also been unusually willing (and able) to change his generic stripes. With unflagging devotion, Gardner stuck to the formulas of his lawyer-detective (Doug Selby and Donald Lam are also lawyers, though the latter was debarred), and Ian Fleming would stick with equal firmness to the conventions of his spy hero. Spillane succeeded first with a detective, then with a spy. He even converted his detective into a spy. And he was far more willing to experiment with non-series protagonists. Over a third of his books employ one-time heroes.

Spillane may be the most daring of the supersellers; his achievement is certainly the most disturbing. There is something admirable in Gardner's dogged iteration of his fables of New Deal individualism and optimism while Fleming's commitment to ethical hedonism and geopolitical Manicheism is at least intelligible and, in any event, is qualified by its application in the fantastic and often parodic world of James Bond. The moral myth which provides a context for the action of Spillane's heroes is neither as decent as that which guides Perry Mason nor as definite as that which governs James Bond. The very ease with which Spillane makes the transition from private eye to counterintelligence agent to hood is most disquieting, for the same voice affirms the values of each. Private revenge, national salvation, gangsterism, and vigilantism are levelled by this equation. The survival value of toughness becomes an end in itself, to be justified on an ad hoc basis by appeals *against* a particular enemy (never *for* an articulate principle)—against killers or Communists, pimps or homosexuals, blackmailers or drug dealers. Spillane's protean career is thus to some extent the result of his radical failure to establish positive values in his fiction.

This failure finds its symbol in another of Spillane's distinctions. Although reticent about his private life, he has actively promoted himself as the prototype of his tough-guy hero. All three supersellers obviously embodied their personal fantasies in their protagonists. Fleming posed for a publicity photograph in which he holds a Bondian Beretta to his lips, and Gardner played the role of the judge in the last show of the Perry Mason television series (even in his younger years, the stocky, bespeckled Gardner could not have cast himself as Mason). But Spillane has gone the furthest to identify himself with his hero. In the 1963 feature film of *The Girl Hunters,* he actually played out his fantasy in celluloid. The back cover of the novel contains a publicity photo from the movie and the accompanying announcement, "Author Mickey Spillane plays the part of Mike Hammer in the motion picture THE GIRL HUNTERS." Spillane has, additionally, lent his voice and his image to various other promotions of his hero, most recently in the publicity surrounding the 1983 telemovie.

There may be sound commercial reasons for these attempts to confound the artist with his art, but the resulting confusion of reality points again to the egocentric nature of the value system implicit in Spillane's vision of the world. Gardner can refer to an objective set of values embodied in the Anglo Saxon institutions of justice and in the complex of social prejudices commonly identified as middle-class morality (what Gardner would call "square shooting"). Fleming too can call upon a set of verifiable standards—the practices of statecraft and the principles of epicureanism. Action in Spillane's world is sanctioned by no such external rules; instead, its justification depends solely upon the force of personality of the actor. The film of *The Girl Hunters* symbolizes this ethical solipsism: self is all. The creator plays his own creation.

In the fairy tales of Spillane-Hammer, the Big Bad Wolf is the narrator, and he justifies his depredations honestly by referring to the requirements of his own appetites. Hunger may be a legitimate motive for action. Certainly it will appeal to an action-starved audience. But it remains an unstable virtue. The wolf would be hard pressed to debate morality with the three little pigs. In the fiction of Gardner and Fleming, the nature of justice *is* a topic for discussion. Mason and Bond are prone to self-doubt and self-defense, and they express their qualms frequently in dialogues with their secretaries and comrades. The mission of Mike Hammer is questioned only once, in *One Lonely Night,* and there, significantly, the debate takes place entirely within the mind of Hammer himself. He is a knight for whom loneliness is a necessity. It is his very alienation from any shared community values that enables him to justify his violent actions as ends in themselves. The ultimate criticism of the ethos of Spillane's fictional world must be that it is literally undebateable.

3

Ian Fleming

The problem of achieving justice divides naturally into three aspects: epistemological (who has done what), ethical (conclusive judgments upon agents and actions), and practical (fitting punishments to crimes). These aspects roughly correspond to the offices of the detective, the jury, and the judge. The American hard-boiled detective tends frequently to usurp the second office. Though Perry Mason nominally accepts the authority of the jury, he invariably preempts an important element of its judgment. But though Mason concludes who is guilty, he leaves it to a jury to apply community values in the determination of how guilty. Even homicide, a capital offense, has its degrees. And Mason never infringes upon the third office, that of sentencing criminals according to a jury's evaluation of their guilt.

Mike Hammer confidently arrogates all three offices, preempting both jury and judge. He knows, judges, and executes. But Tiger Mann, the secret agent, is significantly less comprehensive (though no less confident) in his claims. His primary office is practical: acting on the knowledge and the judgment of others, he must enforce justice in his world. The secret agent novel generates suspense not through who's and why's, but through how's and when's. Knowledge is the conclusion of the detective's work; it is the premise of the secret agent's. The essential truths are contained in his assignment; hence, the convention of distant, godlike agency heads—Tiger Mann's Martin Grady, Matt Helm's Mac, James Bond's M. Chesterton's

The Man Who Was Thursday is, in this regard, the archetypal secret agent novel: Sunday, the ultimate agency head, *is* God.

There are secret agents and there are secret agents. Not all Controls are divine, as John le Carré has shown, nor does the surrender of judgment lead inevitably to the sublime self-confidence of Tiger Mann. But the tradition out of which the next superseller emerged was the one that made politics as clearcut as the detective story had made ethics. In the latter, murder is simply wrong; in the former, my country is simply right. James Bond looks backward to the naive chauvinisms of John Buchan's Richard Hannay or "Sapper's" Bulldog Drummond. M is an unquestionable authority. Bond is not without intelligence, but he employs his resources—mental and physical—toward a predestined end. He is a tactician, not a strategist; a foot soldier, not a general and certainly not a prime minister.

Insofar as Bond is a secret agent and not a detective, he may seem unlikely company for Mickey Spillane or Erle Stanley Gardner. His concern is national security, not homicide; his exercises are prophylactic, not investigative or retributive. And he is, of course, English, not American. And yet his consanguinity with Hammer and Mason is unmistakable. When Kingsley Amis wished to defend the Bond novels against the charge that they pandered to prurient sadistic and sexual appetite, an invidious comparison with Spillane's fiction seemed natural. Bond is cold; Hammer is hot (Bond's adventures are narrated in the third person; Hammer's in the first); both are violent, sensual, self-assertive creatures. Both forcefully command the attention of the willing women and the unwilling men whom they encounter. Both are philanderers; both are executioners.

To the extent that he belongs to the fleshly school of popular literature, Bond seems so much further from the middle-class pieties of Perry Mason. But the distance between London and Los Angeles is abridged by several considerations. The most significant of these is Bond's commitment to a judicial organization. Like Mason, Bond is a reluctant, even rebellious bureaucrat, but a bureaucrat nonetheless. Like Mason, he lives for the excitement of exceeding the rules, but, like Mason, he acknowledges in principle the authority of a governmental system. Related to this acknowledgment is an interest in systems and institutions generally. Mike Hammer is consumed by his own passions; little of the objective, external world finds admission to his narratives. Mason and Bond attend meetings, initial memorandums, study dossiers and transcripts. And Mason shares to some degree Bond's technological curiosity. Gardner inserts in his narratives brief informative lectures, often on matters of legal precedent or forensic medicine, but also upon matters like cameras, eyeglasses, prospecting, or the buoyancy of a duck. The Bond novels are filled with extraneous information—on places, on weapons, on customs, on the rules of card games. Finally, Mason and Bond are more peripatetic. Mason's cases take him to a variety of homes and offices, but he also finds himself in the mountains or the desert, or at sea. He travels as far north as San Francisco, and he flies several times to Las Vegas and at least once to New Orleans. Bond's excursions of course carry him around the world.

It is in the matter of style that Fleming differs most from his two predecessors. All three supersellers wrote necessarily in an accessible prose. Gardner's is the most ordinary; Spillane's the most distinctive; and Fleming's the most literate. Gardner's prose is almost militantly banal, yet it is eminently serviceable in communicating a quick flow of dialogue and action. Spillane's tough, idiosyncratic rhetoric conveys much of the crucial personality of the narrator. The disagreeableness and the redundancy of Spillane's message have often caused his medium to be underrated. Fleming's upper-middle-class upbringing supplied him with a different approach to his writing. He was no more of a blockhead than Gardner or Spillane: he too wrote for money. But he also had in mind the exam-

ples of friends like Somerset Maugham and Raymond
Chandler. The result was a prose not as sensitive as that of
his friends, but clearly more sophisticated than that of the
other supersellers. He attempts to vary the language of his
narrative according to character and context, and even
attempts to reproduce dialect. Most importantly, Fleming
has a degree of self-consciousness as a writer that is missing in Gardner and Spillane. He is capable of irony; they
are not. A small sign of his different ambitions appears in
his decision to compose titles for each of his chapters.

Dionysiac of the Atom Age

Ian Lancaster Fleming, born May 28, 1908, was the
grandson of a Scottish millionaire and the son of a
member of parliament. If Gardner idealized middle-class
values and Spillane exploited proletarian chic, then Fleming represents the image of the nouveau aristocrat. He was
educated at Eton (withdrawing prematurely), Sandhurst
(expelled), Munich (a term of language study), and
Geneva (another term of languages). After failing the
Foreign Office examination, Fleming joined the Reuters
News Agency, serving with some distinction as a foreign
correspondent in Moscow in 1933. In the years before the
war he also enjoyed some success as a banker and a
stockbroker. Fleming apparently led a sybaritic existence
as a bachelor. He read widely in contemporary literature,
and he invested substantially in books, founding the
"Fleming Collection" of first editions marking "milestones
of human progress" since 1800. (In 1955 he became
the proprietor and publisher of the journal, *The Book
Collector.*)

At the outbreak of World War II, Admiral John Godfrey, the Director of Naval Intelligence, selected Fleming
to serve as his personal assistant. Fleming's primary responsibility was to coordinate the various activities of the
Naval Intelligence Division, but he also proposed strate-

gies of his own (some of them quite fantastic) and even participated in some nonhazardous covert operations in Lisbon and New York. Never actually a secret agent, Fleming did gain some experience of the "secret service" through his term with Naval Intelligence. Admiral Godfrey is frequently cited as one of the models for M.

Following the war Fleming held several important positions on the editorial staff of *The London Times*. He regularly spent his long winter vacations at Goldeneye, his estate in Jamaica, and there in 1952 he composed *Casino Royale*. He explained that he had undertaken the novel to "take my mind off the shock of getting married at the age of forty-three."[1] Fleming, the handsome, fitfully melancholic womanizer, had married Anne Rothermere. The marriage was a happy one, and every winter until Fleming's death from cancer in 1964, the Flemings returned to Goldeneye where Fleming would devise a new challenge to the ingenuity and endurance of 007.

Gardner's literary apprenticeship occupied a decade and filled thousands of pages of manuscript. Spillane practiced in the slicks, the pulps, and the comic books. *Casino Royale* was Fleming's very first attempt in fiction. He was a well-read gentleman, and he had considerable experience as a journalist, but as a creative writer he was an utter novice. And his sense of himself as a writer was most ambivalent. Fleming was undoubtedly concerned about commercial success. From the beginning, he haggled over terms with his publisher; he worried about his sales figures; he solicited recommendations from famous friends; he campaigned for positive book reviews. He often spoke deprecatingly of the Bond series, dismissing his hero as "the cardboard booby" and professing to be merely writing "the same book over and over again."[2] But despite this pose of the mercenary hack, Fleming obviously took great care to research the backgrounds of his novels. He set himself the difficult task of preparing new scenes of action for each adventure, and he held himself to a fairly high standard of accuracy in the depiction of these scenes. The contrast with Gardner's consistently nebulous Los Angeles and Spillane's consistently impressionistic New York City does credit to Fleming's conscientiousness. He once declared his intention to write the "spy story to end all spy stories," and he never entirely forgot his ambition.

Unlike Perry Mason and Mike Hammer, James Bond rose slowly to the status of superseller. The first novels attracted an expanding audience, but not until the late fifties did sales begin to accelerate toward the millions. By 1963 the total figure was forty million. The appearance of the film of *Doctor No* in the same year (and of *From Russia, with Love* and *Goldfinger* in the following year) further enhanced sales. By the end of 1965, all of the Bond books were supersellers.

The sources of Bond's sudden appeal, especially in America, are many. The launching of Sputnik in 1957 awakened the country to a technological threat which made Bond's combination of exceptional expertise and exceptional character seem a more appropriate counterforce that the ham-fisted anti-intellectualism of Mike Hammer or the legal niceties of Perry Mason. The well-publicized careers of actual spies—Burgess and MacLean (1954), Colonel Abel (1957), Oleg Penovsky (1962), Francis Gary Powers (1962), Kim Philby (1963)—focused attention upon this aspect of the Cold War, and events such as the Hungarian rebellion (1956), the Berlin Wall and the Bay of Pigs (1961), and the Cuban Missile Crisis (1962) emphasized that the Cold War was indeed a reality. President Kennedy's inclusion of Bond on his list of favorite reading helped his popularity, as did pulpit denunciations of sex, snobbery and sadism. And Bond no doubt benefited from the general vogue for things British in the decade of the Beatles and Carnaby Street.

But ultimately Bond's appeal—even more clearly than that of Mason or Hammer—derives from the fairy-tale quality of his adventures. Fleming himself recognized as much: "Bond is really a latter-day Saint George. He *does* kill dragons after all."[3] Despite his carnal appetites, Bond

For millions of moviegoers Sean Connery epitomized James Bond himself. He appeared in more of the film versions of Fleming's novels than any other actor. Here he is shown with Honor Blackman in the popular *Goldfinger*.

is a chivalric hero who rides out to vanquish a grotesque villain embodying social and moral evil—contemporary totalitarianism as well as traditional vices like pride and covetousness. He may be a Lancelot rather than a Galahad, but he rides for queen, country and the liberal tradition. He is a warrior on a modern battlefield. Missiles and nuclear weapons figure constantly in the foreground of his missions. Single-handedly (with a technical assist from Q Branch and occasional help from local accomplices) Bond again and again rescues a damsel, slays a monster, and averts a holocaust.

Banco: Casino Royale

Like the other supersellers, Fleming relied upon a set of stereotypes—characters, settings, actions—to guarantee the consistency of his product. The reader could expect of a Bond novel at least one pliant female (and could even predict how she would trim her fingernails) and at least one master villain (usually distinguished by physical deformity); he could expect exotic locations, reported with guide-book reliability; he could expect gambling, torture, and explosions. Most of all, he could expect excess in the depiction of these elements: the characters must be very pliant or very villainous; the settings very exotic (or very esoteric); the torture very painful; the explosions very big.

To satisfy this expectation, Fleming was compelled to produce the illusion of considerable variety. His books are superficially much more heterogeneous than those of Gardner or Spillane. Fleming also experimented with the shape of his narratives, abandoning the simple, linear plot developments favored by Gardner and Spillane and employing flashbacks and shifting points of view. Fleming tested the possibilities of the short story, and even made a noble, novel-length effort to use a first person narrator other than the hero himself.

It is not then possible to epitomize the James Bond novel

in any single example. Nonetheless, most of the standard features are at least implied in the first Bond book, *Casino Royale* (1954). The single most important feature—the character of the hero—is clearly displayed. Bond is less active than usual in *Casino Royale*. He shoots no one; he never even poses a physical threat to anyone. But despite his reputation, based in part upon the frenetic and often pointless activity of the films, Bond is the least aggressive of the three superselling heroes. Motion is a panacea in the Mason and Hammer series; confrontation—verbal for Mason, physical for Hammer—is a pleasure as well as a methodology. Bond is something of a reluctant combatant, often suspicious of his own motives and weary of conflict. The relentless enthusiasms of the American heroes give way to an intermittent desire to withdraw from engagement.

Casino Royale opens with a hint of Bond's awareness of his own limitations:

> The scent and smoke and sweat of a casino are nauseating at three in the morning. Then the soul-erosion produced by high gambling—a compost of greed and fear and nervous tension—becomes unbearable, and the senses awake and revolt from it.
>
> James Bond suddenly knew that he was tired. He always knew when his body or his mind had had enough, and he always acted on the knowledge. This helped him to avoid staleness and the sensual bluntness that breeds mistakes.[4]

Bond's withdrawal here is strategic: he must conserve his energy for the next day's tournament. But it suggests a sophisticated self-awareness that contrasts with the more naive debuts of Mason and Hammer. *The Case of the Velvet Claws* opens with a portrait of the lawyer as fighter barely able to contain his eagerness to enter the next round. Mike Hammer bursts into the first paragraph of *I, the Jury*, taking complete command of the scene. The energies of Mason and Hammer are inexhaustible; restoratives like eating and sleeping comprise at most commas in the rush

of their narratives. Bond, to the contrary, begins by withdrawing, pausing briefly on his way out to reconnoiter the
play of his assigned antagonist, Le Chiffre. On his return
to his hotel he interprets a coded confirmation of his mission, and after satisfying himself that his room has not
been searched, he falls asleep.

The next two chapters consist of flashbacks that identify
both the antagonist and the assignment. Le Chiffre is a
Soviet ("Redland") agent, the undercover paymaster of an
important Communist-controlled French trade union. He
has been speculating with union funds, investing in a chain
of brothels. When the French government closed the
brothels, he lost some fifty million francs. He has now
taken his remaining capital—twenty-five million francs—
to the casino at Royale-les-Eaux on the English Channel,
intending to recoup his losses at the baccarat tables. Bond's
mission is to ruin Le Chiffre by winning the twenty-five
million francs. He is not equipped to cheat: in order to
frustrate a French Communist, British Intelligence is simply willing to gamble twenty million francs of its own resources on the luck of its top agent. Fleming attempts to
give credibility to this improbable project by presenting it
through a series of memos from "Head of S." (i.e., of "the
section of the Secret Service concerned with the Soviet
Union") to M. Head of S. describes Le Chiffre's current
circumstances, offers his "Proposed Counter-operation,"
and appends a brief dossier on Le Chiffre and an outline
of the history and the organization of SMERSH, the Soviet
anti-espionage agency.

The next fifteen chapters cover less than a day and nar-
rate all the primary action of the plot. The story line opens
with a morning consultation between Bond and his French
counterpart, Mathis. Bond joins Mathis for lunch. There
he meets his unwanted assistant, Vesper Lynd. As Bond
leaves the restaurant, he is nearly assassinated by two
bomb-carrying Bulgarians. Their clumsiness and a fortuitous tree protect Bond from the explosion. Bond
changes his clothes and proceeds to the casino. Using a

"favorite gambit," he wins over a million francs at roulette. At the table he meets Felix Leiter, the CIA agent who cooperates with Bond in five other novels as well. Bond returns to his hotel, showers, then escorts Vesper Lynd to dinner. After dinner they return to the casino and Bond takes his seat at the baccarat table opposite Le Chiffre. He wins several banks, then loses everything. Felix Leiter rescues him with a loan of thirty-two million francs "with the compliments of the USA." Despite a threat on his life, Bond proceeds quickly to bankrupt Le Chiffre. He returns Leiter's money and cleverly hides his own in his hotel room.

Le Chiffre reacts to his defeat by kidnapping Vesper Lynd from the restaurant where she and Bond are celebrating his victory. Bond pursues Le Chiffre in his Bentley, but a lever in Le Chiffre's Citroën releases a carpet of steel spikes which send Bond's car crashing along the bank of the road. Bond is captured and carried to Le Chiffre's villa, tied to a chair, tortured and threatened with castration unless he reveals where he has hidden the money. At the last minute, an agent from SMERSH enters, executes Le Chiffre for his misappropriation of funds, and, having no orders regarding Bond, merely slices the initial letter of his organization on the top of Bond's right hand. A most unlikely deus ex machina thus concludes a most improbable drama.

The nine remaining chapters comprise a lengthy denouement. Bond never enjoys the superhuman resilience of Mickey Spillane's irrepressible heroes, but his recovery in *Casino Royale* is especially realistic. He is in the hospital several days before he can even speak to Mathis, and it is a week before he permits himself to see Vesper. Over the course of several weeks he regains his strength. He consummates an affair with Vesper and sees signs of a long-lasting emotional commitment. One morning he awakens to find that she has committed suicide and left him a note confessing that she has been a double agent working for the Russians.

Some of the standard Bond formulas appear in *Casino Royale* only in rudimentary form. Bond's brief (four-page) high-speed chase of Le Chiffre's car anticipates the more spectacular pursuits (and flights) in later novels. Unpressured travel, an even more common Bond stereotype, is missing entirely from *Casino Royale*. Bond is often a hound or a hare, but on most of his journeys he travels first class. Fleming was generally fascinated with modes of transportation. His careful accounts of Bond's expeditions on trains and ships and planes constitute a predictable feature of each novel.

The unfortunate Bulgarians are the victims of the first of many explosions in Fleming's novels. Three times there is the threat of a nuclear detonation; more often the explosive is a conventional one—Bond blows up a yacht in the Caribbean, or a warehouse in Mexico, or a castle in Japan. Bombs are a common weapon in spy fiction, but rarely are they as ubiquitous as they are in Fleming's novels. In *Moonraker* the villains attempt to use dynamite to send a section of the White Cliffs of Dover crashing down on the sunbathing Bond. This sacrilege may suggest a reason for the prevalence of bombs in Bond's adventures. They are the emblem of the violent, anarchic forces that seem to threaten civilization in the nuclear age. The crisis which normally confronts Bond is not murder, but mass murder. The villains are not discriminate wielders of knife, pistol, or poison; they are indiscriminate terrorists whose natural weapon is the bomb. The violence done to the White Cliffs symbolizes the destructive violence directed against the foundations of English society.

A portion of every Bond novel is devoted to bureaucratic routine. Bond is after all a civil servant. He does not make alienation the badge of his individualism. He operates in the context of information and instructions that necessitates a systematic organization—Her Majesty's Secret Service. Bond is usually restive when bound to his desk, reading and writing reports, or performing night duty at headquarters, but the desk and the file cabinet are as essential to his identity as are the Beretta and the customized Aston Martin.

In *Casino Royale*, bureaucratic routine appears in the flashback chapters and consists of Head of S.'s memoranda and Bond's short interview with M. In the later novels, formal briefings present the necessary background data. Often Bond consults with outside experts —on missile ballistics, on diamonds, on gold, on heraldry, on Japan. These detailed orientations serve to anchor the fantastic plots in mundane, civil-service reality. Just as Perry Mason referred continuously to the statutes of the California legal code, so Bond plants himself solidly in the procedures of a modern bureaucracy.

One of the most famous of the Bond formulas—"high gambling"—is mentioned in the first paragraph of *Casino Royale* and receives archetypal treatment in Bond's confrontation with Le Chiffre. Luck is an inevitble feature of nearly all popular literature. It is a cheap and natural plot lubricant and it also intimates that there is indeed a divinity that shapes our ends. It is reassuring when a villain earns his own destruction; it is somehow even more comforting when his fall is at least partly accidental. Fairy tales know this truth. So did Ian Fleming, and his particular genius lay in embodying the insight in those almost autonomous scenes where good and evil—Bond and his adversary—confront one another in a game of chance. In *Casino Royale*, Bond's victories—both the minor success at roulette and the triumph at baccarat—are entirely due to good fortune. In later examples of the formula—games of bridge, canasta, chemin de fer, blackjack, golf—an element of skill may enter the equation, but always they provide a ritualistic occasion for Bond to demonstrate that the gods are on his side.

Bond spends much of his dinner with Vesper Lynd explaining to her the rules of the ritual (i.e., of baccarat). This serves the practical function of enabling the reader to follow the succeeding action at the casino, but it also emphasizes Bond's addiction to rules in general. Bond is a conservative: his attitudes are conventional and his behavior is comme il faut. Cheating is one of the most abhorrent of vices in his world. Bond, like Perry Mason, knows that rules and laws are beneficient institutions and that if they are upheld they will ultimately—providentially—benefit the good and diminish the evil.

Bond's dinner with Vesper institutes another famous formula: epicurean self-gratification. Bond encourages Vesper to ignore the column of prices. She complies: "Well, I'd like to start with caviar and then have a plain grilled rognon de veau with pommes soufflés. And then I'd like to have fraises des bois with a lot of cream" (p. 47). Bond knowingly supplements her order with a demand for "plenty of toast" (" 'The trouble always is,' he explained to Vesper, 'not how to get enough caviar, but how to get enough toast with it' "). He continues with his own order.

> I myself will accompany Mademoiselle with the caviar; but then I would like a very small tournedos, underdone, with sauce Béarnaise and a coeur d'artichaut. While Mademoiselle is enjoying the strawberries, I will have an avocado pear with a little French dressing. (p. 47)

After accepting a recommendation from the sommelier (and explaining its wisdom to Vesper), Bond offers an apology.

> "You must forgive me," he said. "I take a ridiculous pleasure in what I eat and drink. It comes partly from being a bachelor, but mostly from a habit of taking a lot of trouble over details. It's very pernickety and old-maidish really, but then when I'm working I generally have to eat my meals alone and it makes them more interesting when one takes trouble. (p. 48)

Vesper respects Bond's sentiments, but he has been ridiculed by critics who usually associate his fastidiousness in food and drink—his vodka martini, shaken, not stirred, with a twist of lemon—with the more general matter of his "snobbery." James Bond always knows exactly what he likes, and he always has the resources to order whatever it may be. In this regard, he embodies the ideal of a consumer society.

The pleasure Bond takes in possessing and consuming material objects has several significances. In part it is simply the prerogative of the hero to live well—very well. In part it serves to make Bond's world seem concrete. The brand names Bond endorses are those the reader might find, if not among his own toiletries or in his own garage, then on the shelves of a nearby store or on the lot of a nearby dealer. Gardner sought to render his hero timeless by eliminating all local references. Fleming aims at the opposite effect. He binds his hero in his time, in a matrix of brand names and detailed menus. Mason knows the would-be eternal laws of California; Bond knows the right wine to go with tournedos or the right cologne for a long evening at the casino. The two types of knowledge are radically different—one transcendent, the other immanent—but both represent power to their possessor. Mason uses his knowledge of the law to discover justice; Bond uses his knowledge of the ways of the world to enforce justice.

"Snobbery" is one of three charges consistently directed against Bond since 1958, when critic Paul Johnson first issued the famous alliterative indictment. "Sex" ("the mechanical, two-dimensional sex-longings of a frustrated adolescent") and "sadism" ("the sadism of a schoolboy bully") are the other two; both are also represented by formulas. Bond's liaison with Vesper Lynd is more complex than most of his sexual affairs, but Vesper is a typical Bond woman. She wears no makeup, is lightly tanned, possesses "fine breasts," prefers wide belts. Bond finds her attractive, but initially resents her as an unnecessary distraction. When she is kidnapped by Le Chiffre, his primary response is one of irritation at her stupidity. But when they meet again in the hospital, Bond feels a desire for her that relieves his fears that he might have lost his masculinity. Desire evolves into love.

Like all Bond women, Vesper is not a virgin, nor has she

ever been married. Like many of the others, she is an agent of the opposition, and like them she falls suddenly and totally in love with Bond. Unlike the others however she cannot manifest her love by betraying her old allegiance. (Bond's damsels often come to the rescue of their St. George.) Vesper has been working for the Soviets because they have held her old lover hostage. Now her love for Bond has made her situation impossible. She is being followed by SMERSH. By remaining silent, she endangers herself and Bond; by speaking, she loses Bond's love. She commits suicide.

Bond, who at first disparaged the girl, then used her to verify his revived masculinity, has fallen in love and proposed marriage. The last nine chapters of *Casino Royale* represent for him an idyll of recovery and romance that is shattered by the revelations of Vesper's suicide note. Bond weeps, then suppresses all emotion:

> He saw her now only as a spy. Their love and his grief were relegated to the boxroom of his mind. Later, perhaps they would be dragged out, dispassionately examined, and then bitterly thrust back with the other sentimental baggage he would rather forget. Now he could only think of her treachery to the Service and to her country, and of the damage it had done. His professional mind was completely absorbed with the consequences. (p. 143)

As he drove to her rescue following her kidnapping, Bond had dismissed Vesper as "the silly bitch." Romance had altered his perception, but the novel closes with Bond on the phone to "the outside liaison officer" in London:

> "This is 007 speaking. This is an open line. It's an emergency. Can you hear me? . . . Pass this on at once: 3030 was a double, working for Redland . . . .
> "Yes, dammit, I said 'was.' The bitch is dead now." (p. 144)

Bond's recovery and infatuation had provided a dramatic contrast to the cold-bloodedness of the preceding action —the bombing, the baccarat, the torture. In the end, however, cold-blooded professionalism reasserts itself. Bond must will himself into emotional indifference. The abruptness and bitterness of his last words are a measure of the price he pays for his success as a secret agent. They express his condition as accurately as Mike Hammer's last words in *I, the Jury* express his. For Bond, it is not easy.

The third formula which consistently outraged Bond's critics is the sadistic inflicton of pain. Chapter 17 of *Casino Royale*, "My Dear Boy," comprises the quintessential example of this formula. Le Chiffre has Bond stripped and tied to a seatless armchair. He sits opposite Bond with the handle of a carpet-beater on his knee, the trefoil under Bond's chair. When Bond still refuses to divulge the location of his winnings, Le Chiffre strikes upward with the carpet-beater. "The result was startling":

> Bond's whole body arched in an involuntary spasm. His face contracted in a soundless scream, and his lips drew right away from his teeth. At the same time his head flew back with a jerk showing the taut sinews of his neck. For an instant, muscles stood out in knots all over his body, and his toes and fingers clenched until they were quite white. Then his body sagged, and perspiration started to bead all over his skin. He uttered a deep groan. (pp. 92–93)

This is only the first of many strokes. The torture is revolting; so is Le Chiffre's attitude: " 'You see, dear boy?' He smiled a soft, fat smile. 'Is the position quite clear now?' " (p. 93). Le Chiffre's phrases, "dear boy," "my dear boy," combined with a reference to his paternal tone ("Le Chiffre spoke like a father") and his obvious design to castrate Bond through the torture or, failing that, with the carving knife he has at hand, make the scene into an obscene parody of an Oedipal situation. Nearly all the villains who torture Bond also patronize him.

This sort of episode constitutes Fleming's notorious sadism. Bond is always the victim or the witness. Elegance and ingenuity usually characterize these scenes. Pain becomes an artistic effect. Later villains, such as Mr. Big, proclaim as much. Le Chiffre is a more naive artist, but even though he lacks the refined motives of his successors, he is typical in his careful arrangement of the trap and his thoughtful selection of the instruments. Fleming avoids the brutal, spontaneous violence of Spillane's novels, the smashed noses, snapping bones, and dislodged teeth. Suffering and death are always components of a larger, well-designed plot. Pain may be extreme in Bond's world, but it is not accidental.

The artists of pain in *Casino Royale* are Le Chiffre and the anonymous SMERSH assassin who shoots him and who neatly initials Bond's hand. Le Chiffre is of course the principal villain, a common stereotype in melodrama that Fleming transformed into a series of transcendent personifications of evil. This antagonist is the most memorable figure in each book. Le Chiffre is only an embryonic version of the sublime adversary Bond normally encounters. His major flaw is his desperaton: Le Chiffre is the only one of Bond's opponents to start from a position of weakness. And his office—that of paymaster—lacks the grandeur and the independence of the later villains. Mr. Big, Hugo Drax, Dr. No, Goldfinger: all are ultimately servants of the Soviet state, but effectively they reign over ambitious organizations of their own. Le Chiffre's only subordinates are the few accomplices necessary to threaten Bond in the casino and to capture him after the car crash.

Nor does Le Chiffre more than hint at the physical and psychological peculiarities that characterize the sublime villains. He does indulge in one habit that offends Bond's sensibilities. Le Chiffre uses a benzedrine inhaler: "He inserted the nozzle of the cylinder, with an obscene deliberation, twice into each black nostril in turn, and luxuriously inhaled the benzedrine" (p. 60). And his features are, at the very least, disagreeable. Bond studies "the wide expanse of white face surmounted by the short abrupt cliff of reddish brown hair, the unsmiling wet red mouth, and the impressive width of the shoulders" (p. 61). The reddish hair *is* typical. It is shared by Hugo Drax and Auric Goldfinger.

According to tradition, it is also shared by the devil. Iconographic subtleties are not, however, necessary to make the point that Bond's larger-than-life adversaries are avatars of The Adversary. Pride is the besetting sin of the principal villains. They attempt to set themselves up as secular gods, determining the course of history. Again, Le Chiffre only foreshadows later developments, but he too clearly presumes too much in trusting his fate to the fall of the cards. And in a curious parallel to the effect of Satan's punishment of Job, he provokes a crisis of faith—of faithlessness—in James Bond.

This crisis occurs during the period of Bond's recovery, emerging through his dialogue with his comforter, Mathis. He begins by explaining the origins of his doubts:

> "When I was being beaten up," he said, "I suddenly liked the idea of being alive. Before Le Chiffre began, he used a phrase which stuck in my mind: 'playing Red Indians.' He said that's what I had been doing. Well, I suddenly thought he might be right. (p. 108).

"Red Indians" is a self-deprecatory phrase Bond will apply to his profession at several points in his career. It is, in fact, Fleming's private name for the actual commando force—No. 30 Assault Unit—that he organized and directed for Naval Intelligence during World War II.[5] Fleming recognized and mocked the element of childish adventure in the mentality of men at war, but the mentality is nonetheless real and necessary in that grand game. In a sense, Bond must mature into acceptance of this childish vision.

He continues for the moment to disparage it. "When one's young," he informs Mathis, "it seems very easy to distinguish between right and wrong; but as one gets older it becomes more difficult" (p. 108). During the war he had had no scruples about performing the two assassinations which earned him his double-0 prefix. But he no longer has the confidence to assume the justice of his cause. "The villains and heroes get all mixed up" (p. 109). Additionally, even firm values seem timebound: today's conservatism fifty years ago "would have been damn near called communism." The only certain value that Bond can affirm is the private one espoused by Mike Hammer, "personal revenge." Bond even argues that the devil has had a bad press and that Le Chiffre may have had his redeeming social value.

Mathis's response consists largely of worldly sarcasm at Bond's sophistries. He appeals partly to authority: M will tell Bond about the villains who would destroy Bond, his friends, and his country. Primarily he appeals to pragmatism—"personal experience":

> And now that you have seen a really evil man you will know how evil they can be, and you will go after them to destroy them in order to protect yourself and the people you love. You won't wait or argue about it. You know what they look like now and what they can do to people. . . . You may want to be certain that the target really is black; but there are plenty of really black targets around. (pp. 112–13)

Mathis has ironically referred to his own childish inability to understand Bond's arguments ("I am a child, an absolute child in these matters"), but again the point is that the child's view of saints and dragons is the accurate, useful one. A hero must believe in the existence of "really black targets."

Bond does not concede; the chapter, "The Nature of Evil," ends inconclusively. It takes Vesper's suicide to restore the child in Bond.

> How soon Mathis had been proved right, and how soon his own little sophistries had been exploded in his face!
> While he, Bond, had been playing red Indians through the years (yes, Le Chiffre's description was perfectly accurate), the real enemy had been working quietly, coldly, without heroics, right there at his elbow. (p. 143)

Bond now embraces his vocation with enthusiasm: "Well, it was not too late. Here was a target for him, right to hand. He would take on SMERSH and hunt it down" (p. 144). The sentiment is not far from that which redeems Mike Hammer in *One Lonely Night*. In SMERSH Bond discovers evil's name and local habitation. The principal villains in five of the next six novels will be affiliated in some fashion with SMERSH. Unlike Mike Hammer, Bond will continue to have doubts about his profession—he will even again consider resigning—but always he will carry on against the definite evils which threaten his community.

Damsels and Dragons

Live and Let Die (1954) contains in ideal form nearly all of the Bond conventions: the villain is sublime; the girl is uncomplicated; the locations are exotic; the pursuits are melodramatic. Though the premise of *Casino Royale* was improbable, the characters and actions were not. Le Chiffre, Bond, and Vesper are trapped in unusual circumstances, but they respond to events more or less as a-dults would—with desperation, courage, disillusionment, affection, despair. The premise of *Live and Let Die* is not only improbable, it is specifically childish, involving as it does pirates and buried treasure. Fleming achieves here the prototype of his standard synthesis of extravagant caricature and careful verisimilitude—the moral vision of a child and a discerning eye for the textures of the modern world.

The bureaucratic routine of instructing Bond on the nature of his assignment again occurs in a flashback. M lectures briefly on the subject of pirates and treasure, then informs Bond that doubloons apparently from the hoard of Bloody Morgan have been turning up inexplicably in the hands of blacks in Florida and Harlem. The source of the coins seems to be Jamaica, hence the involvement of the British Secret Service. The suspected smuggler is Mr. Big.

"Mr. Big," said M, weighing his words, "is probably the most powerful Negro criminal in the world. He is . . . the head of the Black Widow Voodoo cult, and believed by that cult to be the Baron Samedi himself. . . . He is also a Soviet agent. And finally he is, and this will particularly interest you, Bond, a known member of SMERSH."[6]

Bond thus has personal as well as professional motives for carrying out his mission.

Bond arrives in New York City and is pleased to find Felix Leiter representing the CIA. The two friends make an evening tour through Harlem. Through the device of a vanishing nightclub table, Mr. Big takes them captive. He interrogates Bond, testing the truth of Bond's answers by the reactions of Solitaire, a telepath and Mr. Big's fiancée. Solitaire signals to Bond her sympathy with him and then confirms his cover story. As a warning, Mr. Big has one of his lieutenants slowly break the little finger of Bond's left hand. While being led away, Bond manages to break free and to kill three of Mr. Big's men.

Bond and Leiter decide to investigate the Florida end of Mr. Big's network. Solitaire flees Mr. Big and joins Bond on the Silver Meteor to St. Petersburg. Although detected by Mr. Big's minions, who launch a bazooka attack on Bond's compartment, Bond and Solitaire arrive safely. Bond and Leiter reconnoiter Mr. Big's St. Petersburg operation, Ourobouros, Inc. ("Live Worm and Bait Merchants"). Later, Leiter makes a covert entry which leads to his losing an arm and a leg to a shark ("He disagreed with something that ate him"). Bond makes his own entry, and this time Mr. Big's agent falls to the sharks ("Bond heard one terrible snuffling grunt as if a great pig was getting its mouth full"). But meanwhile Mr. Big has kidnapped Solitaire and carried her to his island—the Isle of Surprise—off the coast of Jamaica.

Bond flies to Jamaica and secures the cooperation of the Secret Service's local representative, Strangways. He also obtains the assistance of the Caymen Islander, Quarrel, who supervises Bond's aquatic training. The night before

Mr. Big's boat is scheduled to leave the Isle of Surprise, Bond swims across the channel and manages to attach a limpet mine to its hull before he is captured by Mr. Big's guards. Mr. Big boasts of his accomplishments and announces his intention to tie Bond and Solitaire to a paravane (a mine-sweeping device) which will be dragged behind the departing yacht. Their flesh will be lacerated by a coral reef and then consumed by shark and barracuda. Fortunately the limpet mine explodes just as the paravane reaches the reef. The sharks feed on Mr. Big; Bond and Solitaire share the "fortnight's passionate leave" granted to Bond by M.

Mr. Big is a villain in the grand style. He is a grotesque physical specimen.

> It was a great football of a head, twice the normal size and very nearly round. The skin was grey-black, taut and shining like the face of a week-old corpse in the river. It was hairless, except for some grey-brown fluff above the ears. There were no eyebrows and no eyelashes and the eyes were extraordinarily far apart. (p. 44)

Six and a half feet tall, 280 pounds: Bond reports that Mr. Big radiates power and intellect. The talisman of voodoo adds to his awesomeness.

Like most of Bond's antagonists, Mr. Big justifies his villainy with an articulate, perverse philosophy. He begins with a statement of boredom: "I am prey to what the early Christians called 'accidie,' the deadly lethargy that envelops those who are sated" (p. 51). He has sought to overcome this boredom by exploring the esthetics of villainy. "Mister Bond, I take pleasure now only in artistry, in the polish and finesse which I can bring to my operations. It has become almost a mania with me to impart an absolute rightness, a high elegance, to the execution of my affairs" (p. 52). He aspires to be the Cellini of crime. Therefore he declines to murder Bond crudely—"it would give me no aesthetic pleasure to blow a hole in your stomach"—and instead orders the neatly broken finger. And therefore, on the Isle of Surprise, he elects to execute Bond and Solitaire through the imaginative device of the paravane.

Bond diagnoses Mr. Big as a "raving megalomaniac." Megalomania, not surprisingly, is the pathological condition of all of Bond's sublime adversaries. They all possess the insane self-confidence of Mr. Big.

> In due course, as in the developing history of other races, there will appear Negroes great and famous in every other walk of life. . . . It is unfortunate for you, Mister Bond, and for this girl, that you have encountered the first of the great Negro criminals. . . . I prefer to regard myself as one who has the ability and the mental and nervous equipment to make his own laws and act according to them rather than accept the laws that suite the lowest common denominator of the people. (p. 145)

Of course, such megalomania facilitates plot clarity by compelling the villain to parade his achievements and his intentions before his captive audience.

What is surprising however is that these megalomaniacs should choose to subordinate themselves to SMERSH. After serving with the OSS during World War II, Mr. Big spent five years in Moscow. It is to finance SMERSH operations that he smuggles the gold coins into the U.S. But he does not allude to these services in his analyses of his own greatness. The two motives—self-aggrandizement and political subversion—are more convenient than compatible. The SMERSH connection supplies a necessary legitimacy to Bond's assignment, but it remains essentially irrelevant to the confrontation between Bond and a self-sufficient embodiment of diabolic evil.

Mr. Big, the enemy, is black (as is Quarrel, the ally). Le Chiffre was "a mixture of Mediterranean with Prussian or Polish strains." Hugo Drax, in the next Bond novel, is German. All of Bond's enemies (and, for that matter, most of his allies and his women) are foreigners (i.e., non-British). Xenophobia is a not unnatural ingredient in spy fiction, but it does further distinguish the genre from that of detective fiction. The moral of the latter is that the evil exists among us. Even in Spillaine's *One Lonely Night*, with its malignant Russians, the ultimate villain is an American traitor. In spy fiction, the evil comes from outside; it is inherently alien to our peaceful community. Mr. Big's blackness merely emphasizes his difference from "us." In fact his power and intellect are the equal of that of any of the later Caucasian or Oriental villains Bond encounters. Bond was not immune to racism (cf. his comments on Koreans in *Goldfinger*), but he expresses interest, not condescension, in his dealings with American blacks.

Solitaire is the ideal Bond girl. She is physically as attractive as Vesper Lynd, but she also possesses two new qualities that recur frequently in Bond's women. When she meets Bond, she has a history of rejecting men. Mr. Big informs Bond, "She will have nothing to do with men. That is why, in Haiti, she was called 'Solitaire'" (p. 48). Her second distinction is her instantaneous infatuation with Bond. The romance between Bond and Vesper evolved over a period of weeks. Before Bond ever speaks to Solitaire, she falls so deeply in love with him that she abandons both the powerful Mr. Big and her lifetime aversion to men. Fleming went to great lengths to render plausible his monstrous, maniac villains; he was content to leave unexplained his implausibly complaisant women. Only twice—in *Casino Royale* and the extraordinary *The Spy Who Loved Me*—does he treat a woman's emotional attachments with any seriousness.

Fleming always treats seriously the backgrounds of his novels. A continental casino was familiar territory; Harlem and St. Petersburg were not, and Fleming made a conscientious effort to verify his facts. On the flyleaf of his bound copy of the manuscript of *Live and Let Die*, he noted proudly: "All the settings are based on personal experience and I spent a whole night in Harlem with a detective from the 10th Precinct verifying my geography, etc." He also endeavored to authenticate his material on Bloody Morgan, on Caribbean fishing ("based on my own experi-

ence and on the findings of the U.S. Navy Department"),
and on St. Petersburg ("is just like I say it is").[7] The
Jamaican material was available at his doorstep: *Live and
Let Die*, like all the Bond novels, was composed at Goldeneye, Fleming's Jamaican estate.

Fleming had a journalist's eye for detail. His one night
in Harlem hardly qualified him as an expert, yet he was
able to gather a sense of the landmarks (Sugar Ray's nightclub, Ma Frazier's restaurant, the Savoy Ballroom) and
signs of the special atmosphere (advertisements for hair-
straighteners, "shops devoted to lucky charms and various
occultisms"). The latter details especially suggest an alien
culture where brown eyes are always watching the white
men and where Mr. Big might indeed exploit a reputation
for voodoo powers.

Yet despite an endorsement from Raymond Chandler
("I had a drink with Raymond Chandler last night and he
said that the best bit of *Live and Let Die* was the conversation between the two Negroes in Harlem, which he said
was dead accurate"[8]), Fleming's ear for the American ver-
nacular, black or white, was dubious.

> "Don' waste yo' breff," said the Negro who had been giving
> the orders. "Take da Limey away." He addressed Bond's
> guard. "Mr. Big's waiten." He turned to Leiter. "Yo' kin tell
> yo' fren' goodbye," he said. "Yo' is unlikely to be seein' yo'
> selves agin." (p. 43)

Chandler presumably had his tongue in his cheek. Neither
the syntax nor the diction ("Limey"!) corresponds to Black
English. Fleming tries to alter the monotone of his narrative
by superimposing conventional indications of dialect—
"don'," "yo'," "breff." But only the pronunciations have
changed, not the idiomatic rhythms and usages of the language. An eye for surfaces enabled Fleming to construct
convincing images of strange scenes, but the defect of his
ear (and his failure to recognize the defect: Fleming surely
did not have his tongue in his cheek when he reported

Chandler's compliment) demonstrates his inability to penetrate the nature of strange characters.

A new formula introduced in *Live and Let Die* and repeated regularly thereafter is the training episode. Under Quarrel's direction, Bond prepares diligently for his swim to the Isle of Surprise. Every day for two weeks Bond swims a mile, runs a mile, studies the waters and reefs, and listens to Quarrel lecture on the habits of marine life. Bond accepts the necessity of exertion and instruction. Unlike Mike Hammer, Bond is not a natural hero; he must practice to be superhuman. The reader identifies with Hammer to reassure himself that he contains within himself the knowledge and the strength to make things right; he identifies with Bond to reassure himself that he contains within himself the potential to acquire the knowledge and the strength to make things right.

One other new feature emerges in *Live and Let Die* which distinguishes Fleming's novel series from those of Gardner and Spillane. Felix Leiter makes his second appearance (of six). All series require a central corps of continuing characters—Perry-Della-Paul; Mike-Velda-Pat. The corresponding corps in the Bond series consists of Bond, M, and, in minor roles, the secretaries of the Secret Service, Miss Moneypenny, Loelia Ponsonby, Mary Goodnight. But Fleming also tries to unify the Bond saga through a cast of intermittently appearing outsiders. Leiter is the most prominent of these, but they also include Quarrel and Strangways, Mathis, Assistant Commissioner Vallance of Scotland, and Mr. DuPont (*Casinao Royale* and *Goldfinger*). Ernst Stavro Blofeld is the unique instance of a repeating principal villain. Bond is the superselling hero most haunted by his own past.

Moonraker (1955) reassembles most of the established Bond conventions. The first third of the novel takes place in an exclusive London club and represents a full-scale rendition of the gambling formula. The remainder transpires at a British rocket base near Dover, where the villain,

Sir Hugo Drax, plots to avenge Germany's defeat in World War II. Both scenes are English: *Moonraker* is the only novel in which Bond, with the express consent of the prime minister, operates entirely within the boundaries of the United Kingdom.

If the plot prohibits Fleming from exploiting a foreign locale, he compensates by portraying in detail the esoteric environment of Blades, "still the most exclusive club in London." The four chapters devoted to Blades are usually taken as the apotheosis of Fleming's snobbery. The food is the finest; the servants are unequaled; only brand-new currency is paid out on the premises; the newspapers are neatly ironed before being placed in the reading room. M invites Bond to Blades for a meal which is an epicurean delight. Once again, Bond's definite tastes in fine food serve as a key to his character. After hearing Bond's confident order (smoked salmon, lamb cutlets, peas and new potatoes, asparagus with Hollandaise sauce, a slice of pineapple), M remarks "Thank heavens for a man who makes up his mind."[9] Bond may lack the sublime self-confidence of Mike Hammer (or of the typical Bond villain), but he does know himself. Confronted with a choice, he never hesitates. And of course his taste is impeccable.

M has brought Bond to Blades because a fellow club member, Sir Hugo Drax, seems to be cheating at cards. Drax, popularly acclaimed as England's "saviour," is a millionaire who has offered to spend his private resources developing a "super atomic rocket" which would make England "safe from war for years." (p. 17). M is intensely embarrassed at the thought that the nation's hero might cheat at bridge. Bond agrees to verify the accusation and, should it prove true, to resolve the difficulty without diminishing the hero. He spends an afternoon boning up on bridge in *Scarne on Cards,* training even for an amateur mission. After briefly observing Drax's play, Bond confirms the charge and prepares his retaliation. By switching decks, Bond outcheats the cheater with a bridge hand which Fleming fully diagrams. Bond wins £15,000; Drax, recognizing that he has been detected, concedes with ill grace but no public loss of honor.

The main espionage action begins the following day when a security officer at Drax's rocket base is murdered. Bond undertakes the urgent assignment of protecting Drax's forthcoming test launch from the possibility of Soviet interference. He can rely on the assistance of Gala Brand, another British undercover agent already installed at Drax's base (and the only girl not to succumb to Bond's charms). The remainder of Drax's personnel are German technicians whom he has recruited for his project. Bond discovers a number of suspicious anomalies. The most dramatic sign of foul play occurs when a portion of the chalk cliffs are dynamited, nearly killing Bond and Gala.

Sir Hugo Drax is actually Graf Hugo von der Drache, a former SS Oberleutnant. During the Battle of the Bulge, Drache, through a remarkable coincidence, was able to assume the identity of a dead English soldier, Hugo Drax. He now proposes to avenge the defeat of the Reich by arming his test missile with a Soviet atomic warhead and redirecting its flight toward central London. Drax is another of the sublime villains. Superficially he differs greatly from Mr. Big. Mr. Big combined size with suavity. Drax is an extreme vulgarian. Nicknamed "Hugger," he has a "short braying laugh" and he chews his fingernails. His face has been permanently disfigured by wartime injuries; his bloodshot left eye is larger than his right; his upper jaw is prognathous. He has tight reddish hair and cultivates a bushy mustache and long whiskers. He is, in short, a red demon to Mr. Big's black.

Bond calls Drax a "great hairy-faced lunatic." Like Mr. Big, he is a megalomaniac. Drax captures Bond after leading him on a high-speed chase on the London-Dover road. He cannot resist treating Bond to a full account of his motives and his accomplishments. He pours contempt upon the English: "I loathe and despise you all. You swine! Useless, idle, decadent fools, hiding behind your bloody white cliffs while other people fight your battles" (p. 149).

At least one Englishman is not useless or idle (a bit decadent, perhaps). Bond escapes his captivity, resets the guidance gyros on the rocket, redirecting it to its original North Sea target, and saves the nation. And more: just prior to the launch, Drax had broadcast an ironic farewell to England and then, to the amazement of the radio commentators, had rushed his men into a submarine which appeared suddenly at the base. Somehow the very fast Soviet sub manages to reach the North Sea target area and to surface just where and just as the rocket descends. Thus St. George Bond manages unwittingly once again to annihilate the Dragon (Drax).

Mr. Big's discovery of the treasure of Bloody Morgan was fortuitous. The two crucial events in the life of Graf Hugo—his transformation into Drax and his death—are all but impossible. His pointless cheating and his gigantic private contribution to Britain's nuclear deterrent are almost probable by comparison. But this is the great game of the Bond novels: the delicate blending of apparently contrary modes, farce and melodrama. The narrative presents with equal gravity verifiable facts and ridiculous actions. Bond listens with identical credulity to a learned exposition of the principles of rocket propulsion and to a radio announcer's excited coverage of the descent of Drax's rocket. Though he lacks the moral vision or the artistic commitment of Jonathan Swift, Fleming's technique is not far from that employed by Swift in *Gulliver's Travels*. Fleming too forces extremes of exactness and exaggeration to cohabit productively in his narrative. Fleming however was not a satirist. Sweetness, rather than light, was his aim.

Having dressed one villain in the trappings of voodoo and another in the uniform of a Nazi, Fleming chose to outfit the villain of *Diamonds Are Forever* (1956), Seraffimo Spang, as a cowboy: Spang makes his debut "in full Western costume down to the long silver spurs on his polished black boots." Fleming adds, "Mr. Spang should have looked ridiculous, but he didn't."[10] Unfortunately appearances are deceiving. Seraffimo Spang *is* pretty ridiculous.

Certainly the Spangled Mob which he and his brother Jack run is far less impressive than Mr. Big's black network or Drax's gang of reprobate Nazis. The greed of Seraffimo Spang is gaudy, but not diabolic.

The plot of *Diamonds Are Forever* concerns a major diamond smuggling operation which moves from British West Africa to London to New York and finally to the Spangled Mob headquarters in Las Vegas. M assigns Bond to infiltrate this pipeline as a London-New York City courier. Bond impersonates a petty thief who has been conscripted for this role by the smugglers. Watched over by his attractive London contact, Tiffany Case, Bond delivers his consignment of diamonds to Michael (Shady) Tree in New York and receives the first installment of his fee. He is to obtain the remainder by placing a bet on a fixed race at Saratoga. Bond runs into Felix Leiter, who with a steel arm and a limp has been demobbed from the CIA and now works for the Pinkertons. Coincidentally, Leiter has been investigating fixed horse races at Saratoga, in the very race to which Bond has been directed, focusing on the very horse Bond was told to back. Leiter takes Bond to Saratoga and succeeds in upsetting the fix.

Bond is now sent to Las Vegas to recover the remainder of his fee. Tiffany happens to join him on his flight west. Bond wins his prearranged fee, then persists in winning an additional fifteen thousand dollars. His temerity leads to a high-speed chase at the end of which Bond is captured and carried to Spectreville, Seraffimo Spang's completely restored western ghost town. After a brief interrogation, Spang turns Bond over to his goons, Wint and Kidd, for a "Brooklyn stomping. Eighty per center." Tiffany revives Bond and they flee the town on a railroad handcar. Spang pursues them in his locomotive, which Bond manages to derail. Bond and Tiffany return to New York and sail for England. The progress of the love affair is interrupted by Wint and Kidd. Bond kills the thugs and casts their bodies overboard.

Even such a compact synopsis suggests the presence of

the standard formulas: eccentric villains, infatuated girl (Tiffany, like Solitaire, is initially averse to men, having been gang-raped at sixteen), capture and torture, bureaucratic routine (M's call for 007, informative lectures on the diamond trade), gambling (horse racing, blackjack, roulette), exotic scenes (Saratoga, Las Vegas), pursuits (by car and by locomotive). But there is a strange lack of animation in Fleming's disposition of these conventions. The evocations of Saratoga and Las Vegas represent Fleming at his journalistic best, but the rest of the narrative lacks the extravagance or the coherence of his better novels. The fault lies primarily in the conception of the villains. Leiter tries to manufacture respectability for the Spangs: "You may not have a very high opinion of American gangsters. Compared with SMERSH, for instance, and some of the other people you've been up against. But I can tell you these Spangled boys are tops. They've got a good machine, even if they do have funny names" (p. 53). But neither the characterizations nor the designs of the Spang brothers are very intimidating. They never seem to be in control of events.

The novel also suffers from a sequence of three separate and unintegrated climaxes. In the first, Seraffimo's locomotive crashes spectacularly into the Spectre mountains. In the second, the repulsive Wint and Kidd are slipped quietly into the sea. The third takes place on the western African veldt where the diamond pipeline (and the novel) began. Jack Spang attempts to make one final collection by helicopter and is blasted from the sky by Bond. This succession of disparate climaxes—one on land, one at sea, and one in the air—tends to dissipate the dramatic effect of the conclusion. Still, the separate scenes of the novel are engaging in themselves. Fleming took the subject of diamonds seriously enough to produce in the following year a journalistic account of British efforts to control smuggling in Africa (*The Diamond Smugglers*, 1957).

From Russia, With Love (1957) also lacks a dominating,

megalomaniac villain at its center, but critics have agreed in rating it among the best of the Bond novels. In it M and Bond confront their direct opposites, the representatives of SMERSH. Rosa Klebb and Red Grant are imposing figures in themselves, but their power derives from the organization they serve. Like M and Bond, they are civil servants appointed to execute the policies of their government. The struggle between the two competing bureaucracies shapes the narrative.

Part One of the novel, the first ten chapters, establishes the character of the Soviet bureaucracy. Entitled "The Plan," it introduces the principal officers and agents and reproduces the minutes of the conference at which the

Ian Fleming's debonair James Bond attracted considerable movie interest on both sides of the Atlantic. In *From Russia, with Love* (1964, United Artists) Sean Connery, the original 007, fends off pursuit by a Russian agent, played by Lotte Lenya.

conspiracy against Bond is formulated. The head of SMERSH is Colonel General Grubozaboyschikov (referred to by Fleming as General G.). The Chief of the Committee of State Security, General Serov, relays to General G. a directive from the Praesidium calling for "a conspicuous act of terrorism to be carried out in enemy territory within three months."[11] General G. convenes a meeting of his fellow intelligence chiefs at which Bond is selected as the target for assassination. The details of the plot are left to Rosa Klebb, head of Otdyel II, the department of SMERSH in charge of Operations and Executions. General G. and Rosa Kleb consult Kronsteen, a chess grandmaster and SMERSH strategist. Rosa selects as the instruments of the plot Red Grant, the top SMERSH assassin, and Tatiana Romanova, a minor but beautiful SMERSH functionary. Instead of locating the source of evil in the deformed personality of a single individual, *From Russia, With Love* distributes responsibility throughout a bureaucratic machinery.

Not all of the apparatchiks are colorless organization men. The senior officials do engage in typical maneuvers to extend their territories and to evade responsibility for mistakes. General G. is a bureaucrat of this sort. Kronsteen is a passionless thinking machine. But Rosa Klebb and Red Grant are pathological cases. Rosa is a grotesque, power-hungry, amoral creature with apparent lesbian inclinations. Red Grant is a homicidal maniac with a compulsion to kill on nights of the full moon. The account of the conspiracy that emerges from the conferences of these monstrous bureaucrats in Part One of *From Russia, With Love* resembles Milton's description of Pandemonium in the first books of *Paradise Lost*. Like Satan's parody of the Heavenly Host, SMERSH is a demonic inversion of Her Majesty's civilized Secret Service.

Tatiana Romanova is the fruit with which SMERSH hopes to tempt James Bond. The plot calls for Tatiana to inform British agents that she will defect to the west, bringing with her an invaluable decoder, but only if Bond will meet her in Istanbul. She claims to have fallen in love with his photograph in the SMERSH files. Tatiana is not aware that the plans also call for both her and Bond to be assassinated in France. This act of terrorism will presumably destroy the myth of British invincibility—the myth, as General Vozdvishensky (R.U.M.I.D.) puts it, "of Scotland Yard, of Sherlock Holmes, of the Secret Service."

This reassuring myth is one of the appeals of the Bond series: a small band of dedicated professionals see the world as it really is and act ceaselessly to forestall any subversion of Western—English—civilization. It is especially gratifying to see the enemy concede the myth. At General G's conference, a variety of suitable targets for terrorism are mentioned. Italy and Spain are dismissed ("not yet ripe for revolution"); France is "tempting," but most of its secret services have already been penetrated; the Americans, though they have "the biggest and richest service," "have no understanding for the work." But the English?

> Their Security Service is excellent. . . . Their agents are good. They pay them little money . . . but they serve with devotion. Yet these agents have no special privileges in England, no relief from taxation and no special shops such as we have. . . . It is perhaps the Public School and University tradition. The love of adventure. But still it is odd that they play this game so well, for they are not natural conspirators. (p. 35)

The English then are the proper nation for attack, and James Bond, remembered for his exploits against Le Chiffre, Mr. Big, and Hugo Drax, is the proper target. The very mention of his name elicits an unprintable obscenity from General G.

The long prologue in Moscow is followed by a brief counterportrait of the Heavenly Bureaucracy in London. Chapter 1 describes the self-indulgent morning routine of Red Grant. Chapter 11 describes the more spartan routine of James Bond. Bond is bored. Tiffany Case has left him and married. He now suffers the "accidie" which had afflicted Mr. Big. Nonetheless, he performs the necessary paperwork, even serving on a Committee of Inquiry inves-

tigating the Burgess and Maclean scandal. The tedium of
Bond's office contrasts with the scheming and the lunacy
that pervades the Soviet bureaucracy. The British Secret
Service is a responsive organization, not a provocative one.

M and Bond receive Tatiana's proposal with appropriate
disbelief, but decide that they cannot pass up the opportunity. Q Branch equips Bond with a specially designed
attaché case, and he flies to Istanbul. There he meets
Darko Kerim, Head of T. Bond immediately senses a sympathy with Kerim. Bond's most intimate male friends are
almost uniformly non-English, even non-Aryan: Quarrel,
Darko Kerim, Marc-Ange Draco (Corsican), Tiger Tanaka
(Japanese). Felix Leiter is the only exception, and he is
more a hale-fellow-well-met than a soul mate.

Darko Kerim presides over a third sort of bureaucracy.
Russia has its intriguing malcontents; England has its
faithful civil servants; Kerim has his loyal family: "Common blood is the best security" (p. 105). He is, Bond decides, "an exuberant shrewd pirate" ("the rare type of man
that Bond loved" [p. 100]). He takes Bond to a gypsy camp
where they observe a wrestling match between two girls,
and Bond accompanies him when he assassinates a Soviet
agent who has twice attempted to assassinate him. Kerim is
a fatalist and a hedonist: "Perhaps they will put on my
tombstone 'This Man Died from Living Too Much' " (p.
104). Fleming as well as Bond seems to have envied this
epitaph. When Kerim is finally killed by a SMERSH agent,
his family organization retaliates by blowing up the Soviet
embassy in Istanbul.

Fleming exercises his journalistic eye on two special settings in *From Russia, With Love*: Istanbul, which he had
recently visited on assignment for *The Sunday Times*, and
the Orient Express. Pursuant to her instructions, Tatiana
refuses to fly out of Istanbul; instead, she demands that
Bond accompany her and the decoder on the famous train
ride across the Turkish, Greek, Yugoslavian, Italian, Swiss,
and French borders. Bond's compliance with this whim
costs Darko Kerim his life, but it enables him to develop a
romantic relationship with Tatiana. As the train finally

passes through the Simplon Tunnel, Red Grant, disguised as a British agent, makes his move. He shoots Bond, but as he prepares to execute Tatiana, Bond draws a concealed knife from his attaché case and kills the assassin. (Grant's expert marksmanship had sent the bullet into the gunmetal cigarette case Bond had carefully placed over his heart.) When Bond, accompanied by Mathis, proceeds to arrest Rosa Klebb in Paris, he receives a dangerous wound that influences the opening of his next adventure.

In *From Russia, With Love,* Fleming produced a coherent narrative without the unifying device of a principal villain. Rosa Klebb, the sadistic martinet who comest closest to filling that role, dominates the chapters in which she appears, but these chapters are few. The primary structure of the narrative depends upon the competition between the two antithetical bureaucratic systems—the perverted schemers of the east and the upright, self-reliant defenders of the west. Bond's thoughts on Darko Kerim amplify the contrast:

> He reflected briefly on the way the Russians ran their centres—with all the money and equipment in the world, while the Secret Service put against them a handful of adventurous, underpaid men, like this one, with his secondhand Rolls and his children to help him. Yet Kerim had the run of Turkey. Perhaps, after all, the right man was better than the right machine. (p. 114)

The sentiment expressed in the last sentence, though neglected by the Bond filmmakers, is shared by all the supersellers. A right-minded man can always beat the machine.

The titles of the next two Bond novels—*Doctor No* and *Goldfinger*—indicate a return to the central, sublime villain. A megalomaniac with vague connections to SMERSH undertakes a nefarious project with worldwide repercussions. In the first, Dr. No threatens to misdirect and on occasion even to capture American missiles launched from Cape Canaveral; in the second, Goldfinger plots to rob the gold repository at Fort Knox. The immediate victim of both conspiracies is America, but the hero who rides to the rescue is British. The two novels probably epitomize the popular conception of James Bond.

In *Doctor No* (1958), Fleming added a sinister oriental to his gallery of villainous cowboys, blacks, apparatchiks, and mad Nazi scientists. Dr. No is tall, thin, possesses a pair of steel pincers in place of his amputated hands, and his eyeballs emit a dull ting when he taps them (contact lenses). He has built himself a fortress on his Caribbean island, Crab Key. There, under cover of a guano factory, he pursues his anti-American scheme. Dr. No fits exactly Fleming's stereotype of the principal villain. After he captures Bond and his current girl, Honeychile Rider, Dr. No delivers a complete statement of his grand accomplishments and ambitions. Then he turns to the matter of torture. Mr. Big saw pain as an art form; Dr. No sees it as a science. In one experiment he proposes to kill Honeychile Rider by staking her naked body to the rocks on front of a swarm of hungry crabs. In a second he proposes to test Bond by sending him through a deadly obstacle course that includes an electrified grid, a hot zinc tunnel, a nest of tarantulas, and a giant squid.

Dr. No's sadistic designs, like those of all of Fleming's villains, are refined and dispassionate. Even when they are not functional—Dr. No is not trying to force information from his victims—they are not motivated by crude lusts. Men in Spillane's fiction seem to obtain intense satisfaction out of smashing noses; they slobber as they watch naked women being whipped. Mr. Big and Dr. No find pain interesting, but they make a show of being superior to deriving direct gratification from its infliction. Dr. No even makes the fatal mistake of not observing the outcome of Bond's passage through his obstacle course.

As a result he suffers one of the most original deaths in fiction. After Bond escapes from the course, he struggles up a hillside and observes Dr. No supervising the loading of one of his guano ships. Bond sneaks into the loading crane and shifts the flow of guano onto Dr. No, who is suffocated beneath a mountain of green cormorant dung.

Other noteworthy aspects of the novel include the reappearance of Quarrel, from *Live and Let Die,* and Bond's battle with a dragon. Bond returns to train at the same house he and Quarrel had occupied when preparing for the engagement against Mr. Big. When Bond and Quarrel reach Crab Key, they encounter a flame-breathing monster, actually an armor-plated contrivance employed by Dr. No to frighten away intruders. Bond has already cast himself in a romantic role—"He admitted to himself that this adventure excited him. It had the right ingredients—physical exertion, mystery, and a ruthless enemy. He had a good companion. His cause was just."[12] Now he has a perfect opportunity to play St. George. This time however the mechanical dragon wins, incinerating Quarrel and swallowing Bond and Honeychile Rider.

Honeychile has the primary qualifications of a Bond girl. She is beautiful and she has kept away from men since being raped at age fifteen. She is unusually naive. A child of nature, she briefly overwhelms the worldly Bond with a series of questions like those posed to Job by the Whirlwind:

> Have you ever seen a praying mantis eat her husband after they've made love? Have you ever seen the mongoose dance? Or an octopus dance? How long is a humming bird's tongue? Have you ever had a pet snake that wore a bell round its neck and rang it to wake you? . . . . (p. 75)

Disconcerting moments like these suggest Fleming's ambition to be more than a fiction factory. Honeychile's questions intimate an entirely new perspective on the world. Her moment passes; she submits to Bond's more sophisticated vision of human reality. But Fleming has implied the existence of an alternative.

The bureaucratic routine which opens *Doctor No* illustrates two principles of Fleming's practice in the Bond series: continuity and authenticity. M assigns Bond to the investigation of two missing agents in the Caribbean (Strangways and his assistant) in part to allow him to recuperate fully from the effects of the injury received from

Rosa Klebb at the end of *From Russia, With Love*. M has little sympathy for 007's discomfort: "Bond had made a mistake and he had suffered for it" (p. 16). The mistake had been to carry a silenced pistol which had caught in its holster when Bond tried to arrest Rosa Klebb. Fleming had learned from an actual small arms expert that a Beretta was an inappropriate weapon for a secret agent, and so he took the occasion to have M call in Major Boothroyd, the armorer. Bond sulkily accepts Boothroyd's recommendations of the Walther PPK and the Smith and Wesson Centennial Airweight, and thus goes into action suitably armed.

Goldfinger (1959) is Fleming's most notorious synthesis of fact and farce. He took great care to substantiate the details of Auric Goldfinger's monumental plot against the gold repository—Operation Grand Slam—even inserting a map of Fort Knox into the text. Goldfinger carefully compiles statistics and calculates the weight of the bullion; he collects uniforms to disguise his assault force, procures a deadly poison to annihilate the local population, acquires an atomic bomb to blast open the vault, and even arranges to rendezvous with a Soviet submarine at Norfolk, Virginia. Yet the entire escapade occupies only the final third of the narrative. When he captures Bond at the end of the second part, Goldfinger recites an aphorism: "Mr. Bond, they have a saying in Chicago: 'Once is happenstance. Twice is coincidence. The third time it's enemy action.' "[13] The three parts of the novel are each identified with one of these three times.

"Happenstance" takes place in Miami, where Bond is changing planes after destroying an opium-smuggling ring in Mexico. He accidentally encounters Mr. Du Pont, a slightly vulgar American businessman who had shared Bond's table at baccarat in *Casino Royale*. Mr. Du Pont asks for Bond's assistance in exposing a card cheat, Mr. Goldfinger. The situation clearly echoes the Blades episode in *Moonraker*. Bond even enjoys a gourmet meal with Mr. Du Pont. The game this time is canasta. Bond quickly discovers Goldfinger's method of cheating and forces him to make full restitution.

There is nothing coincidental about Bond's second encounter with Goldfinger, "Coincidence." The Bank of England has become concerned about a "gold leak." During an informative lecture delivered by a bank expert on the ways of gold, Bond learns that Goldfinger is one of the wealthiest men in the world and that he may well be implicated in the leak. Therefore, with M's approval, Bond arranges a "coincidental" meeting with his adversary at the royal St. Marks golf course at Sandwich. Ten thousand dollars is wagered on the outcome of a round of golf; Goldfinger cheats; Bond out-cheats. When, two days later,

Like all Bond films, *Goldfinger* had its wild moments of hi-tech mayhem. Bond is as usual unfazed as billionaire Auric Goldfinger (Gert Frobe) happily contemplates the interesting possibilities of a laser beam in the 1965 film (United Artists).

Goldfinger crosses to the continent with his Rolls Royce Silver Ghost, Bond pursues in his special Aston Martin, equipped with its homer device. The chase proceeds across France. Bond picks up a girl who is also following Goldfinger, and the parade ends at Goldfinger's Swiss industrial plant, where Bond and the girl are captured and "Enemy Action" begins.

The main attraction of the novel is the character of Bond's antagonist. Goldfinger, like Hugo Drax, is exposed first as a person, then as a villain. He is a cheater, and worse, a man who cheats not out of necessity but out of his contempt for his victims. Unlike the blustering Drax, Goldfinger is scrupulously proper in his behavior. Too proper. Bond disparages the mechanical, textbook precision of Goldfinger's golf swing and even faults the man's faultless attire: "Goldfinger had made an attempt to look smart at golf and that is the only way of dressing that is incongruous on a links. . . . It was as if Goldfinger had gone to his tailor and said, 'Dress me for golf—you know, like they wear in Scotland' "(p. 66). Goldfinger also affects an epigrammatic style: "Money is an effective winding sheet" (p. 96), "law is the crystallized prejudices of the community" (p. 97), "riches . . . may not make you friends but they greatly increase the class and variety of your enemies" (p. 126). It is his snobbery that apparently motivates Goldfinger to spare Bond's life and to employ him as his English secretary in Operation Grand Slam.

Auric Goldfinger is, naturally, a megalomaniac, but his mania has the added fillip of a gold fetish. Yet despite his extreme vanity and his extreme avarice, Goldfinger, like Mr. Big, subordinates himself to SMERSH, serving as the organization's banker. And Goldfinger is himself something of a crypto-bureaucrat. To implement Operation Grand Slam, he enlists the support of a half dozen major American mobsters, convening them in a formal strategy session, complete with a typed agenda. Goldfinger's perversions of parliamentary procedure—a dissenter is summarily executed—align him with the other two bureaucracies of evil, SMERSH itself and SPECTRE (*Thunderball*).

Goldfinger includes most of the Bond formulas. Two deserve special notice. Pussy Galore, the girl who abruptly betrays Goldfinger out of love for Bond, is almost a caricature of her type: a tough lesbian gangster who was raped as a child by her uncle. She explains her unexpected conversion: "I never met a man before" (p. 191). Bond promises to cure her with Tender Loving Care. There is a touch of the absurd also in the brief torture scene. In an effort to discover Bond's true identity, Goldfinger turns him over to the painful ministrations of his remarkable Korean servant, Oddjob. This is unexceptional. But he reinforces Oddjob's persuasions by tying Bond to a steel table and setting a circular saw blade to advance inexorably up between his legs. The allusion to one of the stock situations of early cinematic melodramas emphasizes the surreal quality of Goldfinger's villainy.

An insight into the character of James Bond is suggested in a casual bit of self-analysis recorded at the beginning of *Goldfinger*. Bond is slightly repelled by the ostentatious lifestyle of Mr. Du Pont. "It was the puritan in him that couldn't take it" (p. 20). "Puritan" seems an unlikely adjective to apply to James Bond, the noted epicurean. It would seem equally inapplicable to the sophisticated club man, Ian Fleming. Yet Fleming's biographer asserts that he was "essentially a puritan and an idealist."[14] All of the supersellers, heroes and authors, whatever their excesses, seem to have reserved a certain puritanical attitude toward worldly values. This agreement is surely not coincidence. At least through the middle third of the century, the American mass audience demanded that even its sensualist heroes acknowledge in some degree the outlook of John Calvin. Velda's vaunted virginity and Bond's episodes of revulsion at his own self-indulgences are among the obvious signs of this acknowledgment.

The Bond book for 1960 was not a novel, but a collection of five short stories, *For Your Eyes Only*. Two of the

stories, "From a View to Kill" and "Risico," are
straightforward secret-agent adventures. In the first,
Bond uncovers a Soviet espionage project outside Paris; in
the second, he explodes a Soviet-supported heroin smuggling operation in Italy. The title story, "For Your Ey(
Only," involves the assassination of a brutal ex-Nazi in
Vermont. The morality of the piece is complicated by the
fact that two of the villain's victims were personal friends
of M. M feels obliged to debate with Bond the ethics of
ordering retaliation.

The other two tales are more unusual. "The Hildebrand
Rarity" takes place in the Seychelles Islands. A wealthy,
coarse American collector is pursuing a rare tropical fish.
He is callous toward nature, cruel to his wife, and grossly
insulting to Bond and to Bond's native friend. Someone—the wife or the friend—kills the bully by slipping the
preserved fish down his throat while he sleeps. Bond discovers and discreetly disposes of the body; he never learns
the identity of the killer.

Bond is only an accomplice in "The Hildebrand Rarity";
in "Quantum of Solace" he is even less—merely an audience. He listens as the Governor of Nassau fills an after-
dinner hour with the narrative of the marital history of a
young civil servant and his stewardess wife. The dinner
had been tiresome, and Bond expects little of interest from
the governor. But the tale—a domestic drama of infidelity
and bloodless revenge—intrigues him. The wife humiliates the husband, the husband revenges himself, the
couple divorces, the husband declines into ineffectuality,
the wife remarries a millionaire. Fleming neatly manipu-
lates the mood of the story, directing sympathy first toward the husband, then toward the wife. There is even a
final surprise when the governor reveals that the "pretty
chatterbox" who had bored Bond at dinner was this same
victimizing-victimized wife. But most remarkable is Bond's
interest in the tale. Neither Perry Mason nor Mike Hammer could conceivably have sat through such a narrative.
Fleming again hints at his sometime ambition to transcend
his formulas.

In the next Bond novel, he returned to form, redeploying all the familiar conventions. *Thunderball* (1961) is to extortion what *Goldfinger* was to robbery. The main plot concerns an elaborate conspiracy to hijack a NATO warplane carrying two atomic bombs and to demand £100,000,000 in gold bullion as the price for not employing the weapons against British or American targets. The novel was a spectacular success, and remains Fleming's bestselling work. Fleming's own enjoyment of *Thunderball* was marred by a long and expensive court case which resulted in, among other stipulations, Fleming's agreement that all future editions of the novel would contain the title-page note, "This story is based on a screen treatment by K. McClary, J. Whittingham and the author."

The extortion is directed at the west, but the conspirators are not, as hitherto, affiliated with the Soviet Union. Rather, Fleming chose to invent an entirely autonomous bureaucracy of evil, SPECTRE—The Special Executive for Counter-intelligence, Terrorism, Revenge, and Extortion. The brainchild of Ernst Stavro Blofeld, SPECTRE is governed by an executive board comprised of representatives of major European crime organizations: three members of the Mafia, three members of the Union Corse, three former members of the recently disbanded SMERSH, three former members of the Gestapo, three Yugoslavian partisans, three highland Turks. Whereas Goldfinger's American pandemonium was convened as an ad hoc committee with a single item on its agenda, Blofeld's Special Executive coordinates a wide range of illicit activities: the smuggling of gems and drugs, blackmail, espionage, and assassination.

Fleming's three evil bureaucracies are increasingly fantastic. SMERSH, in *From Russia, With Love,* was a fictionalization of what Fleming believed to be an actual, active Soviet agency (the historical SMERSH seems to have been reorganized after World War II). Goldfinger's convocation of gangsters was fanciful, but there was still a slender link to SMERSH to substantiate Goldfinger's designs. SPECTRE is completely removed from political reality—a

corporation from an archcriminal never-never land. At
the same time that John le Carré (*Call for the Dead*, [1962];
The Spy Who Came in from the Cold, [1963]) and Len
Deighton (*The Ipcress File*, [1963]) were leading a reaction
against the romanticized secret agent, Fleming chose to
emphasize the essential political irrelevance of his fables.

But if the source of evil in the Bond series becomes
simply fantastic, Fleming still took care to render the fantasy in such circumstantial detail as to create the illusion of
reality. SPECTRE is superficially no less real than
SMERSH. Fleming gives the exact address of the main
Paris office, describes the operations of the philanthropic
front behind which its Special Executive hides, and records the proceedings of the board meeting chaired by
Blofeld. Fleming seems have been fascinated by the pro-
tocols of evil. C. S. Lewis, in *The Screwtape Letters*, imagined
"the greatest evil" in the modern world being "conceived
and ordered (moved, seconded, carried, and minuted) in
clean, carpeted, warmed, and well-lighted offices by quiet
men with white collars and cut fingernails and smooth-
shaven cheeks who do not need to raise their voice."[15] This
is the image projected by General G., Goldfinger, and—
supremely—by Ernst Stavro Blofeld. This is SPECTRE.
Blofeld, as the chairman of a completely independent
executive board, is the epitome of the bureaucratic Satan.
Goldfinger's greed was in some degree subservient to his
political commitment to the Soviet system. Blofeld's motives are more pure; he has no positive commitments at all.
In *Thunderball* he aims at self-aggrandizement; in his two
later appearances he derives no profit whatsoever from his
destructive schemes. He comes to embody simple motive-
less malignity—simple negation.

This shift in the metaphysical character of the evil which
the Secret Service is assigned to combat has no practical
effect on the action. Fleming describes the hijacking of the
plane and its crash landing in the Caribbean with his usual
close attention to detail. The bombs might be anywhere in
the world, but M, seizing at a straw, sends Bond to the
Bahamas. Bond and Leiter (conveniently reactivated by

the CIA) investigate the only suspicious activity in the area: a well-equipped treasure-hunting project headed by Emilio Largo. The stages of Bond's advance to certainty regarding Largo's complicity give order to the narrative.

Largo, Blofeld's second-in-command, is in charge of retrieving the bombs, concealing them, and if necessary deploying them. He is a large, powerful, sensual, selfish man, neither a genius nor a maniac. In him Bond confronts the nearest thing to a mirror image of himself. Both men are the efficient agents of a higher authority; both rely upon complicated technological support systems (including Largo's specially designed ship and, for Bond, the latest American nuclear submarine); both are gamblers (Largo suffers an expensive loss to Bond in chemin de fer); both are the lovers of the same woman, Dominetta (Domino) Vitali. But Largo is a sadist who tortures Domino with a

This time it is David Niven as the sophisticated 007. Surrounded by a bevy of beautiful women, he coolly faces the camera in Columbia's *Casino Royale* (1967), loosely based on Fleming's first novel.

cigar and an ice cube, and Bond is the savior who sucks sea-egg spines from her foot. Largo is killed while attempting to deploy the first bomb. His death ends the action; Blofeld escapes to hatch new evils.

One of the most entertaining sections of *Thunderball* has not been mentioned. The novel opens with the most remarkable of Bond's training programs—a three chapter excursion to an English health farm, Shrublands. On M's instructions, Bond submits to a regimen of exercise, massage, nut cutlets, and orange juice. He emerges after two weeks unbearably rejuvenated. But, to the relief of his associates, he responds to his assignment in the Bahamas by resuming his normal consumption of cigarettes and alcohol. Bond may be a puritan at heart, but his lungs and liver belong to self-indulgence.

Bond's next adventure confounds expectations. In *The Spy Who Loved Me* (1962) Fleming abstained from nearly all of his profitable formulas. The novel resorts to clichés, but they are not the Bond clichés. Neither Gardner nor Spillane ever attempted such a radical rejection of the premises of his popularity.

The most obvious change occurs in the narrative point of view. For the first (and only) time, Fleming experimented with first-person narration. Moreover the narrator is not, as might be expected, Bond; it is not even a man or a secret agent. Vivienne Michel is a twenty-five-year-old Canadian girl who, after suffering a disastrous nine years in England, is distracting herself with a motorbike tour of America. She narrates the history of her romantic disappointments at length and in a true-confessions style. She has had two lovers, a supercilious Englishman and a cold German. Now, wounded in both her wings (her image), she is rambling through the Adirondacks. To recover her budget, she takes a position as temporary manager of the Dreamy Pines Motor Court.

Unfortunately the owner has arranged to burn down his own motel. The two thugs he has hired arrive and take

Vivienne captive. Sol "Horror" Horowitz is "tall and thin, almost skeletal, and his skin had this gray, drowned look as if he always lived indoors. The black eyes were slow-moving, incurious, and the lips thin and purplish like an unstitched wound."[16] Sluggsy Morant is "a short, moon-faced youth with wet, very pale blue eyes and fat wet lips. His skin was very white and he had that hideous disease of no hair" (p. 73). This pair of cadaverous gargoyles speak a very stylized slang:

> "This is some bimbo! Git an eyeful of those knockers! And a rear end to match! Geez, what a dish!"
>
> "Not now, Sluggsy. Later. Git goin' and look those cabins over. Meantime, the lady's goin' to fix us some chow. How you want your eggs?"
>
> The man called Sluggsy grinned at me. "Scramble 'em, baby. And nice and wet. Like mother makes. Otherwise poppa spank. Right across that sweet biscuit of yours. Oh boy, oh boy!" (p. 74)

Fleming's success at imagining sublime villains did not carry over to his depiction of ordinary criminals. Horror and Sluggsy are the errand boys in the bureaucracy of evil. They are clearly intended as repulsive figures who abuse Vivienne and promise to rape and to kill her, but something clownish in their behavior and their language counteracts the effect.

Parts One and Two of the novel—"Me" (Vivienne) and "Them" (Horror and Sluggsy)—occupy nine chapters; Part Three—"Him"—occupies six. "Him" is of course James Bond, who has been in Toronto trapping a SPECTRE assassin hired by the Soviets to kill a defector. On his way to Washington, D.C., he suffers a flat tire just before reaching the Dreamy Pines. He rescues Vivienne and kills Horror and Sluggsy as they attempt to set fire to the motor court. After a night of love, he departs at dawn before Vivienne awakens. The police arrive in the morning, and a fatherly captain advises Vivienne to have no illusions about the ruthlessness of her rescuer. But as she

mounts her Vespa to leave, she has no doubts about
Bond's heroism: "A secret agent? I didn't care what he did.
A number? I had already forgotten it. I knew exactly who
he was and what he was. And everything, every smallest
detail, would be written on my heart forever" (p. 143).

The Spy Who Loved Me presents a maiden's-eye view of
the contemporary St. George. Vivienne's portrait of Bond
is unequivocal: "Apart from the excitement of his looks,
his authority, his maleness, he had come from nowhere,
like the prince in the fairy tales, and he had saved me from
the dragon" (p. 128). Bond not only slays the dragon, he
restores the maiden's soul: "The scars of my terror had
been healed, wiped away, by this stranger who slept with a
gun under his pillow" (p. 143). And, being Bond, he even
influences her cosmetically. He adds a final postscript to
his farewell note: "PPS. Try Guerlain's 'Fleurs des Alpes'
instead of Camay!" (p. 134). Bond devotes to the fate of a
girl the same virtues—his strength, his knowledge, his
character—that he normally applies to the fate of the
world.

The Spy Who Loved Me is an admirable and even entertaining diversion; *On Her Majesty's Secret Service* (1963) returns Bond to his familiar role. He plays in a casino, races
his Bentley through France, studies an esoteric subject
(heraldry), infiltrates an enemy stronghold, leads a thril-
ling chase down an Alpine ski slope, makes love to two
beautiful girls, and foils a plot to destroy the agriculture of
the United Kingdom.

The plot involves recruiting a number of girls from
important British agricultural districts and supplying each
with an appropriate biological weapon—fowl pest, an-
thrax, Colorado beetle, swine fever. The girls would distribute these plagues in the belief that they were improv-
ing the kind. The perpetrator of the plot is none other
than Ernst Stavro Blofeld, who has assembled the rem-
nants of SPECTRE at his resort atop his Swiss Alp. Blofeld
has become Bond's special nemesis. As the novel begins,
Bond has spent an entire year pursuing leads regarding

Bond in the person of George Lazenby takes aim at pursuing
SPECTRE agents somewhere in the Alps in *On Her Majesty's
Secret Service* (1970, United Artists).

Blofeld's current whereabouts; at the novel's end Bond has an additional, personal motive for continuing the pursuit.

Blofeld is in several respects a peculiar villain. His survival through three novels is unique, as is his independence from political affiliations. In the tradition of the sublime villain he conceived the monumental extortion scheme in *Thunderball*, but he remained distant from the action. He had no occasion to confront Bond directly or to boast about his accomplishments. (He does recite his most recent results to his executive board, but without the passion that illuminated the characters of Goldfinger, Dr. No, Hugo Drax, or Mr. Big.) In *On Her Majesty's Secret Service*, Bond escapes down the slopes just before Blofeld orders his apprehension and so avoids the typical scene in which he is held captive and treated to a rehearsal of the villain's triumphs. And Blofeld's motives do require clarification. Bond's guess that Blofeld might be speculating against the pound on the financial markets seems rather farfetched: "All he has to do is go a bear of sterling or Gilt-Edged. If Mr. Franklin's right . . . our currency'll literally go through the floor—and the country with it." Destroying a nation's agriculture in order to devalue its currency seems an improbably extreme measure.

Not only does Blofeld have no satisfactory reason for sending his plagues against Britain, he allows petty vanity to reveal to the Secret Service what a year of Bond's dogged investigations could not. In order to claim officially the title of Comte Balthazar de Bleuville, he informs the College of Arms in London of his real name (even documenting his ancestry so that there be no mistake about which Ernst Stavro Blofeld is making the application) and he agrees to receive Bond (alias Sir Hilary Bray) as the representative of the College. There is no inheritence or special privilege attached to the title, nor does Blofeld even have a legitimate claim to it. Out of mere snobbery he places his identity at risk. Bond boldly exploits the opportunity and Blofeld barely escapes with his life down a bobsled run.

One of Bond's two girls in *On Her Majesty's Secret Service* belongs to Blofeld's group of prospective disease carriers; the other one is his wife. He meets Madame la Comtesse Teresa di Vicenzo—Tracy—in the same casino where he met Vesper Lynd in *Casino Royale*. Bond proposes marriage to both, but the histories of the two women move in opposite directions. Her love for Bond led Vesper to commit suicide. Tracy is suicidal when Bond first meets her—despondent over the death of her daughter (Tracy, a divorcée, is the only Bond girl to have been married)—but Bond's concern for her and his lovemaking give her a new reason for living. Her grateful father is Marc-Ange Draco, Capu of the Corsican crime syndicate, the Union Corse. Draco is an attractive rogue, somewhat after the fashion of Darko Kerim. As a wedding gift, he supplies Bond with an extra-legal, airborne assault force with which to attack Blofeld's mountaintop resort. In this instance, Bond fights at the side of the dragon (Draco).

Bond absolutely refuses an additional gift of one million pounds. He intends to retain his position and his sense of place. But the marriage is ill-starred. Only hours after the ceremony in Munich, Blofeld manages to kill Tracy while she and Bond are driving to their honeymoon in Kufstein. The novel ends on the pathetic note of Bond holding onto his wife's body and explaining to a policeman:

> "It's all right. . . . It's quite all right. She's having a rest. We'll be going on soon. There's no hurry. You see"—Bond's head sank down against hers and he whispered into her hair—"you see, we've got all the time in the world."

You Only Live Twice (1964) is the least engaging novel in the series. Fleming hides a very weak plot behind an overabundance of travel writing. To prepare for the composition of *You Only Live Twice*, Fleming had conscientiously undertaken a twelve-day tour of Japan. But instead of supplying the background to the melodramatic action, Fleming's expositions of the Japanese lifestyle and world view occupy the foreground of the narrative. The first six-

teen chapters (of twenty-two) consist of Bond's passive
exposure to Japanese customs. Fleming's genuine talent
for incorporating brief informative dissertations into his
plots was not equal to this scale. He could effectively simu-
late expertise in a chapter on diamonds or gold or heraldry, but his views of modern Japan are neither sufficiently
convincing nor sufficiently interesting to justify the space
accorded them.

The premise of the novel is the desire of the British
Secret Service to gain access to Japanese sources of intelligence currently reserved by the CIA. Bond's specific assignment is to negotiate with Tiger Tanaka, head of the
Japanese Secret Service, for the use of an important Soviet
decoding machine, the MAGIC 44. Tanaka claims as the
price of his covert cooperation Bond's services as an assassin. A wealthy European, Dr. Shatterhand, has purchased
a seaside castle in southern Japan and installed within its
walls a "Garden of Death," full of poisonous plants and
animals, carnivorous fish, and boiling geysers. Shatterhand
has quietly encouraged hundreds of suicidal Japanese to
take advantage of his special attractions. The Japanese
government is reluctant to act, so Tanaka, apparently on
his own initiative, wants a foreigner to eliminate Shatterhand. (He nonetheless insists that Bond disguise himself as a Japanese, hence Bond's lengthy schooling in local
Japanese customs.)

Dr. Shatterhand turns out to be Ernst Stavro Blofeld,
undertaking his third and most inexplicable villainy. He
derives no profit from his very expensive garden, nor even
any visible sadistic gratification. His mistress, Irma Bunt,
refers to the garden as a "Disneyland of Death"; Blofeld
boasts that it is an epochal achievement: "It is very difficult
to invent something that is entirely new in the history of
the world. I have done that."[17] Later, after he has at last
taken Bond captive, Blofeld compares himself to Frederick the Great, Nietzsche, and Van Gogh. The man who
organized SPECTRE and conceived of Plan Omega and
who later plotted the destruction of British agriculture
now reveals himself to be a megalomaniac crank who

glories in the role of a necrophiliac Disney. The grandest of the Bond villains proves to be the most hollow.

Blofeld's final alias derives from the nickname of the hero of Karl May's series of boy's books. Much of *You Only Live Twice* seems juvenile. Bond gambles, but not at cards or dice or horses: "It was the old game of Scissors cut Paper, Paper wraps Stone, Stone blunts Scissors, that is played by children all over the world" (p. 11). Bond plays (and beats) Tiger Tanaka; Fleming provides a summary of the rules, as he did for baccarat in *Casino Royale*. Bond is tortured by being placed on the equivalent of a potty—a stone throne through the seat of which a geyser periodically erupts. In the climactic duel between Blofeld and Bond, the one wields a Samurai sword, the other a stave. After some cinematic thrusts and parries, Bond dispatches his archenemy. He then shuts a valve which will cause the castle to explode. He looks around for a means of escape. He notices the helium balloons which Blofeld has been using to advertise his garden.

> A lunatic idea came to him, a flashback to one of the old Douglas Fairbanks films when the hero had swung across a wide hall by taking a flying leap at the chandelier. This helium balloon was strong enough to hold taut fifty feet of framed cotton strip bearing the warning sign! Why shouldn't it be powerful enough to bear the weight of a man? (p. 148)

It is, and Bond floats out to sea.

Children's games, adolescent tortures, Douglas Fairbanks films: Bond has come a long way from the painful realism of *Casino Royale*. The Saint-George-and-the-Dragon motif has become increasingly obtrusive. Tiger Tanaka refers to Bond's task in these terms: "You are to enter this Castle of Death and slay the dragon within" (p. 66). Later, he adds: "But, Bondo-san, does it not amuse you to think of that foolish dragon dozing all unsuspecting in his castle while St. George comes silently riding towards his lair across the waves?" (p. 100). Blofeld dresses himself in a black silk kimono embroidered with golden dragons, "so easily to be derided as a childish fantasy," and he recruits his assistants from the Black Dragon Society, a powerful Japanese secret society. These allusions continue the process of simplifying the morality of Bond's contests. Blofeld eliminated political complications by creating SPECTRE; by creating his Garden of Death he reduces to the simplest one of saint vs. dragon, life vs. death.

But Bond has become a reluctant St. George. Though revived by his visit to Shrublands in *Thunderball,* he began *On Her Majesty's Secret Service* mentally composing a letter of resignation. As *You Only Live Twice* opens, he has "bungled" his two most recent missions, and M considers releasing him from duty. The Japanese negotiation is intended as a final test of his usefulness to the service. Though he does not age physically, remaining perpetually at midlife, Bond's later episodes of incompetence and weltschmerz distinguish him from the omnicompetent, ever-enthusiastic characters of Perry Mason and Mike Hammer. Bond's adventures regress toward childish fantasy, but his character matures in surprising ways.

Bond's emotional evolution is paralleled by the evolving context in which he must act. Perry Mason operates in an eternal Los Angeles; Mike Hammer in an eternal New York. A secret agent must act in actual time and space. Inventions such as SPECTRE reduce this necessity, but even in the late novels Bond must take the real world into account. The Great Britain he serves in 1964 is not the same geopolitical power as the nation he served in 1952. In *Thunderball* (1961) he notices a sign of the social change. He observes an apparently arrogant gesture made by a cab driver:

> The play with the comb, Bond guessed, was to assert to Bond that the driver was really only taking him and his money as a favor. It was typical of the cheap self-assertiveness of young labor since the war. This youth, thought Bond, makes about twenty pounds a week, despises his parents, and would like to be Tommy Steele. It's not his fault. He was born into the buyers' market of the Welfare State and into the age of atomic bombs and space flight.[18]

In *You Only Live Twice,* he listens to Tiger Tanaka's long indictment of the declining British Empire. Though forced to concede much, Bond finally rebels:

> Balls to you, Tiger! And balls again! . . . Let me tell you this, my fine friend. England may have been bled pretty thin by a couple of world wars, our welfare-state politics may have made us expect too much for free, and the liberation of our colonies may have been too fast, but we still climb Everest and beat plenty of the world at plenty of sports and win Nobel Prizes. (p. 66)

Bond's world has changed. The atomic age has altered England's status in the world; the welfare state has altered the quality of life in England itself. Both changes have

Roger Moore appeared as James Bond in several film versions, some of which used little more than the novel title. Here he is kept at bay by the murderous giant Jaws (Richard Kiel) in a train scene from *The Spy Who Loved Me,* a 1977 United Artists release.

been for the worse. But old-fashioned English heroes remain: Edmund Hilary, Francis Crick, James Bond.

After falling into the sea from his balloon, Bond is rescued by Kissy Suzuki, the Ama pearl diver who had provided him with a base of operations against Shatterhand/Blofeld. The days he had spent with her prior to his incursion into the castle comprised a unique pastoral interlude—James Bond in an Oriental arcadia. Bond suffers amnesia as a result of his fall, and Kissy decides to keep him with her on her island. In London, M publishes Bond's obituary in *The Times* (including a threat to prosecute the author of a "series of popular books" on Bond for violations of the Official Secrets Act. Only his disdain for the fictions restrains him).

You Only Live Twice ends with two portentous incidents. Kissy discovers that she is pregnant, and Bond recognizes the word "Vladivostok" and insists upon visiting the place in hopes of recovering his memory. The issue of the first event is never reported; the issue of the second is *The Man with the Golden Gun*.

The last two Bond books—a novel and a collection of previously published short stories—appeared posthumously. Fleming was ill as he composed *The Man with the Golden Gun* (1965) and he did not survive to make planned revisions. The novel as it stands is a slight addition to the series. It lacks many of the expected formulas: there is no gambling, no torture, no gourmet cuisine. There is no sex (there is a girl, Bond's former secretary, Mary Goodnight, but she remains a vague personality). The villain is not sublime. But despite these negatives, *The Man with the Golden Gun* is a satisfactory adventure. The unadorned melodrama of this final Jamaican tale contrasts favorably with the excesses of *You Only Live Twice*.

The novel opens with Bond's return to London after his odyssey across Russia. He has been brainwashed by the KGB and programmed to assassinate M (who, for the first time, is named: Admiral Sir Miles Messervy). Bond's attempt is frustrated; he undergoes rehabilitation; and earns his readmission to the Service by accepting an

Once again Roger Moore as James Bond, linked with Lois Chiles as double agent Holly Goodhead. The movie is *Moonraker* (1979) from United Artists. This still was widely used in publicity and ads for the movie.

assignment to liquidate Francisco (Paco) "Pistols" Scaramanga, "Free-lance assassin mainly under K.G.B. control through D.S.S., Havana, Cuba." With the demise of Blofeld, Bond once again faces a real world agency of evil, the KGB. In an echo of *Casino Royale,* Fleming reproduces the Secret Service dossier on Scaramanga, complete with Freudian analyses of his pistol fetishism and his homosexual tendencies. Like Le Chiffre, Scaramanga is essentially the instrument of others. He is not a megalomaniac schemer, a Drax or a Goldfinger for whom service to the Soviet Union is a necessary but secondary consideration.

But, like the grand villains, Scaramanga is a conspirator. He convenes in Jamaica a board meeting of his own miniature organization. The board's members include a KGB agent, a mafioso, and assorted gangsters. The organization's activities are of regional rather than global significance: drug smuggling, acts of terrorism designed to diminish the Jamaican sugar crop (and thus to raise the value of Cuba's production). Scaramanga's little pandemonium pales by comparison with those of Goldfinger and Blofeld, but it clearly belongs to the same type. Like Goldfinger and Blofeld, Scaramanga dramatically executes a restive member of his board. And like Goldfinger, he employs James Bond as the "manager" of his convention. The reduced scale of his operations is epitomized in Bond's ability to eavesdrop on the meeting through the simple device of holding a champagne glass to a closed door.

Bond receives unexpected assistance from Felix Leiter, once again called to duty by the CIA. The climax of the action occurs when Scaramanga entertains his colleagues by taking them on a train ride through the Jamaican swamps. Midway on the journey he stages a melodramatic charade by having the train roll over a showroom dummy dressed to resemble Mary Goodnight. The play upon the hoary convention of the maiden tied to the tracks is characteristic of Fleming's late novels. The illusion forces Bond to reveal his true identity, and in the gunplay that follows, most of the villains are killed. Leiter, Bond, and Scaramanga are wounded. In the well-played conclusion, Bond outshoots his last adversary.

Octopussy (1965) is a slim volume containing three Bond short stories. In the title story, Bond is sent to Jamaica to arrest a former intelligence officer guilty of theft and murder. In "The Living Delights," Bond is assigned to protect a defector by killing a Soviet assassin across the border in East Berlin. And in "The Property of a Lady," Bond attends a Sotheby auction in order to identify the KGB's Resident Director in London. A central figure in this last story is Maria Freudenstein, a Soviet double agent working in the offices of the Secret Service. Aware of her treachery, the service uses her to pass misinformation to Moscow. An ugly woman, she is only the second double agent to penetrate the service during Bond's tenure. The first was the beautiful Vesper Lynd. The parallel gives an accidental symmetry to the course of Bond's career.

But the career was not over. Fleming died at the peak of Bond's popularity, and his heirs decided to permit the creation to survive the creator. In 1969 Kingsley Amis, author of the admiring and insightful *James Bond Dossier* (1965), was licensed to resurrect Bond in *Colonel Sun*. Amis, writing as Robert Markham, attempted to restore a degree of realism to the melodrama, in part in a conscious reaction against the excesses of the films. The villain is a Chinese Communist colonel who plans a terrorist attack designed to embarrass both the Soviets and the British.

Amis's version of Bond was popular (ten paperback printings in three years), but *Colonel Sun* was not a super-seller. The films upon which Bond's primary appeal had come to depend were moving in the opposite direction— toward the abandonment of any sort of narrative realism. They finally abandoned Fleming's Bond altogether, saving only the titles. This development led to the production of such ersatz Bond books as *James Bond and Moonraker* (1979) by Christopher Wood. In this novelization of the

1979 movie *Moonraker,* Drax operates a fleet of space shuttles in California and schemes to repopulate the planet after first annihilating its present inhabitants.

The 1980s saw a serious third coming of Bond. John Gardner, who in the 1960s authored the Boysie Oakes spoofs of the Bond-style secret agent, has thus far published three continuations of the Bond saga: *License Renewed* (1981), *For Special Services* (1982), and *Icebreaker* (1983). Unlike Amis, Gardner has chosen to emphasize the more fantastic aspects of Bond's assignments. The principal villain in *License Renewed,* for example, is a wealthy, maniac, Scottish nuclear physicist who devises a colossal extorton plot in order to finance his design for safe nuclear energy.

But Bond's various literary reincarnations only comprise footnotes to his history as a superseller. The novels as well as the novelizations now depend upon the audience created by the films. The singular achievement of Gardner, Spillane, and Fleming lay in the ability to reach a mass audience directly and repeatedly. They composed a series of ritualized melodramas in which the right sort of hero overcame the right sort of problem in the right sort of way. In a confused and precarious world, people seek reassurance in ritual and repetition. The fables of Gardner, Spillane, and Fleming served as the secular magic for the literate masses of mid-century America.

Notes

The volume of superseller production has led to a large variety of publication formats: hardcovers, paperbacks, second editions, reissues, book club editions, omnibus editions, book-club-omnibus editions, etc. First editions are only accidentally accessible. The contemporary reader may purchase a current paperback, or take advantage of the vast, indiscriminate second-hand market, or resort to the various hardcovers and omnibuses available in the public library. I have taken all quotations from paperbacks in my possession. To facilitate verification, I have included parenthetically the total number of pages the narrative occupies in my copy.

Introduction

1. All sales figures are from Alice Payne Hackett and James Henry Burke, *80 Years of Best Sellers, 1895–1975,* (New York: Bowker, 1977).
2. *Books In Print, 1982–1983.*
3. Serge Schnemann, "What Russians Read and Don't Read," *New York Times Book Review,* 28 February 1982.
4. Bruno Bettelheim, *The Uses of Enchantment,* (New York: Vintage Books, 1977), 37.
5. Ibid., 9.
6. Ibid.
7. Ibid.

1.   Erle Stanley Gardner

1. Francis L. and Roberta B. Fugate, *Secrets of the World's Best-Selling Writer,* (New York: Morrow, 1980), 99.
2. Dorothy Hughes, *The Case of the Real Perry Mason,* (New York: Morrow, 1978), 250.
3. Fugate, 93.

4. Ibid., 98.

5. Ibid., 99.

6. Ibid., 96–7.

7. Ibid., 221.

8. Erle Stanley Gardner, *The Amazing Adventures of Lester Leith*, ed. Ellery Queen, (New York: Davis Publications, 1980), 3. All references to the Leith tales are to this edition.

9. Erle Stanley Gardner, "Speed Dash," *Atlantic*, #219 (June 1965), 56.

10. Hughes, 102.

11. Fugate, 178.

12. Raymond Chandler, *Selected Letters*, ed. Frank MacShane, (New York: Columbia University Press, 1981), 161–62.

13. Erle Stanley Gardner, *The Case of the Velvet Claws*, (New York: Pocket Books, 1970), 58–9 (of 215).

14. Chandler, 101.

15. Raymond Chandler, *Farewell, My Lovely*, (New York: Knopf, 1940), 20.

16. Erle Stanley Gardner, *The Case of the Sulky Girl*, (New York: Pocket Books, 1950), 187 (of 229).

17. Hughes, 110–11.

18. Erle Stanley Gardner, *The Case of the Glamorous Ghost*, (New York: Pocket Books, 1963), 230 (of 230).

19. Erle Stanley Gardner, *The Case of the Howling Dog*, (New York: Pocket Books, 1954), 127 (of 216).

20. Erle Stanley Gardner, *The Case of the Shapely Shadow*, (New York: Pocket Books, 1963), 128 (of 178).

21. Hughes, 102.

22. Charles W. Morton, "The World of Erle Stanley Gardner," *Atlantic*, 215 (January 1967), 84.

23. Erle Stanley Gardner, *The Case of the Empty Tin*, (New York: Pocket Books, 1966), 275 (of 276).

24. Erle Stanley Gardner, *The Case of the Duplicate Daughter*, (New York: Pocket Books, 1962), 197 (of 197).

25. Erle Stanley Gardner, *The Case of the Caretaker's Cat*, (New York: Pocket Books, 1943), 16 (of 242).

26. Erle Stanley Gardner, *The Case of the Haunted Husband*, (New York: Pocket Books, 1981), 16 (of 199).

27. Julian Symons, *Bloody Murder*, (Harmondsworth: Penguin Books, 1972), 216.

28. Erle Stanley Gardner, *The Case of the Moth-Eaten Mink*, (New York: Pocket Books, 1971), 92 (of 211).

29. Gardner, *The Case of the Howling Dog*, 177.

30. Erle Stanley Gardner, *The Bigger They Come*, (New York: Pocket Books, 1971), 7 (of 197).

31. Erle Stanley Gardner, *Spill the Jackpot*, (New York: Pocket Books, 1962), 165–66 (of 256).

32. Gardner, *Spill the Jackpot*, 166–67.

33. Chandler, *Selected Letters*, 162.

2. *Mickey Spillane*

1. Mickey Spillane, *I, the Jury*, (New York: New American Library, 1947, sixty-second printing), 5 (of 174).

2. Dashiell Hammett, *The Maltese Falcon*, (New York: Vintage Books, 1972), 227.

3. Mickey Spillane, *My Gun Is Quick*, (New York: New American Library, 1957), 144 (of 174).

4. Mickey Spillane, *Survival . . . Zero!* (New York: New American Library, 1971), 70 (of 160).

5. Mickey Spillane, *Vengeance Is Mine!* (New York: New American Library, 1959), 95 (of 142).

6. Mickey Spillane, *One Lonely Night*, (New York: New American Library, 1962), 6–7 (of 176).

7. Mickey Spillane, *The Big Kill*, (New York: New American Library, 1959), 79 (of 152).

8. Mickey Spillane, *Kiss Me, Deadly*, (New York: New American Library, 1952, thirtieth printing), 38 (of 176).

9. Mickey Spillane, *The Girl Hunters*, (New York: New American Library, 1963), 105, 133 (of 189).

10. Mickey Spillane, *The Snake*, (New York: New American Library, 1964), 133 (of 160).

11. Mickey Spillane, *The Deep*, (New York: New American Library, 1962), 119 (of 191).

12. Mickey Spillane, *The Last Cop Out*, (New York: New American Library, 1973), 13 (of 190).

3. *Ian Fleming*

1. John Pearson, *The Life of Ian Fleming*, (New York: Bantam Books, 1967), 175.

2. Ibid., 265, 267.

3. David Cannadine, "James Bond and the Decline of England," *Encounter*, 53 (September 1979), 52.

4. Ian Fleming, *Casino Royale*, (New York: New American Library, 1963), 7 (of 144).

5. Pearson, 111.

6. Ian Fleming, *Live and Let Die*, (New York: New American Library, 1964), 17 (of 159).

7. *The Ian Fleming Collection of 19th–20th Century Source Material Concerning Western Civilization* . . . [Bloomington: Lilly Library Publication Number XII, 1971], 32.

8. Pearson, 244.

9. Ian Fleming, *Moonraker*, (New York: New American Library, 1962), 37 (of 175).

10. Ian Fleming, *Diamonds Are Forever*, (New York: New American Library, 1956, twenty-second printing), 115 (of 160).

11. Ian Fleming, *From Russia, With Love*, (New York: New American Library, 1964), 28–29 (of 191).

12. Ian Fleming, *Doctor No*, (New York: New American Library, 1958, twenty-fifth printing), 64 (of 192).

13. Ian Fleming, *Goldfinger*, (New York: New American Library, 1959, twenty-eighth printing), 123 (of 191).

14. Pearson, 74.

15. C. S. Lewis, *The Screwtape Letters*, (New York: Macmillan, 1961), x.

16. Ian Fleming, *The Spy Who Loved Me*, (New York: New American Library, 1963), 73 (or 143).

17. Ian Fleming, *You Only Live Twice*, (New York: New American Library, 1965), 129 (of 160).

18. Ian Fleming, *Thunderball*, (New York: New American Library, 1961, twenty-third printing), 12–13 (of 188).

Bibliography

Erle Stanley Gardner

I. *NOVELS*

(Unless otherwise indicated, all published in New York by William Morrow)

A. *LESTER LEITH*

Erle Stanley Gardner's The Amazing Adventures of Lester Leith. Ed. Ellery Queen. New York: Davis Publications, 1980.

B. *PERRY MASON*

**The Case of the Velvet Claws.* 1933.
**The Case of the Sulky Girl.* 1933.
**The Case of the Lucky Legs.* 1934.
The Case of the Howling Dog. 1934.
**The Case of the Curious Bride.* 1934.
**The Case of the Counterfeit Eye.* 1935.
**The Case of the Caretaker's Cat.* 1935.
**The Case of the Sleepwalker's Niece.* 1936.
**The Case of the Stuttering Bishop.* 1936.
**The Case of the Dangerous Dowager.* 1937.
**The Case of the Lame Canary.* 1937.

**The Case of the Substitute Face.* 1938.
The Case of the Shoplifter's Shoe. 1938.
The Case of the Perjured Parrot. 1939.
**The Case of the Rolling Bones.* 1939.
**The Case of the Baited Hook.* 1940.
**The Case of the Silent Partner.* 1940.
**The Case of the Haunted Husband.* 1941.
**The Case of the Empty Tin.* 1941.
The Case of the Drowning Duck. 1942.
**The Case of the Careless Kitten.* 1942.
The Case of the Buried Clock. 1943.

*Superseller

219

The Case of the Drowsy Mosquito. 1943.

*The Case of the Crooked Candle. 1944.

*The Case of the Black-Eyed Blonde. 1944.

*The Case of the Golddigger's Purse. 1945.

*The Case of the Half-Wakened Wife. 1945.

*The Case of the Borrowed Brunette. 1946.

The Case of the Fan Dancer's Horse. 1947.

The Case of the Lazy Lover. 1947.

The Case of the Lonely Heiress. 1948.

The Case of the Vagabond Virgin. 1948.

The Case of the Dubious Bridegroom. 1949.

*The Case of the Cautious Coquette. 1949.

The Case of the Negligent Nymph. 1950.

The Case of the One-Eyed Witness. 1950.

The Case of the Fiery Fingers. 1951.

The Case of the Angry Mourner. 1951.

The Case of the Moth-Eaten Mink. 1952.

The Case of the Grinning Gorilla. 1952.

The Case of the Hesitant Hostess. 1953.

The Case of the Green-Eyed Sister. 1953.

The Case of the Fugitive Nurse. 1954.

The Case of the Runaway Corpse. 1954.

The Case of the Restless Redhead. 1954.

The Case of the Glamorous Ghost. 1955.

The Case of the Sun Bather's Diary. 1955.

The Case of the Nervous Accomplice. 1955.

The Case of the Terrified Typist. 1956.

The Case of the Demure Defendant. 1956.

The Case of the Gilded Lily. 1956.

The Case of the Lucky Loser. 1957.

The Case of the Screaming Woman. 1957.

The Case of the Daring Decoy. 1957.

The Case of the Long-Legged Models. 1958.

The Case of the Foot-Loose Doll. 1958.

The Case of the Calendar Girl. 1958.

The Case of the Deadly Toy. 1959.

The Case of the Mythical Monkeys. 1959.

The Case of the Singing Skirt. 1959.

The Case of the Waylaid Wolf. 1960.

The Case of the Duplicate Daughter. 1960.

The Case of the Shapely Shadow. 1960.

The Case of the Spurious Spinster. 1961.

The Case of the Bigamous Spouse. 1961.

The Case of the Reluctant Model. 1962.

The Case of the Blonde Bonanza. 1962.

The Case of the Ice-Cold Hands. 1962.
The Case of the Mischievous Doll. 1963.
The Case of the Stepdaughter's Secret. 1963.
The Case of the Amorous Aunt. 1963.
The Case of the Daring Divorcee. 1964.
The Case of the Phantom Fortune. 1964.
The Case of the Horrified Heirs. 1964.
The Case of the Troubled Trustee. 1965.
The Case of the Beautiful Beggar. 1965.
The Case of the Worried Waitress. 1966.
The Case of the Queenly Contestant. 1967.
The Case of the Careless Cupid. 1968.
The Case of the Fabulous Fake. 1969.
The Case of the Fenced-In Woman. 1972.
The Case of the Postponed Murder. 1973.

(Novelettes)

The Case of the Crimson Kiss. 1971.
The Case of the Crying Swallow. 1971.
The Case of the Irate Witness. 1972.

C. DOUG SELBY, THE D.A.

The D.A. Calls It Murder. 1937.
The D.A. Holds a Candle. 1938.
The D.A. Draws a Circle. 1939.
The D.A. Goes to Trial. 1940.
The D.A. Cooks a Goose. 1942.
The D.A. Calls a Turn. 1944.
The D.A. Breaks a Seal. 1946.
The D.A. Takes a Chance. 1948.
The D.A. Breaks an Egg. 1949.

D. BERTHA COOL AND DONALD LAM
(Pseudonym: A. A. Fair)

The Bigger They Come. 1939.
Turn On the Heat. 1940.
Gold Comes in Bricks. 1940.
Spill the Jackpot. 1941.
Double or Quits. 1941.
Owls Don't Blink. 1942.
Bats Fly at Dusk. 1943.
Cats Prowl at Night. 1943.
Give 'em the Ax. 1944.
Crows Can't Count. 1946.
Fools Die on Friday. 1947.
Bedrooms Have Windows. 1949.
Top of the Heap. 1952.
Some Women Won't Wait. 1953.
Beware the Curves. 1956.
You Can Die Laughing. 1957.
Some Slips Don't Show. 1957.
The Count of Nine. 1958.
Pass the Gravy. 1959.
Kept Women Can't Quit. 1960.
Bachelors Get Lonely. 1961.
Shills Can't Cash Chips. 1962.
Try Anything Once. 1962.
Fish or Cut Bait. 1963.
Up For Grabs. 1964.
Cut Thin to Win. 1965.
Widows Wear Weeds. 1966.
Traps Need Fresh Bait. 1967.
All Grass Isn't Green. 1970.

E. MISCELLANEOUS FIC-
    TION.

*The Clew of the Forgotten Murder
1935.
*This Is Murder. 1935.
Murder Up My Sleeve. 1937.
The Case of the Turning Tide.
1941.
The Case of the Smoking Chimney.
1943.

The Case of the Backward Mule.
1946.
Two Clues. 1947.
The Case of the Musical Cow. 1950.
The Case of the Murderer's Bride
and Other Stories. Ed. Ellery
Queen. New York: Davis Pub-
lications, 1969.
The Amazing Adventures of Lester
Leith. Ed. Ellery Queen. New
York: Davis Publications,
1980.

(A complete bibliography of all Gardner's fiction and nonfiction is available in Ruth Moore's appendix to Dorothy Hughes's biography, *The
Case of the Real Perry Mason.*)

II. SELECTED WORKS ABOUT GARDNER

Fugate, Francis L. and Robert B. *Secrets of the World's Best-Selling Writer.*
New York: Morrow, 1980.
    A useful assembly of materials from the Gardner collection at the
    University of Texas, with good coverage of his work for the pulps
    and a full account of the machinery of the fiction factory.
Johnston, Alva. *The Case of Erle Stanley Gardner.* New York: Morrow,
1947.
    An entertaining, anecdotal account of Gardner at the peak of his
    career.
Kane, Patricia. "Perry Mason: Modern Culture Hero." In *Heroes of
Popular Culture.* Ed. Ray B. Browne. Bowling Green: Bowling Green
University Popular Press, 1972. 125–33.
Hughes, Dorothy. *The Case of the Real Perry Mason.* New York: Morrow,
1978.
    An informative, but uncritical and discursive biography.
Morton, Charles W. "The World of Erle Stanley Gardner." *Atlantic,* 215
(January 1967), 79–91.
Robbins, Frank. "The Firm of Cool and Lam." In *The Mystery Writer's
Art,* ed. Francis M. Nevins, Jr. Bowling Green: Bowling Green Uni-
versity Popular Press, 1970. 136–148.
    Robbins's companion article, "The World of Perry Mason," is avail-
    able only in its original publication: *Michigan Alumnus Quarterly
    Review,* Summer 1950.

Mickey Spillane

I. NOVELS

(Unless otherwise indicated, all published in New York by E.P. Dutton)

A. MIKE HAMMER

*I, the Jury. 1947.
*My Gun Is Quick. 1950.
*Vengeance Is Mine! 1950.
*The Big Kill. 1951.
*One Lonely Night. 1951.
*Kiss Me, Deadly. 1952.
The Girl Hunters. 1962.
The Snake. 1964.
The Twisted Thing. 1966.
The Body Lovers. 1967.
Survival . . . Zero! 1970.

B. TIGER MANN

Day of the Guns. 1964.
Bloody Sunrise. 1965.
The Death Dealers. 1965.
The By-Pass Control. 1966.

C. OTHER

*The Long Wait. 1951.
*The Deep. 1961.
Killer Mine. New York: New American Library, 1968.
The Delta Factor. 1967.
Me, Hood! New York: New American Library, 1969.
The Tough Guys. New York: New American Library, 1969.
The Erection Set. 1972.
The Last Cop Out. 1973.

D. ENGLISH NOVELETTE COLLECTIONS

Me, Hood! London: Corgi, 1963.
The Flier. London: Corgi, 1964.
Return of the Hood. London: Corgi, 1964.

II. SELECTED WORKS ABOUT SPILLANE

Banks, R. Jeff. "Anti-Professionalism in the works of Mickey Spillane." Notes on Contemporary Literature, 3 (1973), 6–8.
——. "Spillane's Anti-Establishmentarian Heroes." In Dimensions of Detective Fiction. Ed. Larry Landrum. Popular Press, 1976. 124–39. A complete survey of Spillane's fiction.
Cawelti, John G. "The Spillane Phenomenon." Journal of Popular Culture, 3 (1969), 9–22.
Fetterley, Judith. "Beauty as the Beast: Fantasy and Fear in I, the Jury." Journal of Popular Culture, 8 (1975), 775–782.
La Farge, Christopher. "Mickey Spillane and His Bloody Hammer." In

Mass Culture: the Popular Arts in America. Ed. Bernard Rosenberg. Glencoe, Ill: The Free Press, 1957. 176–85.
A savage attack on Spillane.

Rolo, Charles J. "Simenon and Spillane: The Metaphysics of Murder for the Millions." In *Mass Culture: The Popular Arts in America.* Ed. Bernard Rosenberg. Glencoe, Ill: The Free Press, 1957. 165–75.

Ruehlmann, William. *Saint with a Gun: The Unlawful American Private Eye.* New York: New York University Press, 1974.

Weibel, Kay. "Mickey Spillane as a Fifties Phenomenon." In *Dimensions of Detective Fiction.* Ed. Larry Landrum. Popular Press, 1976.

Ian Fleming

I. NOVELS

(All editions published in London by Jonathan Cape; in New York by New American Library)

A. JAMES BOND

Casino Royale. 1954.
Live and Let Die. 1954.
Moonraker. 1955.
Diamonds Are Forever. 1957.
From Russia, With Love. 1957.
Doctor No. 1958.
Goldfinger. 1959.
For Your Eyes Only. 1960.

Thunderball. 1961.
The Spy Who Loved Me. 1962.
On Her Majesty's Secret Service. 1963.
You Only Live Twice. 1964.
The Man with the Golden Gun. 1965.
Octopussy, and The Living Delights. 1966.

II. SELECTED WORKS ABOUT FLEMING

Amis, Kingsley. *The James Bond Dossier.* New York: New American Library, 1965.
An interesting, sympathetic analysis of the elements of Bond's popularity.

———. *What Became of Jane Austen? and Other Questions.* London: Cape, 1971.
The essay, "A New James Bond," discussed Bond's appeal and Amis's motives for composing a sequel.

Boyd, Ann S. *The Devil in James Bond.* Richmond, Va: John Knox Press, 1967.

Cannadine, David. "James Bond and the Decline of England." *Encounter*, 53 (September 1979), 46–55.

Eco, Umberto and Oreste del Buono, eds. *The Bond Affair*. Trans. R. A. Dawnie. London: MacDonald, 1966.

Holbrook, David. *The Masks of Hate*. Oxford: Pergamon Press, 1972. Includes a twelve chapter psychoanalytic analysis of *Goldfinger*.

The Ian Fleming Collection of 19th–20th Century Source Material Concerning Western Civilization . . . [Bloomington: Lilly Library Publication Number XII, 1971].

Johnson, Paul. "Sex, Snobbery and Sadism." *New Statesman*, 55 (5 April 1958), 430–2.

Lane, Sheldon. *For Bond Lovers Only*. New York: Dell, 1965.

Pearson, John. *The Life of Ian Fleming*. New York: McGraw-Hill, 1966. An informative, well-written biography.

Richler, Mordecai. *Shovelling Trouble*. Toronto: McClelland & Stewart, 1972.
"Bond" (pp. 55–83) is a full version of an often reprinted, eloquent attack on Bond and Fleming.

Snelling, O. F. *Double O Seven, James Bond: A Report*. New York: New American Library, 1965.

Starkey, Lycurgus M. *James Bond's World of Values*. Nashville: Abingdon Press, 1966.

Zeiger, Henry A. *Ian Fleming: The Spy Who came In with the Gold*. New York: Duell, Sloan, and Pearce, 1965.

SELECTED WORKS OF GENERAL RELEVANCE

Barzun, Jacques and Wendell Hertig Taylor. *A Catalogue of Crime*. New York: Harper and Row, 1971.
Select for special notice ten Masons, six Cool & Lams, and two D.A.s.

Bettelheim, Bruno. *The Uses of Enchantment*. New York: Vintage Books, 1977.

Cawelti, John G. *Adventure, Mystery, and Romance: Formula Stories As Art and Popular Culture*. Chicago: University of Chicago Press, 1976.

Chandler, Raymond. *Selected Letters*. Ed. Frank MacShane. New York: Columbia University Press, 1981.

Contemporary Authors. Detroit: Gale Research, 1967–

Hackett, Alice Payne and James Henry Burke. *80 Years of Best Sellers, 1895–1975*. New York: Bowker: 1977.

Hackett, Alice Payne and James Henry Burke. *80 Years of Best Sellers, 1895–1975*. New York: Bowker, 1977.

Palmer, Jerry. *Thrillers: Genesis and Structure of a Popular Genre.* London: Edward Arnold, 1978.
  Uses Spillane and Fleming as principal examples.
Penzler, Otto. *The Private Lives of Private Eyes, Spies, Crime Fighters, and Other Good Guys.* New York: Grosset and Dunlap, 1977.
Reilly, John M., ed. *Twentieth-Century Crime and Mystery Writers.* London: Macmillan Press, 1980.
Steinbrunner, Chris and Otto Penzler. *Encyclopedia of Mystery and Detection.* New York: McGraw-Hill, 1976.

Film and Television

Gardner, Spillane, and Fleming were not averse to exploiting media other than print that the twentieth century made available to them.

Hollywood was quick to recruit Perry Mason, and Gardner was willing to have his lawyer adapted for radio, television, and even comic strips. As a television hero, Mason dominated Saturday nights for nearly a decade. James Bond's spectacular and continuing success as a cinema hero has by now almost overshadowed his notoriety as a super-seller. Spillane's novels, with their reliance upon the distinctive voice of his overpowering narrators, have proved less amenable to visual treatments, but several movies and two television series (one of them launched in 1984) suggest that he too has had a more than literary appeal.

Erle Stanley Gardner

I. PERRY MASON

Film

Warren William. *The Case of the Howling Dog*. Warner Bros. 1934.
The Case of the Curious Bride. Warner Bros. 1935.
The Case of the Lucky Legs. Warner Bros. 1935.
The Case of the Velvet Claws. Warner Bros. 1936.
Ricardo Cortez. *The Case of the Black Cat* (based upon *The Case of the Caretaker's Cat*). Warner Bros. 1936.
Donald Woods. *The Case of the Stuttering Bishop*. Warner Bros. 1937.

Television

Raymond Burr. *Perry Mason*. CBS. 1957–1966.
Monte Markham. *The New Adventures of Perry Mason*. CBS. 1973.

II. OTHER NOVELS

Film

This Is Murder. Eastern Service Studios. c. 1935.

227

Special Investigator (based on the novelette "Fugitive Gold"). RKO. 1935.
Granny Get Your Gun (based on the Mason novel *The Case of the Dangerous Dowager)*. Warner Bros. 1940.

Television
The Bigger They Come (Cool and Lam). CBS. 1955.
The Court of Last Resort. NBC. 1957–1958.
The D.A. Draws a Circle. NBC. 1971.

Mickey Spillane

I. MIKE HAMMER

Film
Biff Elliott. *I, the Jury.* United Artists. 1953.
Ralph Meeker. *Kiss Me Deadly.* United Artists. 1955.
Robert Gray. *My Gun Is Quick.* United Artists. 1957.
Mickey Spillane. *The Girl Hunters.* Colorama. 1963.

Television
Darren McGavin. *Mike Hammer, Detective.* NBC. 1958–1959.
Stacy Keach. *Murder Me, Murder You* (telemovie). CBS. 1983.
Stacy Keach. *Mickey Spillane's Mike Hammer.* CBS. 1984–

II. OTHER NOVELS

Film
The Long Wait. United Artists. 1954.
The Delta Factor. ACF. 1970.
(Spillane played himself in the film *Ring of Fear,* Warner Bros., 1954)

Ian Fleming

I. JAMES BOND

Film
Sean Connery. *Doctor No.* United Artists, 1963.
From Russia, With Love. United Artists. 1964.
Goldfinger. United Artists. 1965.
Thunderball. United Artists. 1966.
You Only Live Twice. United Artists. 1967.

Diamonds Are Forever. United Artists. 1971.
Never Say Never Again. Columbia. 1983.
David Niven. *Casino Royale.* Columbia. 1967.
George Lazenby. *On Her Majesty's Secret Service.* United Artists. 1970.
Roger Moore. *Live and Let Die.* United Artists. 1973.
The Man With the Golden Gun. United Artists. 1974.
The Spy Who Loved Me. United Artists. 1977.
Moonraker. United Artists. 1979.
For Your Eyes Only. United Artists. 1981.
Octopussy. United Artists. 1983.

Index

All Grass Isn't Green (Gardner), 78
Amazing Adventures of Lester Leith,
  The (Gardner), 27
Amis, Kingsley, 213

Barzun, Jacques, 75
"Bastard Bannerman, The"
  (Spillane), 143–44
Benchley, Peter, 2, 3, 4, 7
bestsellers, 1–6, 8–11
Bettelheim, Bruno, 10–13
Bigger They Come, The (Gardner),
  79
Big Kill, The (Spillane), 128
Big Sleep, The (Chandler), 117
Blackman, Honor, 159
Body Lovers, The (Spillane), 137–38
Bond, James, series, 153–213
  formulas used in, 139, 164–69,
  179–80, 184, 195, 197, 200–02
  and Mike Hammer series,
  compared, 154–55
  and Perry Mason series,
  compared, 154–55
  motion pictures based on, 158,
  159, 185, 193, 199, 203, 209,

211, 213–14, 227
  point of view in, 200
  predictability of, 1–2, 5, 160
  sales of, ix, 3, 5, 158–60
  settings in, 177–78
  violence in, 169–70
Burr, Raymond, 81

Caldwell, Erskine, 4–5
Case of the Black Cat, The
  (Gardner), 69
Case of the Caretaker's Cat, The
  (Gardner), 71
Case of the Cautious Coquette, The
  (Gardner), 75
Case of the Crooked Candle, The
  (Gardner), 50
Case of the Duplicate Daughter, The
  (Gardner), 69–70
Case of the Empty Tin, The
  (Gardner), 69
Case of the Fabulous Fake, The
  (Gardner), 71
Case of the Glamorous Ghost, The
  (Gardner), 60
Case of the Haunted Husband, The
  (Gardner), 86

Case of the Horrified Heirs, The
   (Gardner), 73–75
Case of the Howling Dog, The
   (Gardner), 62, 63, 75
Case of the Lame Canary, The
   (Gardner), 72
Case of the Long-Legged Models, The
   (Gardner), 91–92
Case of the Moth-Eaten Mink, The
   (Gardner), 75
Case of the Shapely Shadow, The
   (Gardner), 64
Case of the Stuttering Bishop, The
   (Gardner), 73
Case of the Substitute Face, The
   (Gardner), 72
Case of the Sulky Girl, The
   (Gardner), 34, 35, 54–70
   action in, 66–68
Case of the Velvet Claws, The
   (Gardner), 33–54, 56, 70
   action in, 44–45, 55, 67
   dialogue in, 39–42
Casino Royale (Fleming), 157,
   160–73
   motion picture based on, 199
Chandler, Raymond, 16, 156
   and Fleming, 178
   and Gardner, 8, 16–23, 39, 41,
   87
   settings of, 42–43
   and Spillane, 117
characterization, 12–13
   in Fleming's works, 7, 153–54,
   161, 170–77, 181, 190–213
   in Gardner's works, 7, 21–22,
   35, 44–46, 51–55, 58, 67,
   71–73, 80, 161
   of hero, 7, 12–13, 28, 31–33,
   in Spillane's works, 7, 100–01,
   104, 110, 120–22, 137, 146–47,
   161

Chiles, Lois, 211
Colonel Sun (Amis), 213
Connery, Sean, 159, 185, 193
Cool, Bertha. *See* Lam-Cool series
*Cops on Campus and Crime in the
   Streets* (Gardner), 71–72
Cortez, Ricardo, 69
courtroom scenes, 35, 54, 61–65

D.A. series, 76–78
Dash, Speed, series, 29
Day the Sea Rolled Back, The
   (Spillane), 93
Deep, The (Spillane), 139–43
Deighton, Len, 8, 198
Delta Factor, The (Spillane), 146–47
detective fiction, rules of, 23–24,
   35
"Detective Story Decalogue, A"
   (Knox), 23
Diamonds Are Forever (Fleming),
   182–84
Diamond Smugglers, The (Fleming),
   184
Doctor No (Fleming), 158, 189–90,
   191
Doyle, Arthur Conan, 28

80 Years of Best Sellers, 1895–1975
   (Hackett and Burke), 3–4
Erection Set, The (Spillane), 144–46
"Exact Opposite, The" (Gardner),
   32
Executioner series (Pendleton),
   128–29
Exorcist, The (Blatty), 2, 7

Fair, A. A. (Gardner pseudonym),
   79
   See also Lam-Cool series
fairy tales, elements of, in crime
   fiction, 10–13, 21–22, 158–60

Farewell, My Lovely (Chandler), 43
Fleming, Ian, 153–213
  and Gardner, compared,
    87–89, 120, 150–52
  life of, 156–57, 212
  motion pictures based on works
    of, 159, 185, 193, 199, 203,
    209, 211
  sales of books by, ix, 3, 5,
    158–60
  and Spillane, compared, 87–89,
    120, 150–52
  style of, 155–56
For Your Eyes Only (Fleming),
  195–96
From Russia with Love (Fleming),
  158, 184–89, 192, 197
  motion picture based on, 185

Gardner, Erle Stanley, 15–89
  and Chandler, compared,
    16–22
  and Fleming, compared, 87–89,
    120, 150–52
  life of, 17–20, 24
  and Ross Macdonald,
    compared, 16–22
  motion pictures and television
    series based on works of, 63,
    69, 73, 81
  nondetective writing of, 15, 20
  prolificacy of, 26, 33, 34
  pseudonyms of, 26, 79
  sales of books by, ix, 2–3, 5–6,
    27, 91–92
  and Spillane, compared, 87–89,
    120, 150–52
  style of, 39–41, 155–56
  writing method of, 24, 26
Gardner, John, 214
Girl Hunters, The (Spillane), 120,
  131–36, 139

  motion picture based on, 135,
    151–52
Goldfinger (Fleming), 189, 192–95,
  197–98
  motion picture based on, 158,
    159, 193

Hamilton, Hamish, 39
Hammer, Mike, series, 153
  and Bond series, compared,
    154–55
  formulas used in, 115–16, 139,
    146
  illogic of, 102, 112–15
  and Mason series, compared,
    92–93, 114
  motion pictures and television
    series based on, 3, 129, 135,
    151–52, 227
  point of view in, 94, 95, 145–46
  predictability of, 1–2, 5
  sales of, 2, 92, 131, 139
  settings of, 95–96, 118–19
  surprise endings of, x–xi, 111,
    115, 119
  themes of, 95–99, 126–27,
    142–43
  violence in, 104–05, 116–17
Hammett, Dashiell, 98, 111–12
Hobson, Thayer, 31, 34
Hornung, E. W., 28, 32–33

"In Round Figures" (Gardner),
  28–30, 33
I, the Jury (Spillane), 94–118, 161
  as homage to *The Maltese Falcon*
    (Hammett), 111–12
  sales of, 2, 5, 7, 92

James Bond Dossier (Amis), 213
Jenkins, Ed, series, 29

Keach, Stacey, 135
"Kick It or Kill" (Spillane), 146
Kiel, Richard, 209
"Killer Mine" (Spillane), 143
"Kiss Me Deadly" (Spillane),
    128–31
  motion picture based on, 129
Knox, Ronald A., 23

Lam-Cool series, 15, 78–87
Last Cop Out, The (Spillane), 147
Lazenby, George, 203
Leblanc, Maurice, 28
le Carré, John, 8, 154, 198
Leith, Lester, series, 27–33
Lenya, Lotte, 185
Lewis, C. S., 198
Live and Let Die (Fleming), 173–79,
    191
London, Jack, 31
Long Wait, The (Spillane), 139–42
  motion picture based on, 141

Macdonald, Ross, 16–22
Maltese Falcon, The (Hammett), 98,
    111–12
"Man Alone" (Spillane), 146
Mann, Tiger, series, 148–50, 153
Man with the Golden Gun, The
    (Fleming), 5, 210–12
Man Who Was Thursday, The
    (Chesterton), 153–54
Mason, Perry, series, 22–23,
    31–34, 92–93, 114, 153–55
  formulas used in, 21, 30, 35,
    46–57, 76–77, 184
  motion pictures and television
    series based on, 63, 69, 73, 81,
    227
  predictability of, 1–2, 5, 21,
    34–35, 70–71
  sales of, 2, 3, 5, 27, 91–92

settings of, 20–21, 42–43, 119
McGavin, Darren, 135
Meeker, Ralph, 129
Me, Hood! (Spillane), 146–47
metaphor, 95, 99–100, 118
Moonraker (Fleming), 164, 179–82,
    211
Moore, Roger, 209, 211
Moore, Ruth, 15
morality in crime fiction, 6–7,
    10–11, 12, 28–33, 46–48,
    171–73, 195–96
My Gun Is Quick (Spillane), 115–18
Mystery of Marie Roget, The (Poe),
    30

1984 (Orwell), 4
Niven, David, 199
Norton, Charles, 68

Octopussy (Fleming), 213
One Lonely Night (Spillane),
    122–26, 151–52
On Her Majesty's Secret Service
    (Fleming), 202–05
  motion picture based on, 203

pace in crime fiction, 66–70, 103
Pendleton, Don, 128–29
Playback (Chandler), 88
plots, 21–25
  complexity of, 30, 44–45, 65
  devices and formulas used in,
    21, 25, 46–57, 59, 76–77,
    115–16, 139, 146, 164–69,
    179–80, 184, 195, 197, 200–02
  predictability of, 1–2, 5, 21,
    34–35, 70–71
  thinness of, 110, 112–14
Puzo, Mario, 2, 4, 7, 147

Queen, Ellery, 26, 27

Quinn, Anthony, 141

Red Harvest, The (Hammett), 141
Robbins, Harold, 3, 4–5, 7

Sayers, Dorothy, 27
Screwtape Letters, The (Lewis), 198
*Secrets of the World's Best-Selling
   Writer* (Fugate), 23, 24
Segal, Erich, 2, 4, 7
Selby, Doug, series, 15
"Seven Year Kill, The" (Spillane),
   146
Snake, The (Spillane), 117, 120,
   131, 133–34, 139
Spillane, Mickey, 91–152
   as actor, 135, 151
   comic books' influence on,
      93–94
   and Fleming, compared, 87–89,
      97–98, 120, 147, 150–52
   and Gardner, compared,
      87–89, 120, 150–52
   motion pictures and television
      series based on works of, 129,
      135, 141, 151–52
   sales of books by, ix, 2, 5, 7, 92,
      131, 148
   sex in works of, treatment of,
      87, 89, 144–45
   style of, 99–100, 155–56
   surprise endings of, x–xi, 111,
      115, 119, 122, 126
   themes of, 142–43
   violence in works of, 144–45
Spill the Jackpot (Gardner), 82–87
Spy Who Loved Me, The (Fleming),
   200–02

   motion picture based on, 209
   structure
      in James Bond novels, 160, 184,
         189
      in Mike Hammer novels, 106,
         109–10
      in Perry Mason novels, 31–32,
         60–62, 65–66
Survival Zero (Spillane), 117,
   138–39, 148
Susann, Jacqueline, 2, 4, 7, 145,
   147
Symons, Julian, 72

Taylor, Wendell, 75
"Thousand to One, A" (Gardner),
   30, 32
Thunderball (Fleming), 5, 197–200,
   208
Tough Guys, The (Spillane), 145–46
"Twenty Rules for Writing
   Detective Stories" (Van Dine),
   23
Twisted Thing, The (Spillane),
   136–37

Van Dine, S. S., 23, 27
Vengeance Is Mine (Spillane),
   119–22

William, Warren, 63
Wood, Christopher, 213
Woods, Donald, 73

You Only Live Twice (Fleming),
   205–10